THE BLIZ...

MW00805414

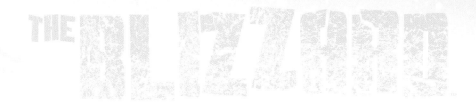

THE BLIZZARD™

GEOFF JOHNS & ANDREA MUTTI
CREATORS

ROB LEIGH
LETTERS

BRIAN CUNNINGHAM
EDITOR

STEVE BLACKWELL
DESIGNER

GHOST machine

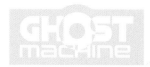

CREATORS

BRAD ANDERSON | JASON FABOK | GARY FRANK
BRYAN HITCH | GEOFF JOHNS | ROB LEIGH | LAMONT MAGEE
FRANCIS MANAPUL | BRAD MELTZER | IVAN REIS
PETER SNEJBJERG | PETER J. TOMASI | MAYTAL ZCHUT

JAMIE IRACLEANOS SVP Development & Production
MICHAEL COTTON VP Publishing & Marketing
COREY SALTER VP Creative & Business Development
REBECCA DOWDY Creative Executive

GHOSTMACHINEPRO.COM

image

ROBERT KIRKMAN Chief Operating Officer | **ERIK LARSEN** Chief Financial Officer | **TODD McFARLANE** President | **MARC SILVESTRI** Chief Executive Officer | **JIM VALENTINO** Vice President | **ERIC STEPHENSON** Publisher / Chief Creative Officer
NICOLE LAPALME Vice President of Finance | **LEANNA CAUNTER** Accounting Analyst | **SUE KORPELA** Accounting & HR Manager | **JIM VISCARDI** Vice President of Business Development | **LORELEI BUNJES** Vice President of Digital Strategy
EMILIO BAUTISTA Digital Sales Coordinator | **DIRK WOOD** Vice President of International Sales & Licensing | **RYAN BREWER** International Sales & Licensing Manager | **ALEX COX** Director of Direct Market Sales
MARGOT WOOD Vice President of Book Market Sales | **CHLOE RAMOS** Book Market & Library Sales Manager | **KAT SALAZAR** Vice President of PR & Marketing | **DEANNA PHELPS** Marketing Design Manager
DREW FITZGERALD Marketing Content Associate | **HEATHER DOORNINK** Vice President of Production | **IAN BALDESSARI** Print Manager | **DREW GILL** Art Director | **MELISSA GIFFORD** Content Manager
ERIKA SCHNATZ Senior Production Artist | **WESLEY GRIFFITH** Production Artist | **RICH FOWLKS** Production Artist | **JON SCHLAFFMAN** Production Artist

IMAGECOMICS.COM

TALES OF THE UNNAMED: THE BLIZZARD. First printing. July 2024. Published by Image Comics, Inc. Office of publication: PO BOX 14457, Portland, OR 97293. ISBN: 978-1-5343-8713-2

GHOST machine

What you're about to read is a tale from the universe of THE UNNAMED. A universe that follows mysterious fable-like figures throughout American history, from the earliest days of the American Revolution to the final days of America's destruction during The Unknown War.

This account occurred on the outskirts of our heroes' lives but is definitively connected to them.

It begins when a group of convicts being transferred to a maximum security prison are stranded in the mountains by an unexplainable storm...and hunted by something even more unexplainable.

This is a story about judgment from both within and without. A peek into the existence of a deadly and strange creature hungry for those who deserve absolute and final punishment.

Bundle up.

It's cold out there.

Geoff Johns

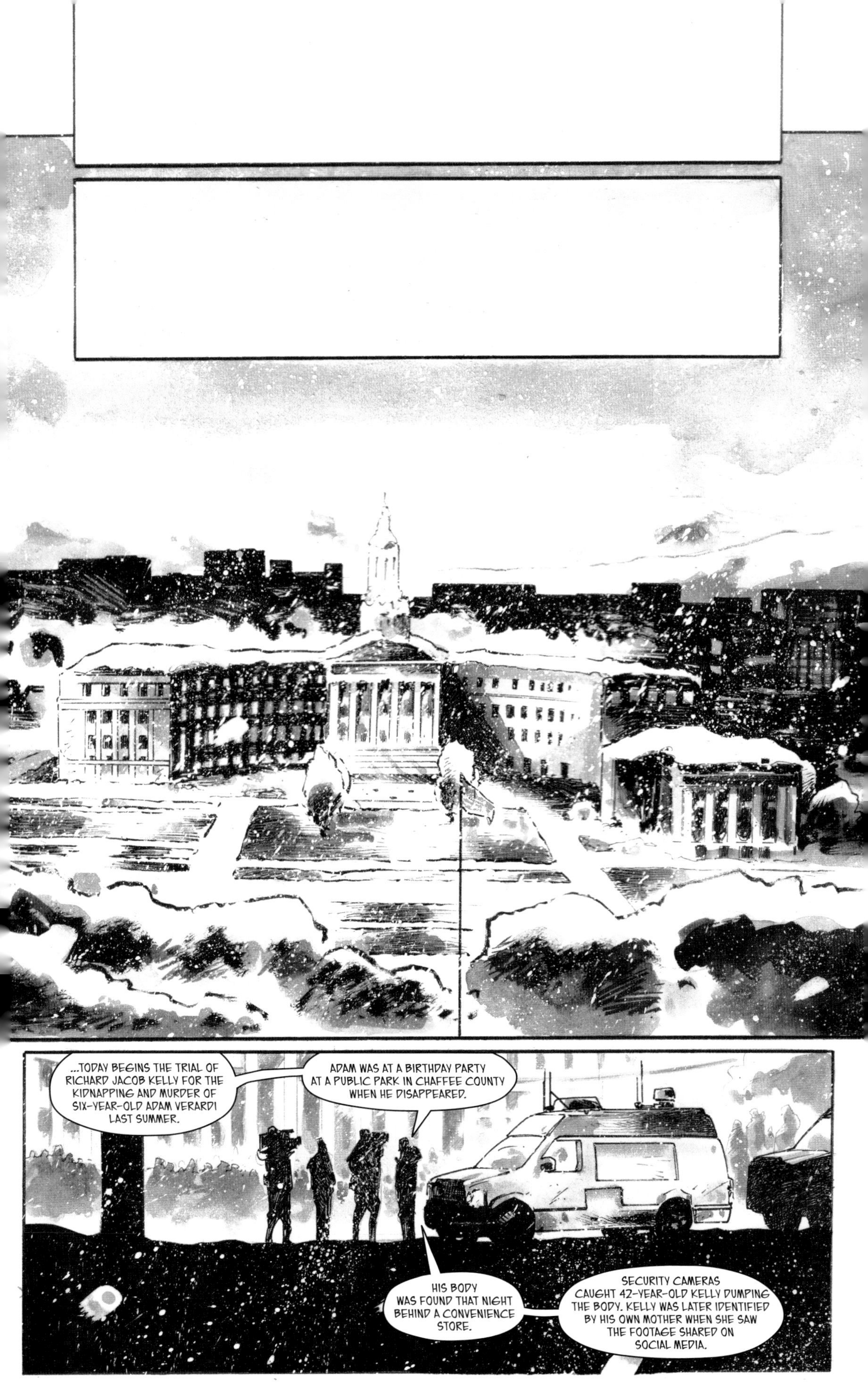
...TODAY BEGINS THE TRIAL OF RICHARD JACOB KELLY FOR THE KIDNAPPING AND MURDER OF SIX-YEAR-OLD ADAM VERARDI LAST SUMMER.
ADAM WAS AT A BIRTHDAY PARTY AT A PUBLIC PARK IN CHAFFEE COUNTY WHEN HE DISAPPEARED.
HIS BODY WAS FOUND THAT NIGHT BEHIND A CONVENIENCE STORE.
SECURITY CAMERAS CAUGHT 42-YEAR-OLD KELLY DUMPING THE BODY. KELLY WAS LATER IDENTIFIED BY HIS OWN MOTHER WHEN SHE SAW THE FOOTAGE SHARED ON SOCIAL MEDIA.

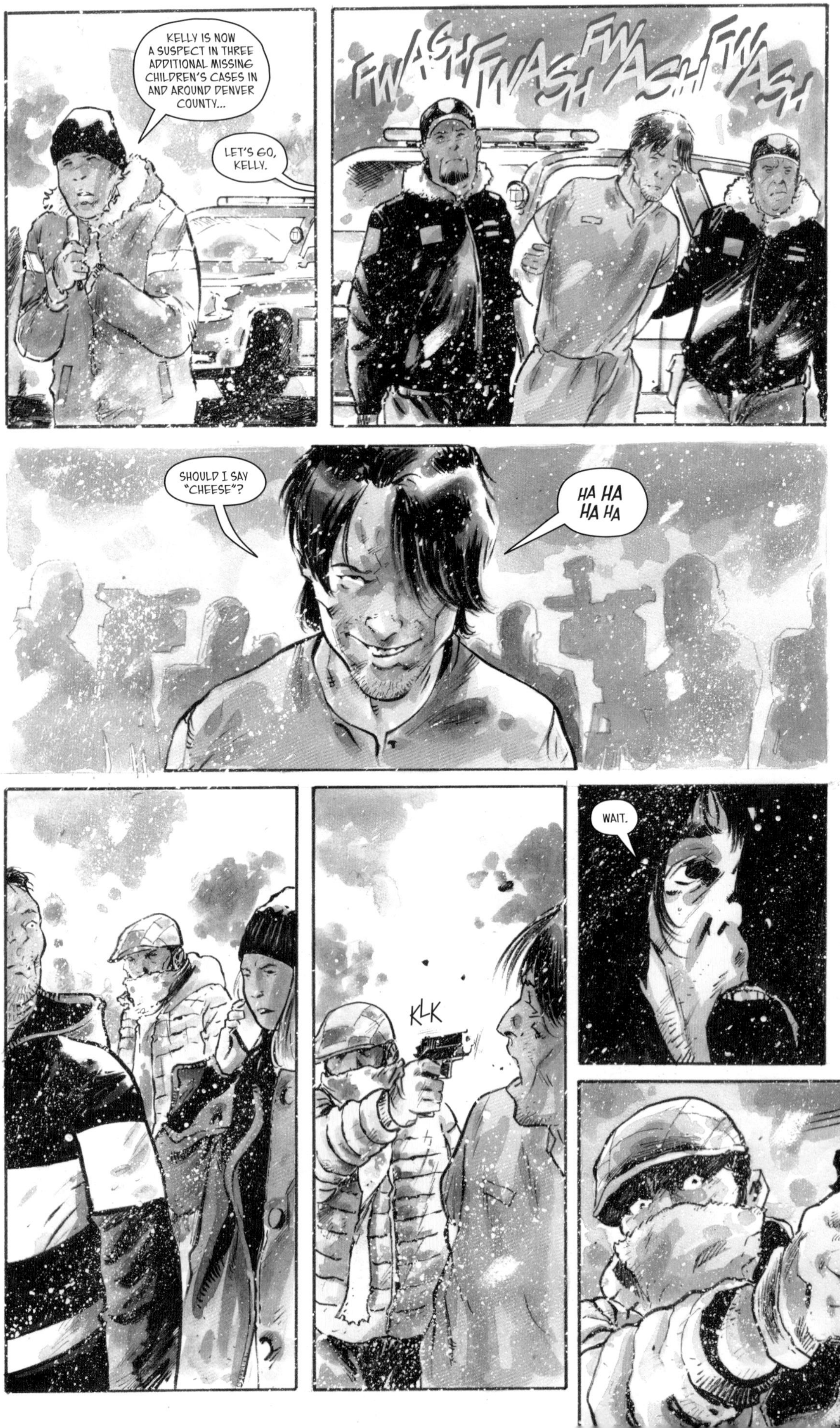
KELLY IS NOW A SUSPECT IN THREE ADDITIONAL MISSING CHILDREN'S CASES IN AND AROUND DENVER COUNTY...
LET'S GO, KELLY.
FWASH FWASH FWASH FWASH FWASH
SHOULD I SAY "CHEESE"?
HA HA HA HA
KLK
WAIT.

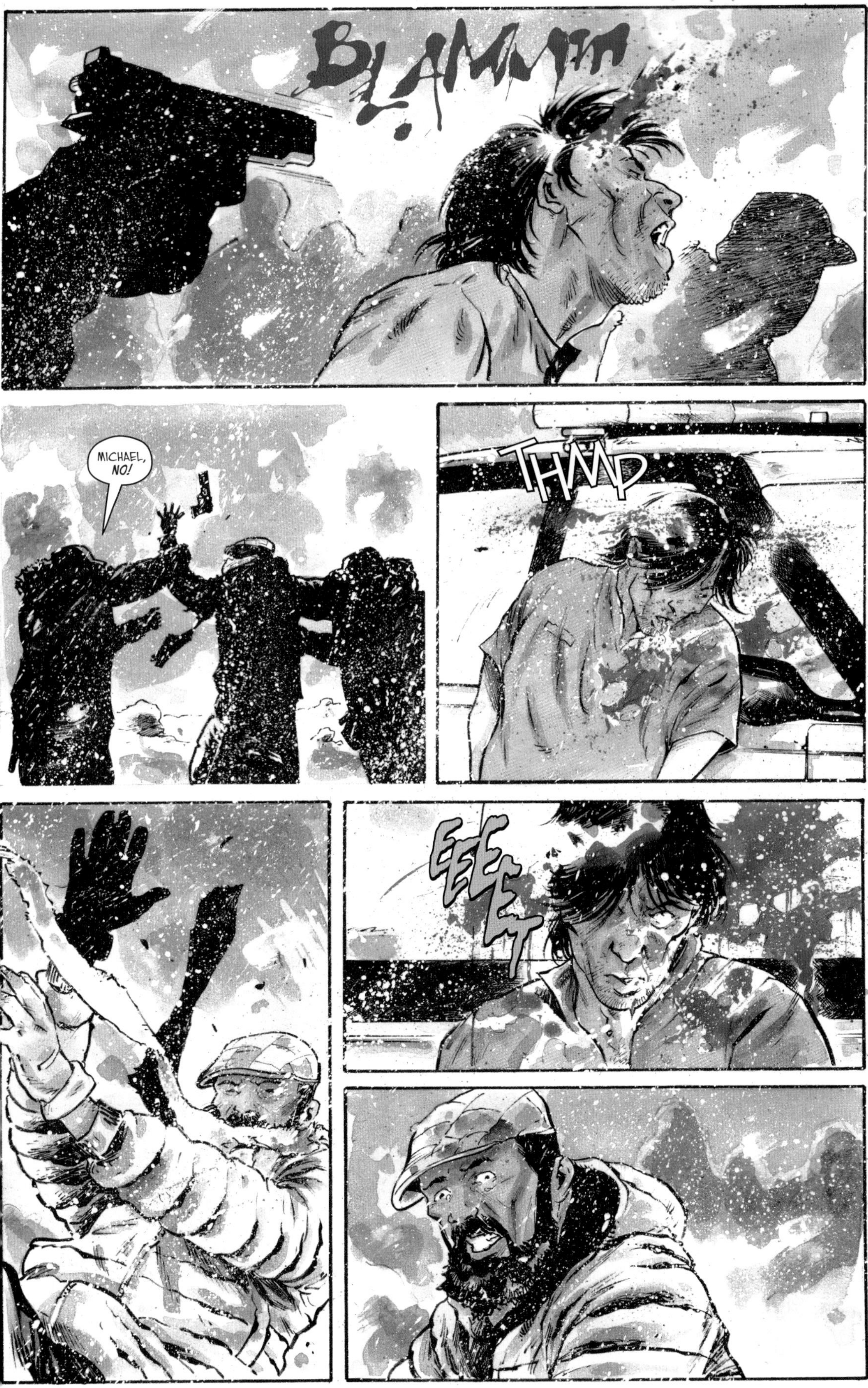
BLAMMM
MICHAEL, NO!
THMP
EEEEET

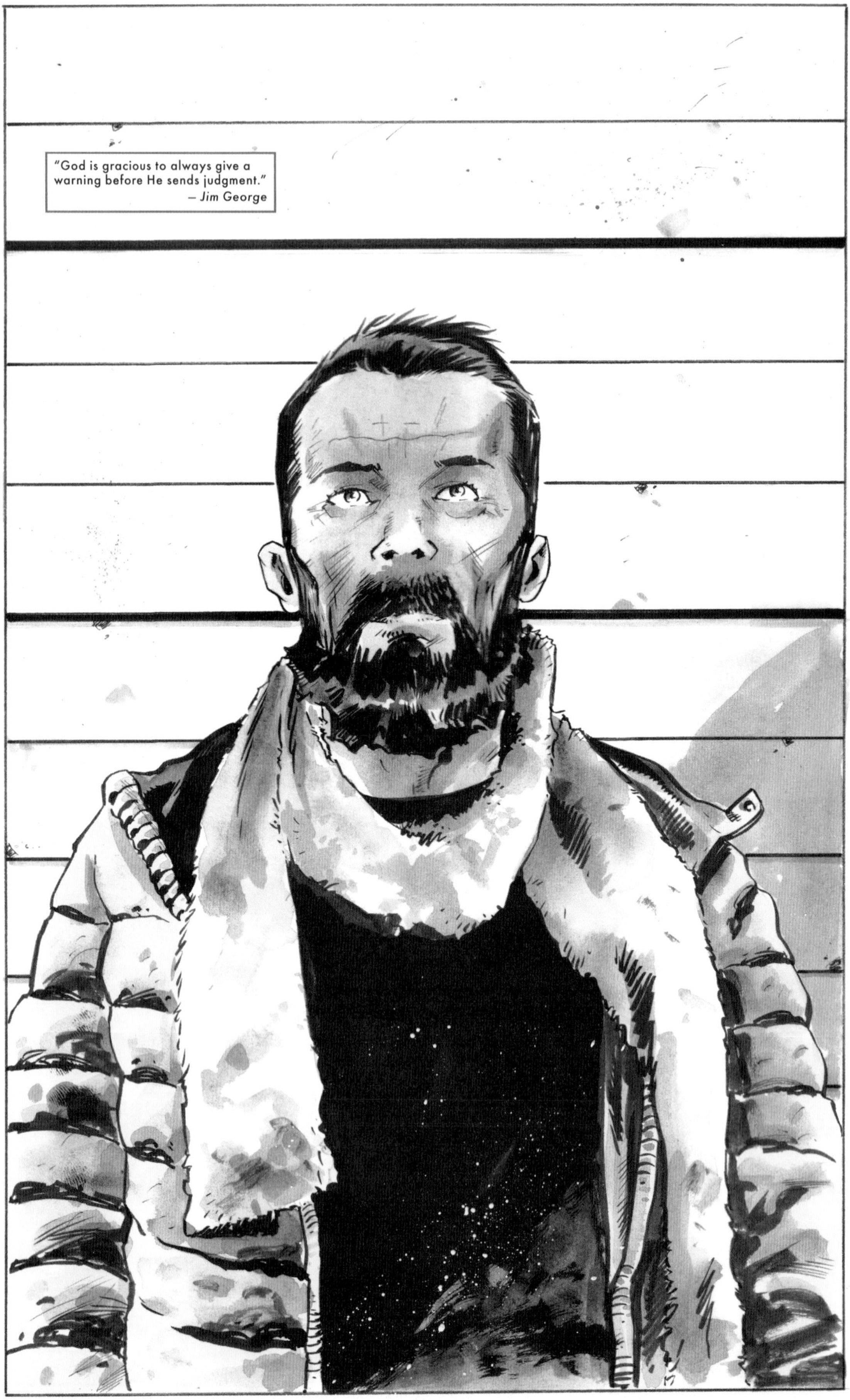
"God is gracious to always give a warning before He sends judgment."
– Jim George

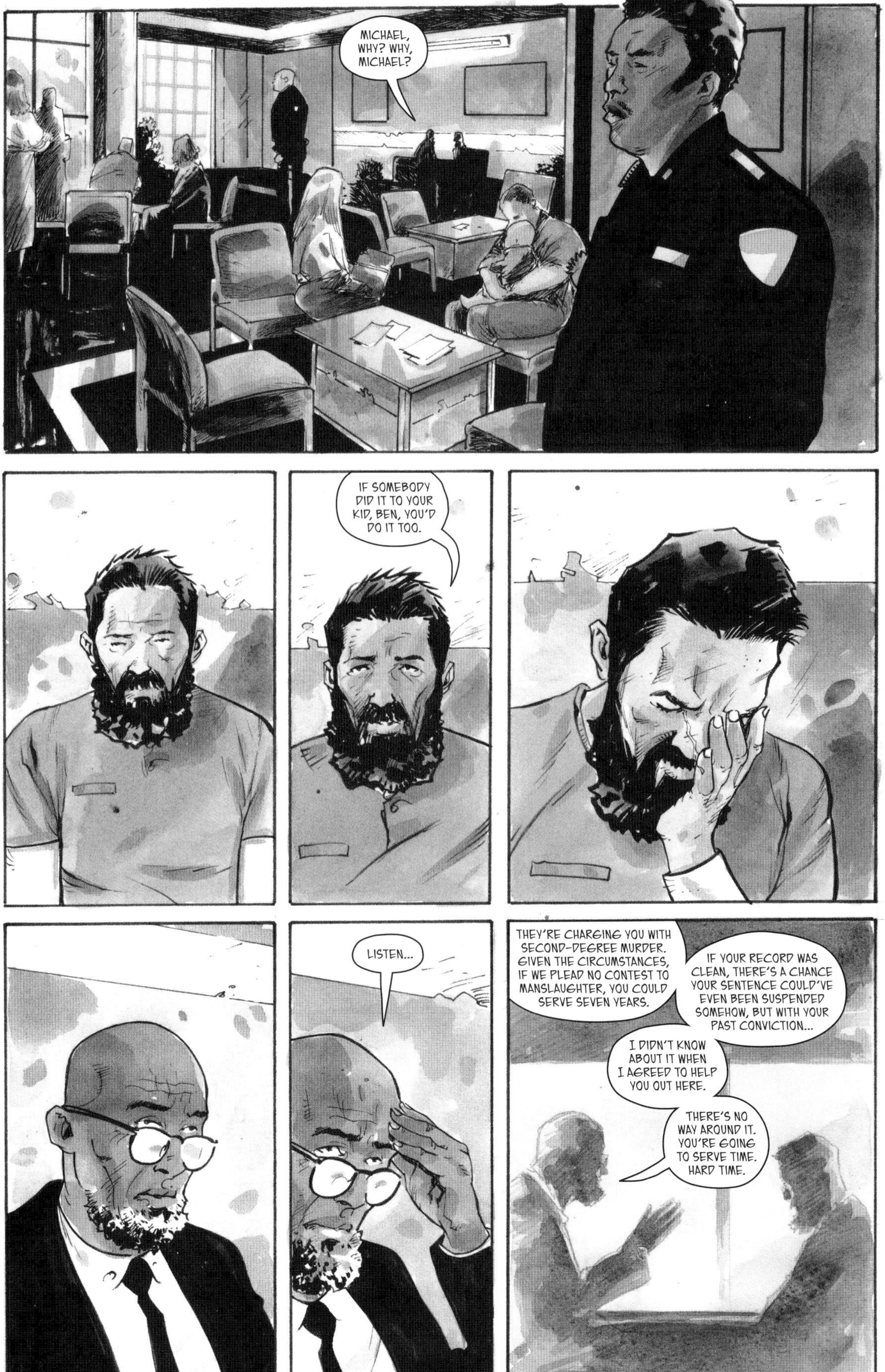
MICHAEL, WHY? WHY, MICHAEL?
IF SOMEBODY DID IT TO YOUR KID, BEN, YOU'D DO IT TOO.
LISTEN...
THEY'RE CHARGING YOU WITH SECOND-DEGREE MURDER. GIVEN THE CIRCUMSTANCES, IF WE PLEAD NO CONTEST TO MANSLAUGHTER, YOU COULD SERVE SEVEN YEARS.
IF YOUR RECORD WAS CLEAN, THERE'S A CHANCE YOUR SENTENCE COULD'VE EVEN BEEN SUSPENDED SOMEHOW, BUT WITH YOUR PAST CONVICTION...
I DIDN'T KNOW ABOUT IT WHEN I AGREED TO HELP YOU OUT HERE.
THERE'S NO WAY AROUND IT. YOU'RE GOING TO SERVE TIME. HARD TIME.

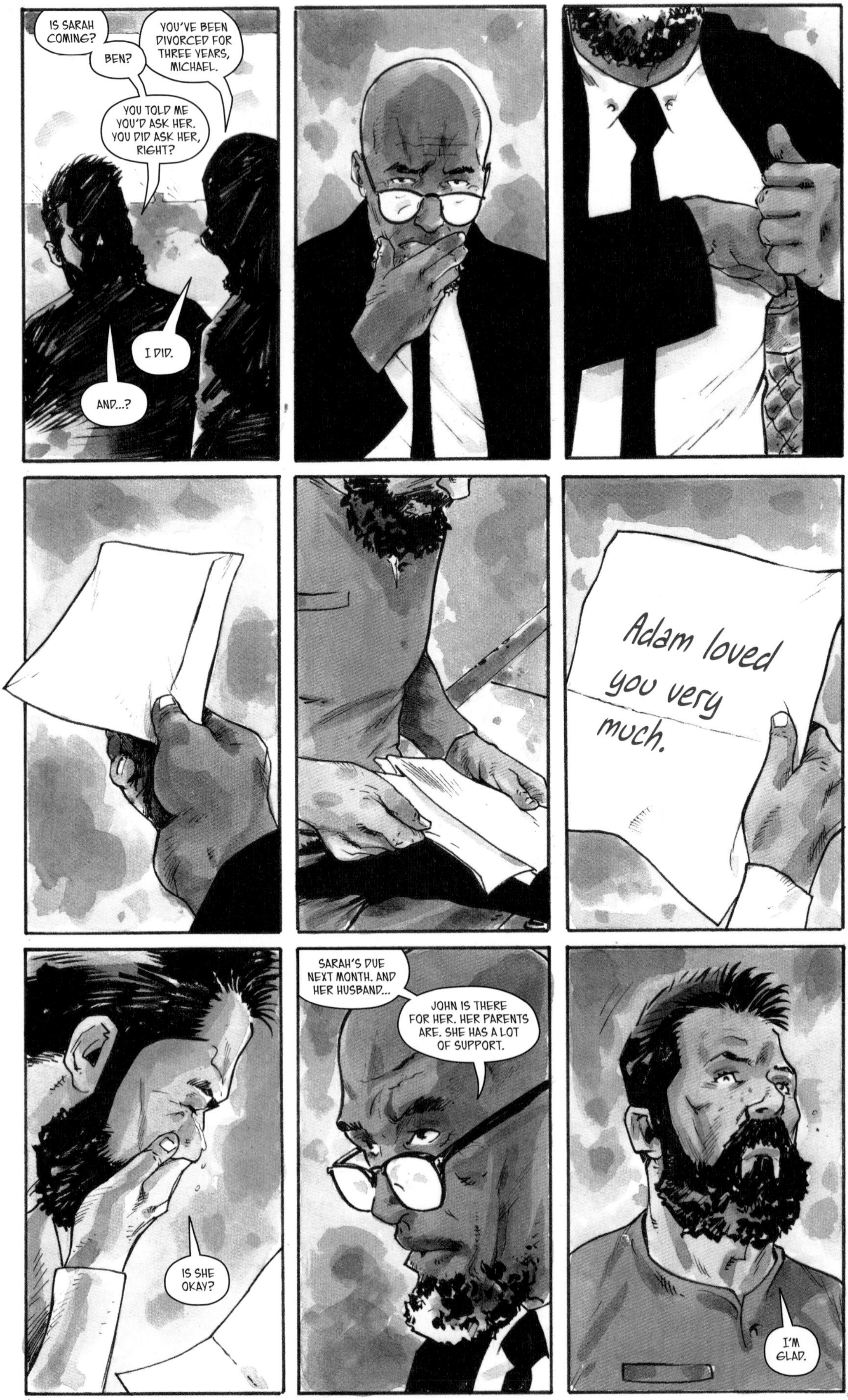
IS SARAH COMING?
BEN?
YOU'VE BEEN DIVORCED FOR THREE YEARS, MICHAEL.
YOU TOLD ME YOU'D ASK HER. YOU DID ASK HER, RIGHT?
I DID.
AND...?
Adam loved you very much.
IS SHE OKAY?
SARAH'S DUE NEXT MONTH. AND HER HUSBAND...
JOHN IS THERE FOR HER. HER PARENTS ARE. SHE HAS A LOT OF SUPPORT.
I'M GLAD.

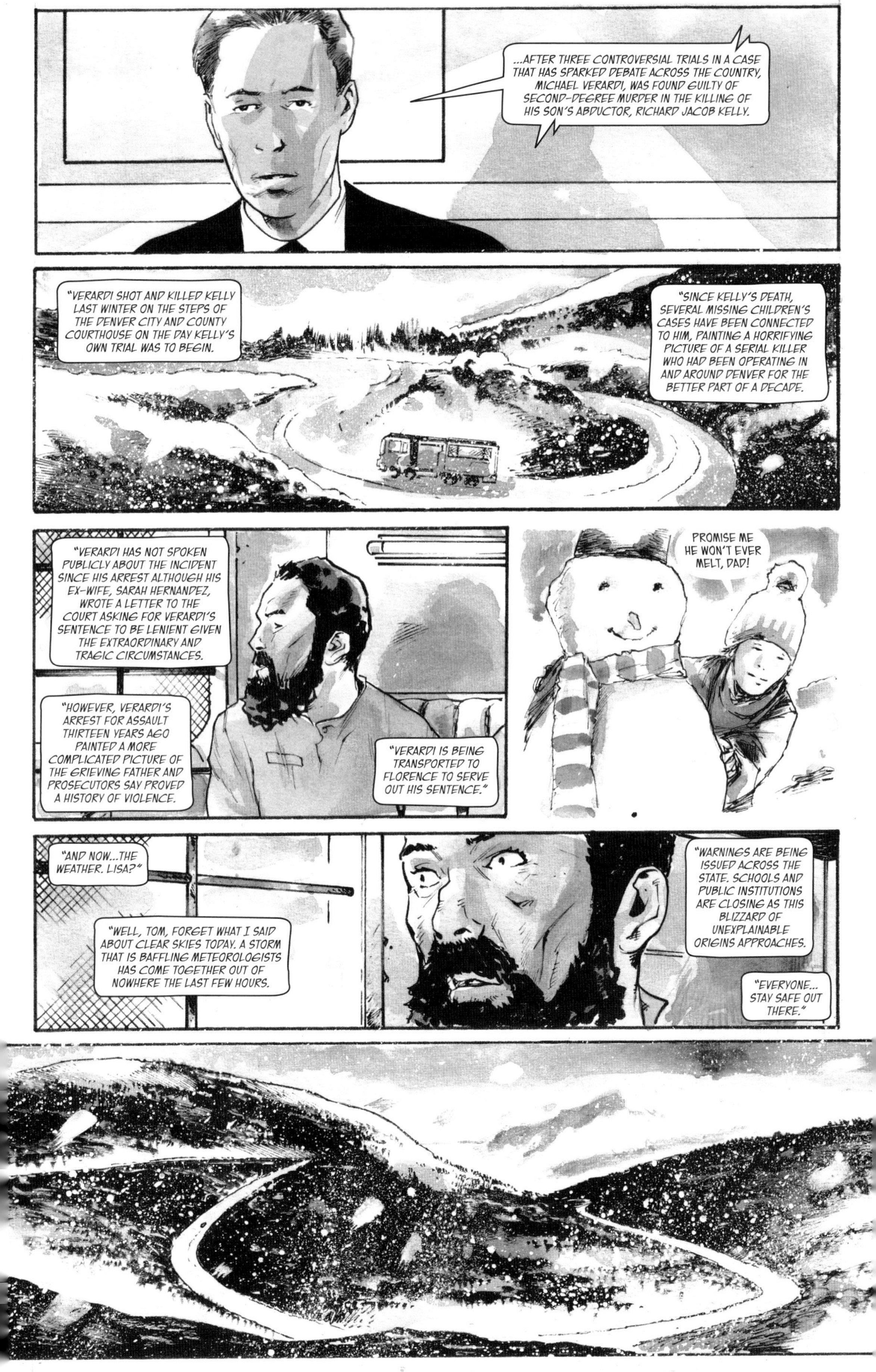
...AFTER THREE CONTROVERSIAL TRIALS IN A CASE THAT HAS SPARKED DEBATE ACROSS THE COUNTRY, MICHAEL VERARDI, WAS FOUND GUILTY OF SECOND-DEGREE MURDER IN THE KILLING OF HIS SON'S ABDUCTOR, RICHARD JACOB KELLY.
"VERARDI SHOT AND KILLED KELLY LAST WINTER ON THE STEPS OF THE DENVER CITY AND COUNTY COURTHOUSE ON THE DAY KELLY'S OWN TRIAL WAS TO BEGIN.
"SINCE KELLY'S DEATH, SEVERAL MISSING CHILDREN'S CASES HAVE BEEN CONNECTED TO HIM, PAINTING A HORRIFYING PICTURE OF A SERIAL KILLER WHO HAD BEEN OPERATING IN AND AROUND DENVER FOR THE BETTER PART OF A DECADE.
"VERARDI HAS NOT SPOKEN PUBLICLY ABOUT THE INCIDENT SINCE HIS ARREST ALTHOUGH HIS EX-WIFE, SARAH HERNANDEZ, WROTE A LETTER TO THE COURT ASKING FOR VERARDI'S SENTENCE TO BE LENIENT GIVEN THE EXTRAORDINARY AND TRAGIC CIRCUMSTANCES.
"HOWEVER, VERARDI'S ARREST FOR ASSAULT THIRTEEN YEARS AGO PAINTED A MORE COMPLICATED PICTURE OF THE GRIEVING FATHER AND PROSECUTORS SAY PROVED A HISTORY OF VIOLENCE.
"VERARDI IS BEING TRANSPORTED TO FLORENCE TO SERVE OUT HIS SENTENCE."
PROMISE ME HE WON'T EVER MELT, DAD!
"AND NOW...THE WEATHER. LISA?"
"WELL, TOM, FORGET WHAT I SAID ABOUT CLEAR SKIES TODAY. A STORM THAT IS BAFFLING METEOROLOGISTS HAS COME TOGETHER OUT OF NOWHERE THE LAST FEW HOURS.
"WARNINGS ARE BEING ISSUED ACROSS THE STATE. SCHOOLS AND PUBLIC INSTITUTIONS ARE CLOSING AS THIS BLIZZARD OF UNEXPLAINABLE ORIGINS APPROACHES.
"EVERYONE... STAY SAFE OUT THERE."

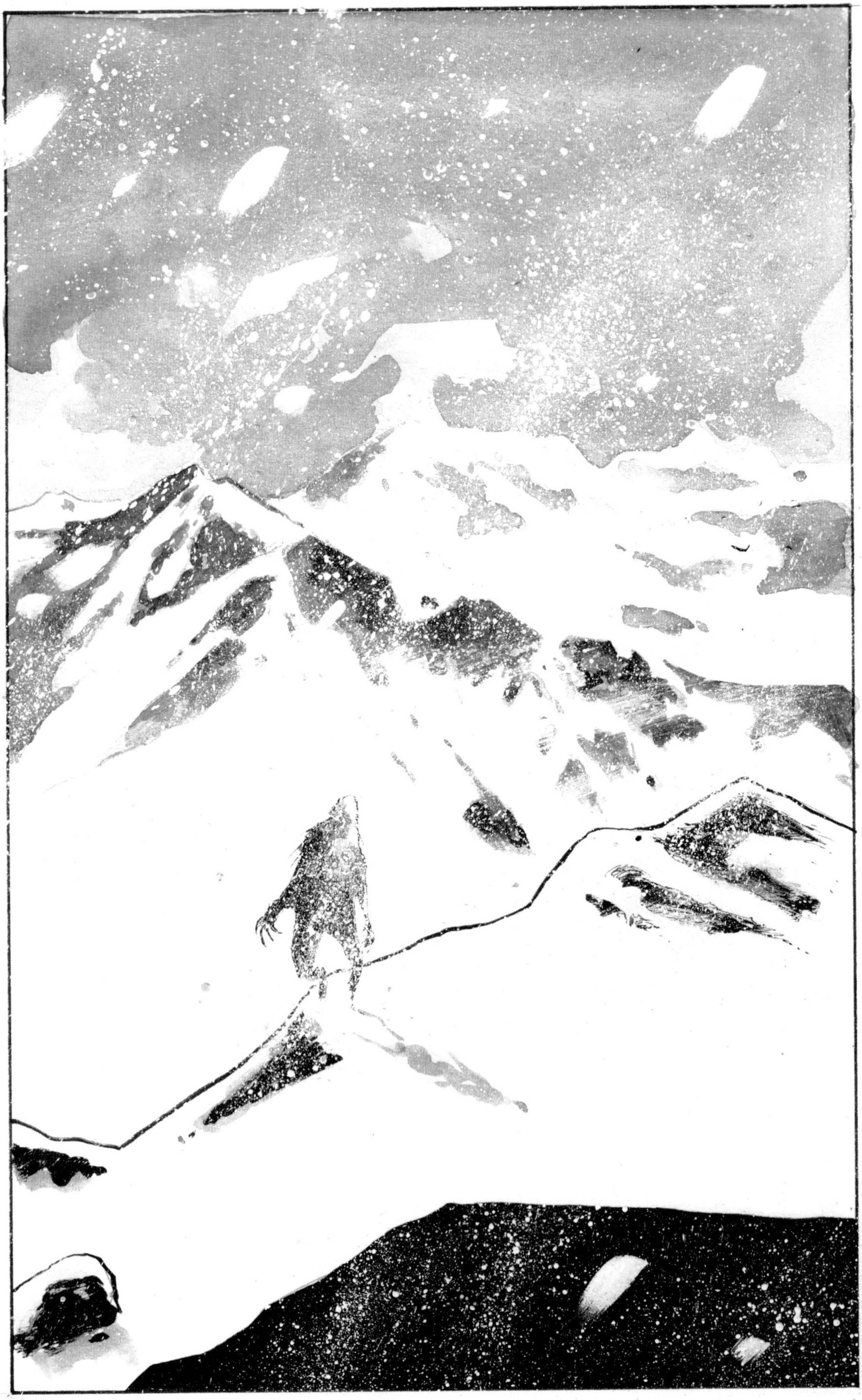

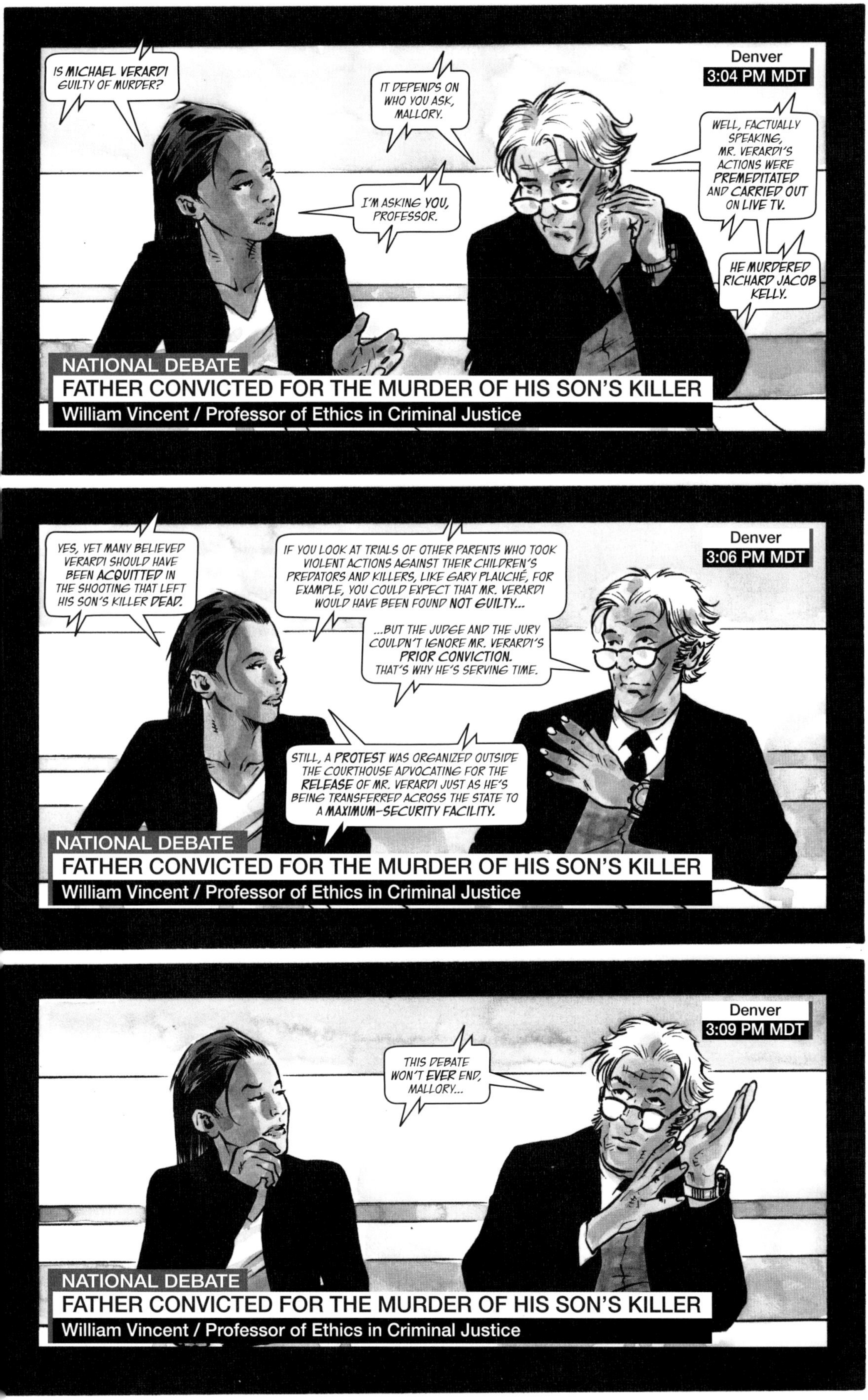

IS MICHAEL VERARDI GUILTY OF MURDER?
IT DEPENDS ON WHO YOU ASK, MALLORY.
I'M ASKING YOU, PROFESSOR.
Denver
3:04 PM MDT
WELL, FACTUALLY SPEAKING, MR. VERARDI'S ACTIONS WERE PREMEDITATED AND CARRIED OUT ON LIVE TV.
HE MURDERED RICHARD JACOB KELLY.
NATIONAL DEBATE
FATHER CONVICTED FOR THE MURDER OF HIS SON'S KILLER
William Vincent / Professor of Ethics in Criminal Justice
YES, YET MANY BELIEVED VERARDI SHOULD HAVE BEEN ACQUITTED IN THE SHOOTING THAT LEFT HIS SON'S KILLER DEAD.
IF YOU LOOK AT TRIALS OF OTHER PARENTS WHO TOOK VIOLENT ACTIONS AGAINST THEIR CHILDREN'S PREDATORS AND KILLERS, LIKE GARY PLAUCHÉ, FOR EXAMPLE, YOU COULD EXPECT THAT MR. VERARDI WOULD HAVE BEEN FOUND NOT GUILTY...
...BUT THE JUDGE AND THE JURY COULDN'T IGNORE MR. VERARDI'S PRIOR CONVICTION. THAT'S WHY HE'S SERVING TIME.
Denver
3:06 PM MDT
STILL, A PROTEST WAS ORGANIZED OUTSIDE THE COURTHOUSE ADVOCATING FOR THE RELEASE OF MR. VERARDI JUST AS HE'S BEING TRANSFERRED ACROSS THE STATE TO A MAXIMUM-SECURITY FACILITY.
NATIONAL DEBATE
FATHER CONVICTED FOR THE MURDER OF HIS SON'S KILLER
William Vincent / Professor of Ethics in Criminal Justice
Denver
3:09 PM MDT
THIS DEBATE WON'T EVER END, MALLORY...
NATIONAL DEBATE
FATHER CONVICTED FOR THE MURDER OF HIS SON'S KILLER
William Vincent / Professor of Ethics in Criminal Justice

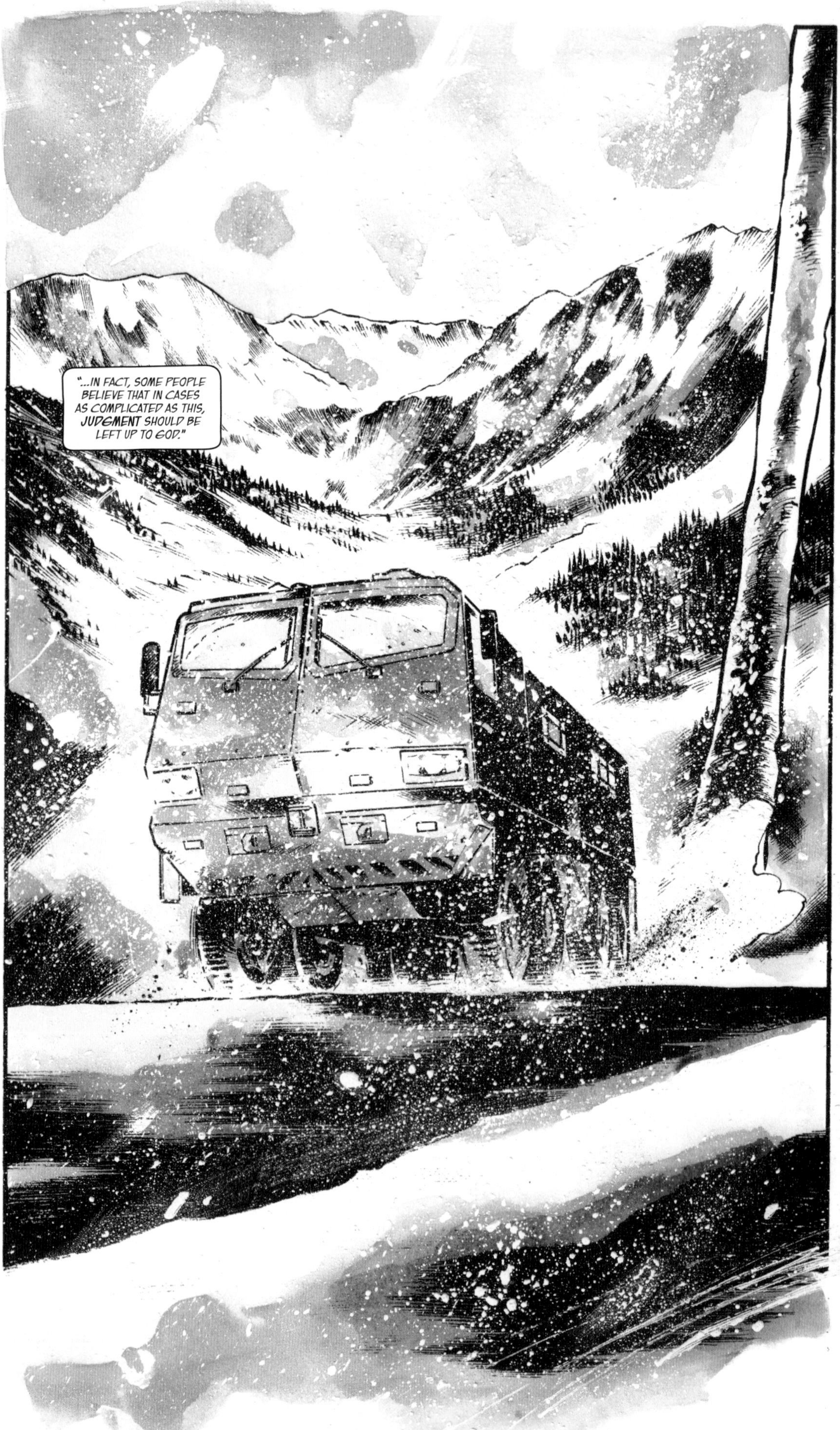
"...IN FACT, SOME PEOPLE BELIEVE THAT IN CASES AS COMPLICATED AS THIS, JUDGMENT SHOULD BE LEFT UP TO GOD."

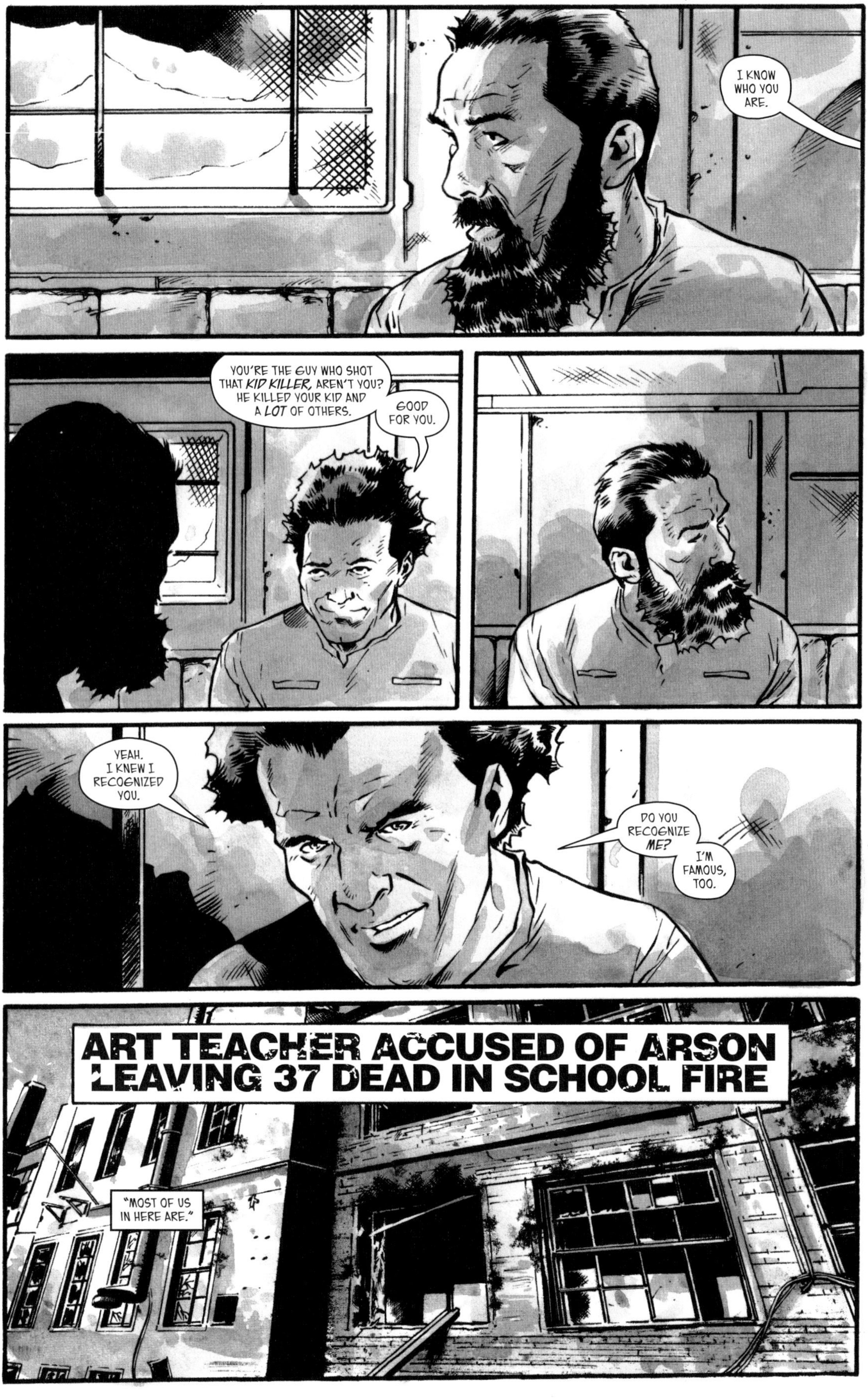
I KNOW WHO YOU ARE.
YOU'RE THE GUY WHO SHOT THAT KID KILLER, AREN'T YOU? HE KILLED YOUR KID AND A LOT OF OTHERS.
GOOD FOR YOU.
YEAH. I KNEW I RECOGNIZED YOU.
DO YOU RECOGNIZE ME?
I'M FAMOUS, TOO.
ART TEACHER ACCUSED OF ARSON LEAVING 37 DEAD IN SCHOOL FIRE
"MOST OF US IN HERE ARE."

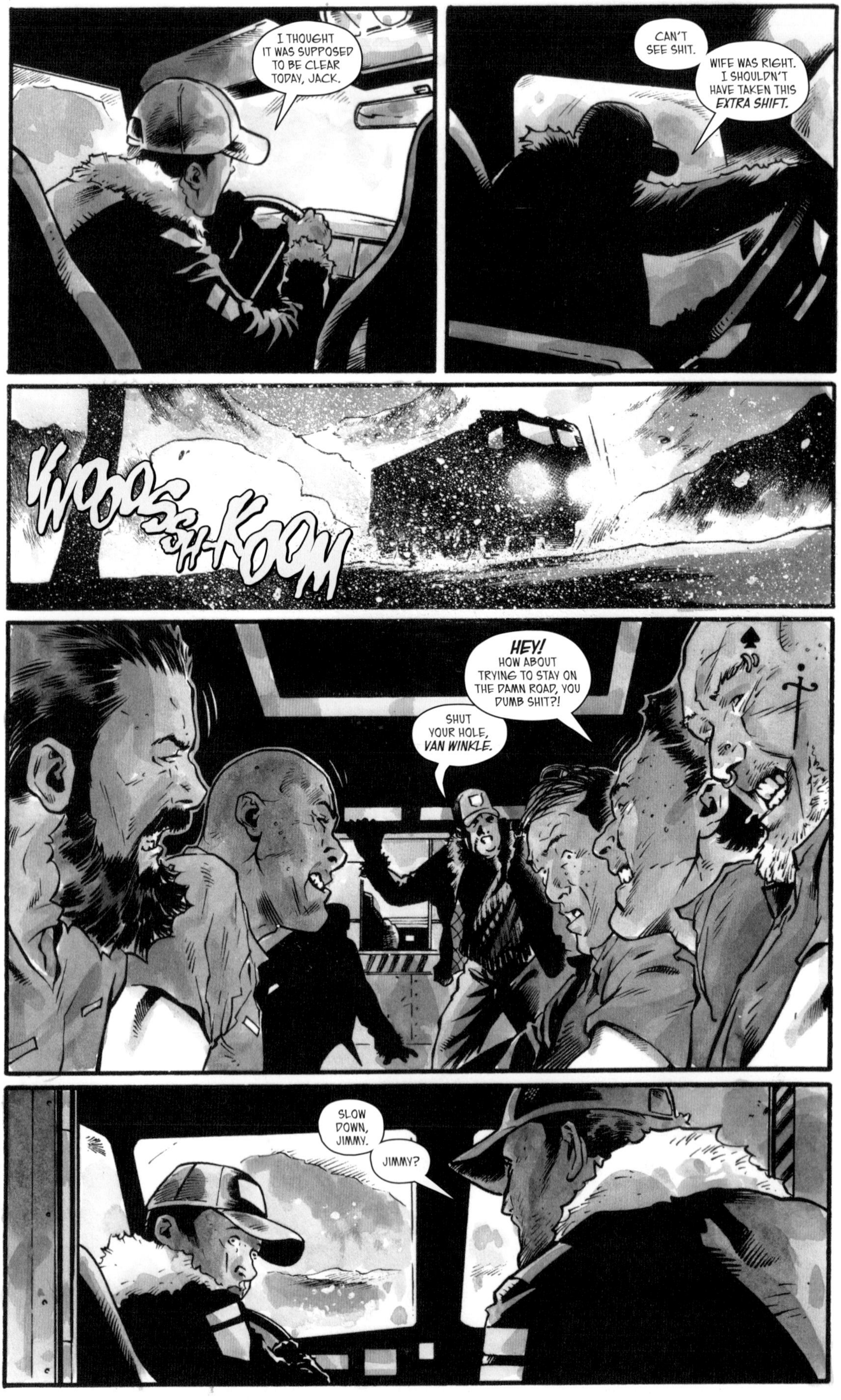
I THOUGHT IT WAS SUPPOSED TO BE CLEAR TODAY, JACK.
CAN'T SEE SHIT.
WIFE WAS RIGHT. I SHOULDN'T HAVE TAKEN THIS EXTRA SHIFT.
KWOOSSH-KOOM
HEY! HOW ABOUT TRYING TO STAY ON THE DAMN ROAD, YOU DUMB SHIT?!
SHUT YOUR HOLE, VAN WINKLE.
SLOW DOWN, JIMMY.
JIMMY?

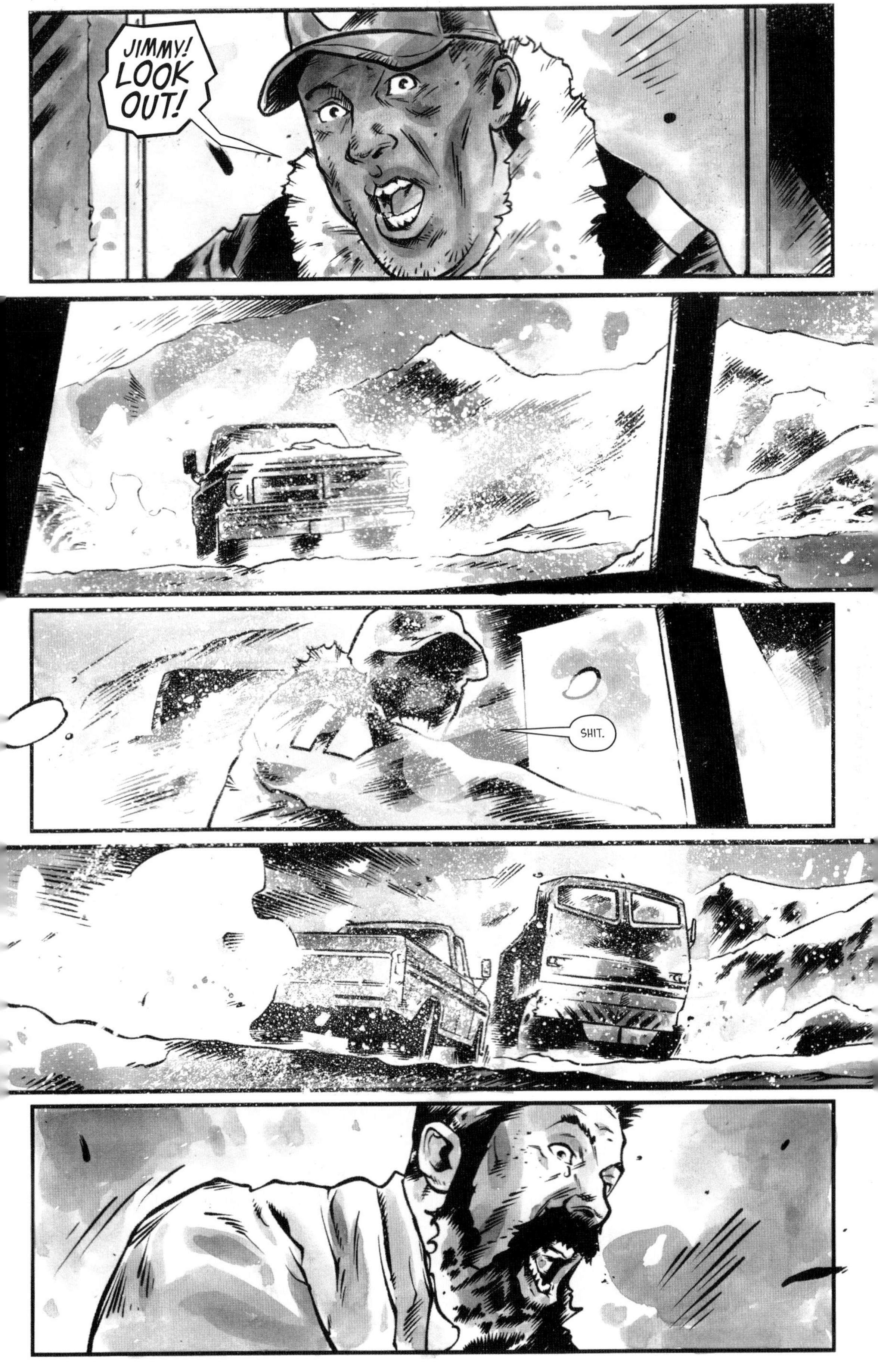
JIMMY! LOOK OUT!
SHIT.

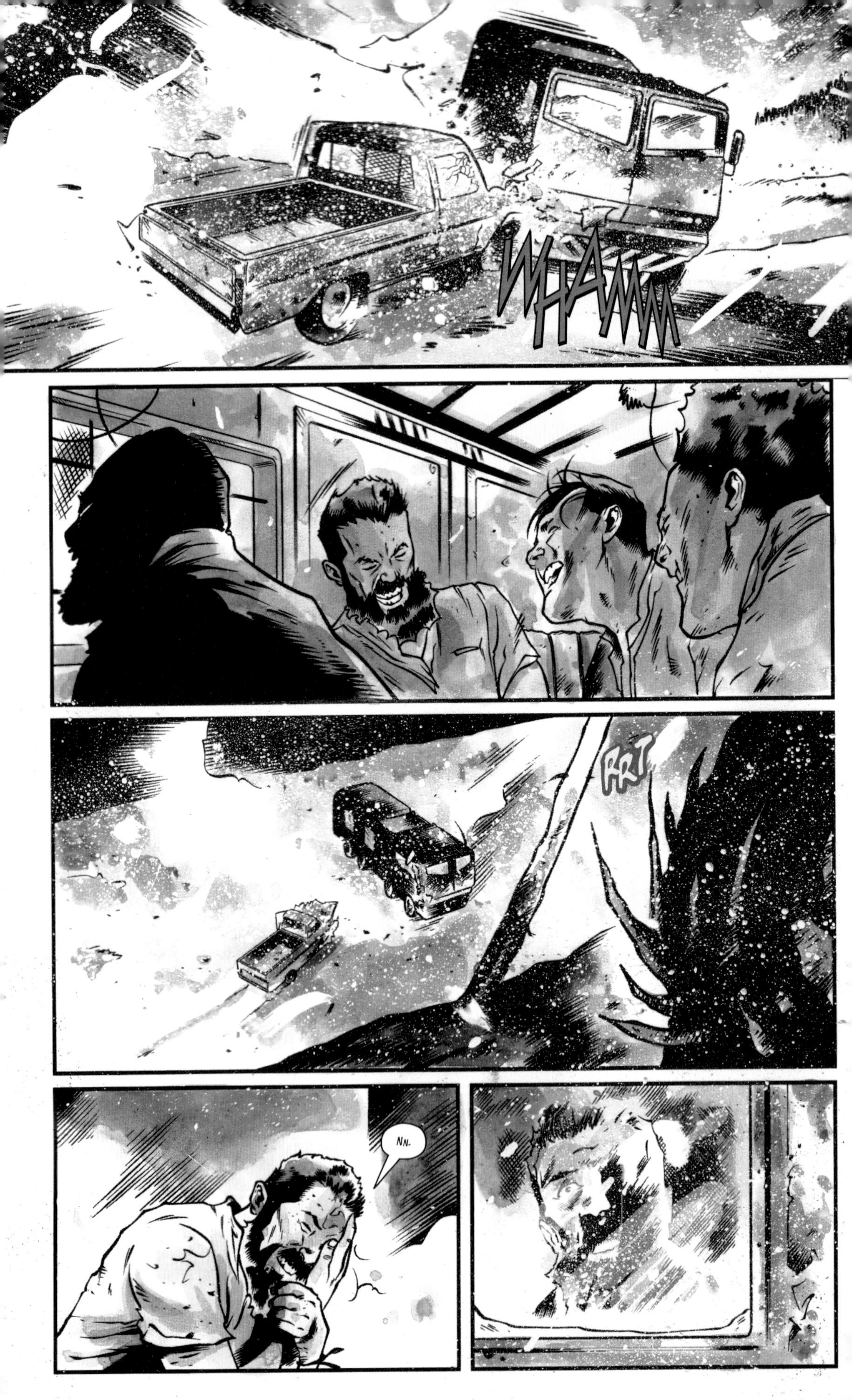
WHAMM
RRT
NN.

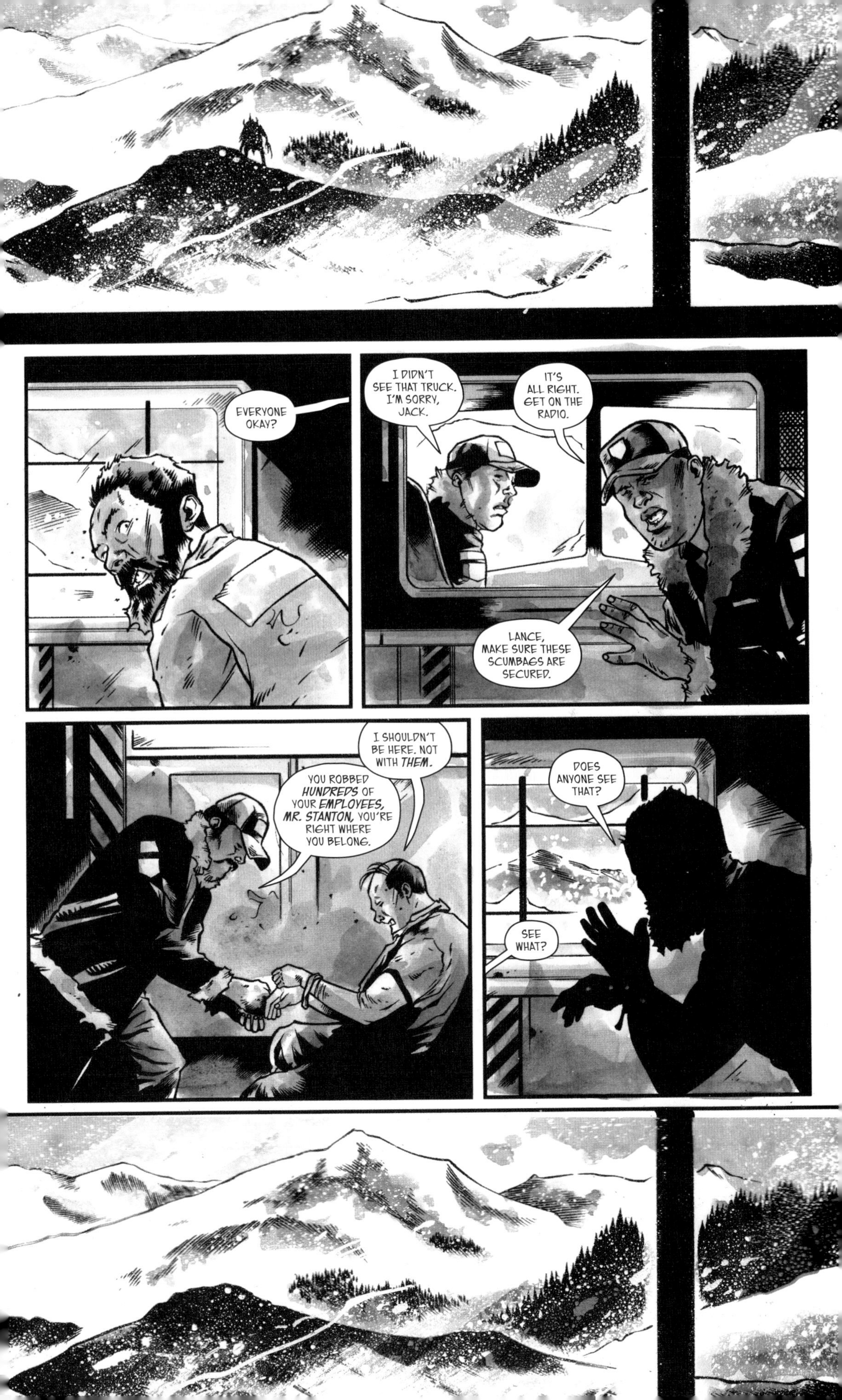
EVERYONE OKAY?
I DIDN'T SEE THAT TRUCK. I'M SORRY, JACK.
IT'S ALL RIGHT. GET ON THE RADIO.
LANCE, MAKE SURE THESE SCUMBAGS ARE SECURED.
I SHOULDN'T BE HERE. NOT WITH THEM.
YOU ROBBED HUNDREDS OF YOUR EMPLOYEES, MR. STANTON, YOU'RE RIGHT WHERE YOU BELONG.
DOES ANYONE SEE THAT?
SEE WHAT?

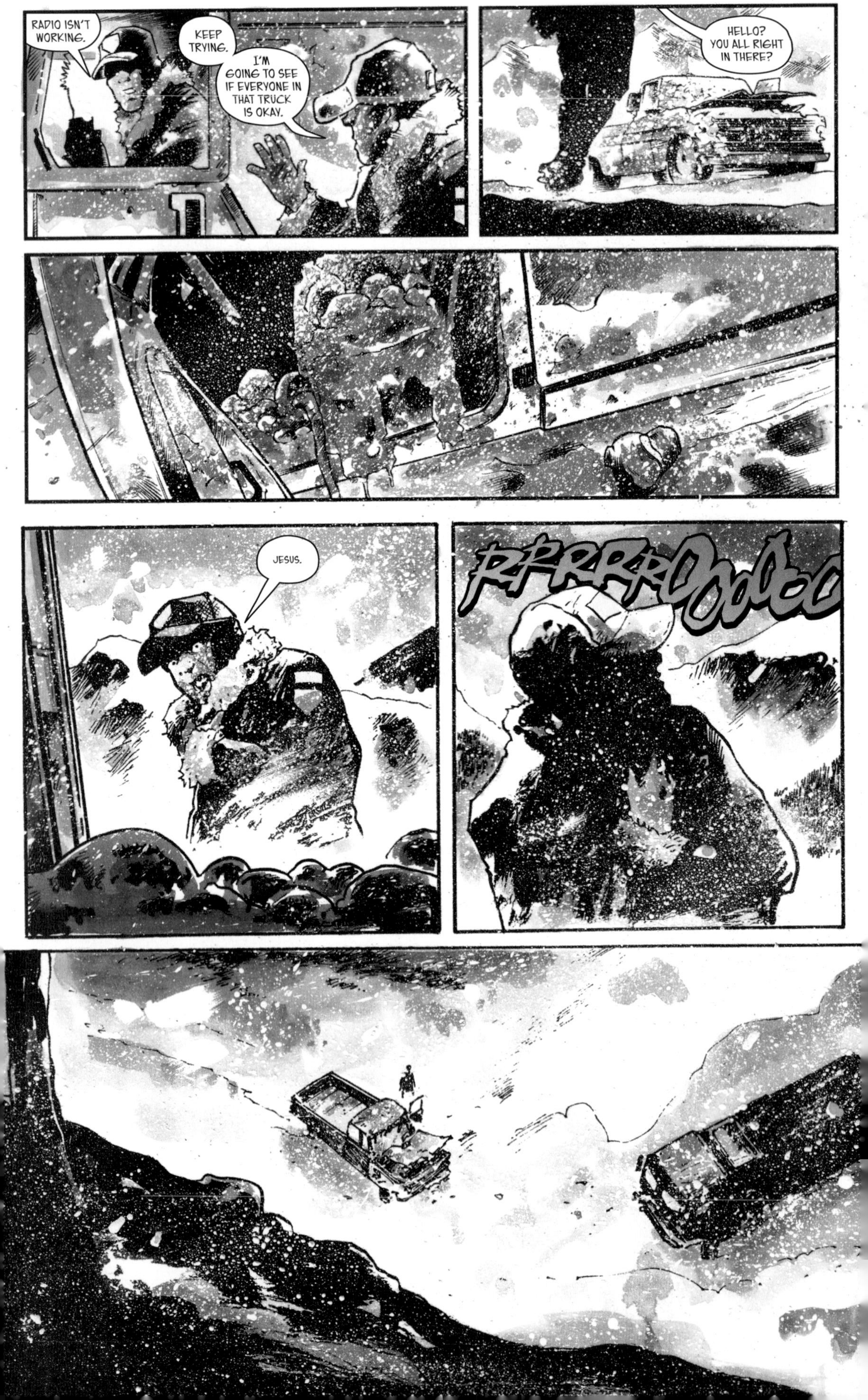
RADIO ISN'T WORKING.
KEEP TRYING.
I'M GOING TO SEE IF EVERYONE IN THAT TRUCK IS OKAY.
HELLO? YOU ALL RIGHT IN THERE?
JESUS.
RRRRROOOOOO

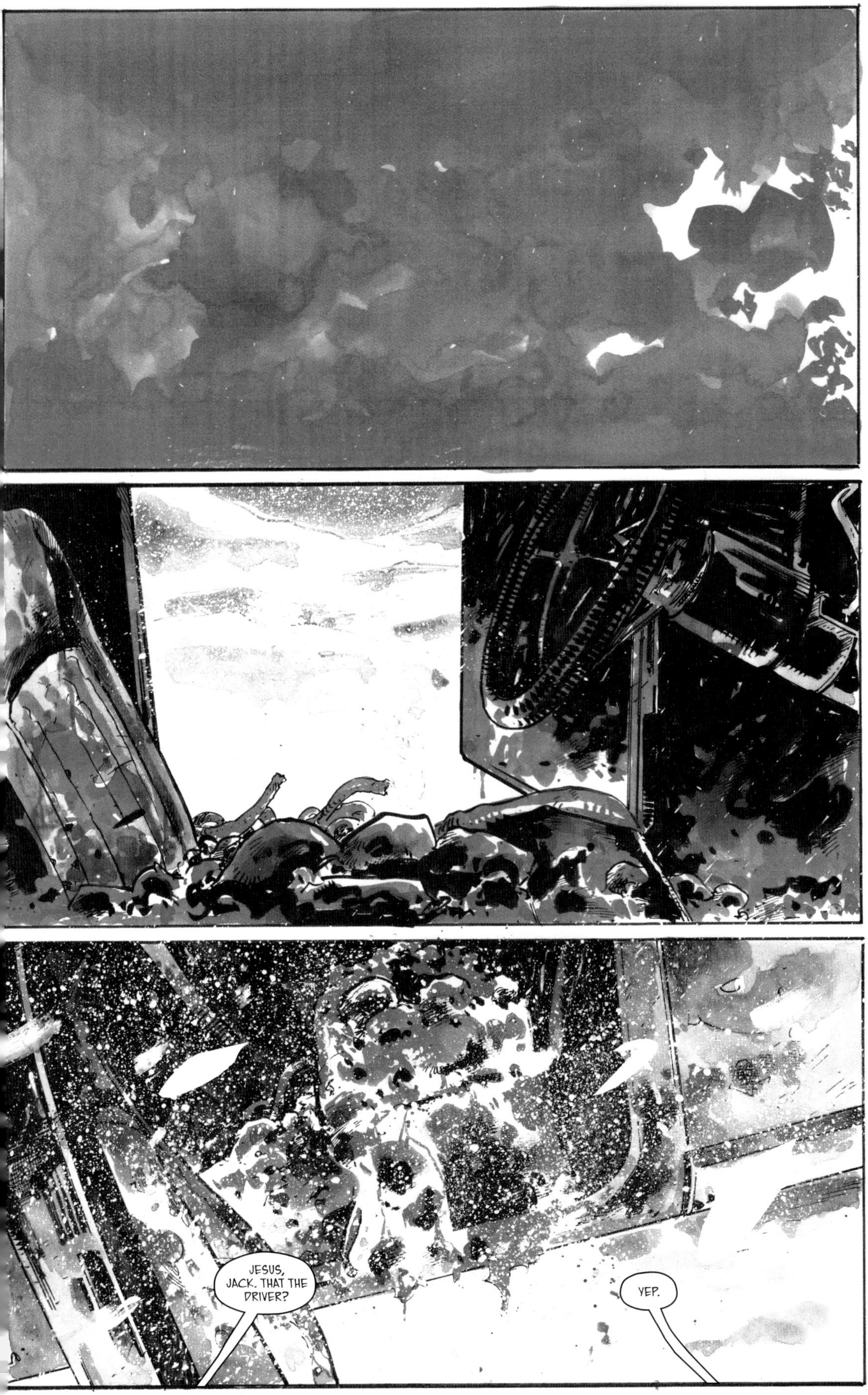
JESUS, JACK. THAT THE DRIVER?
YEP.

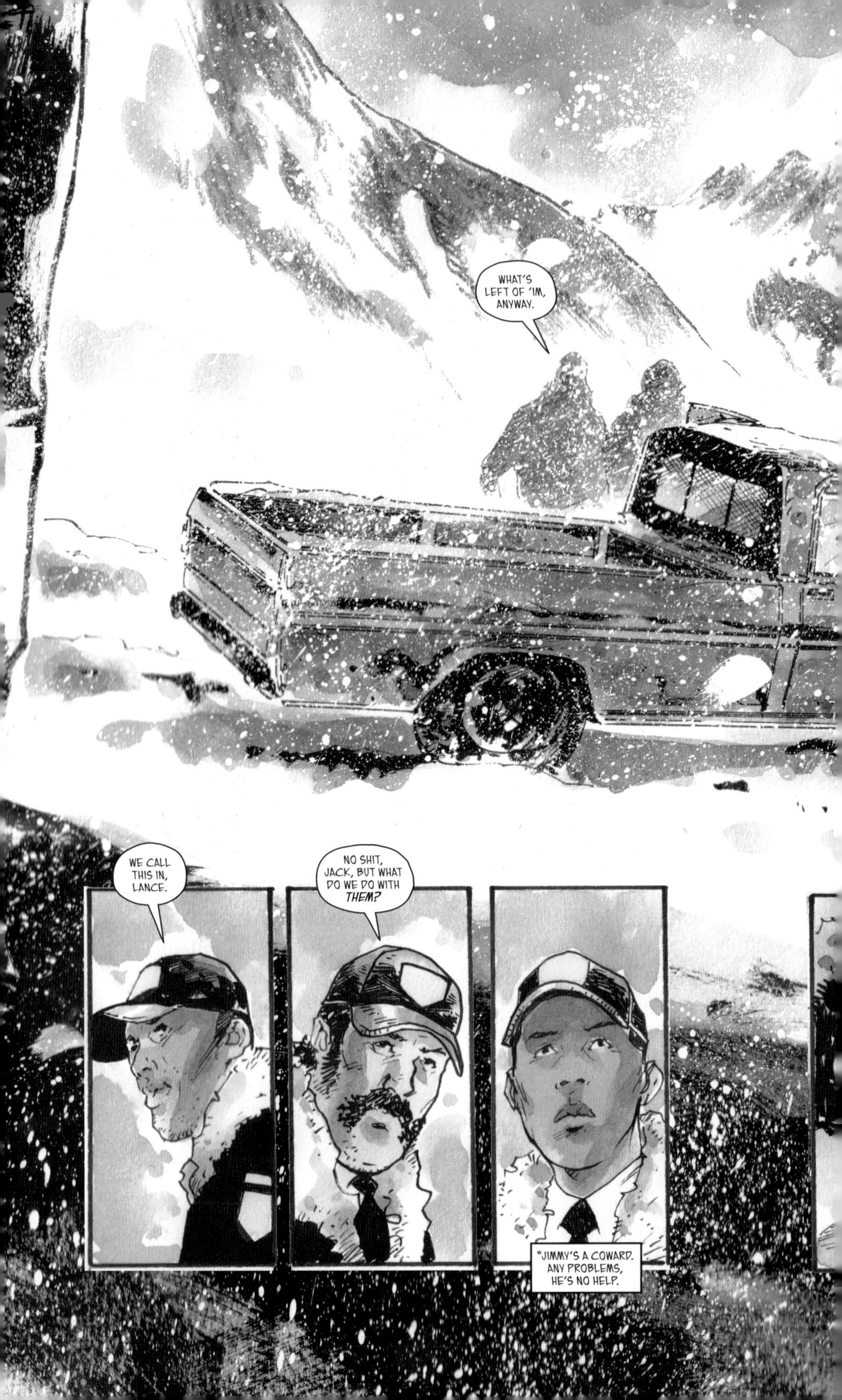
WHAT'S LEFT OF 'IM, ANYWAY.
WE CALL THIS IN, LANCE.
NO SHIT, JACK, BUT WHAT DO WE DO WITH *THEM?*
"JIMMY'S A COWARD. ANY PROBLEMS, HE'S NO HELP.

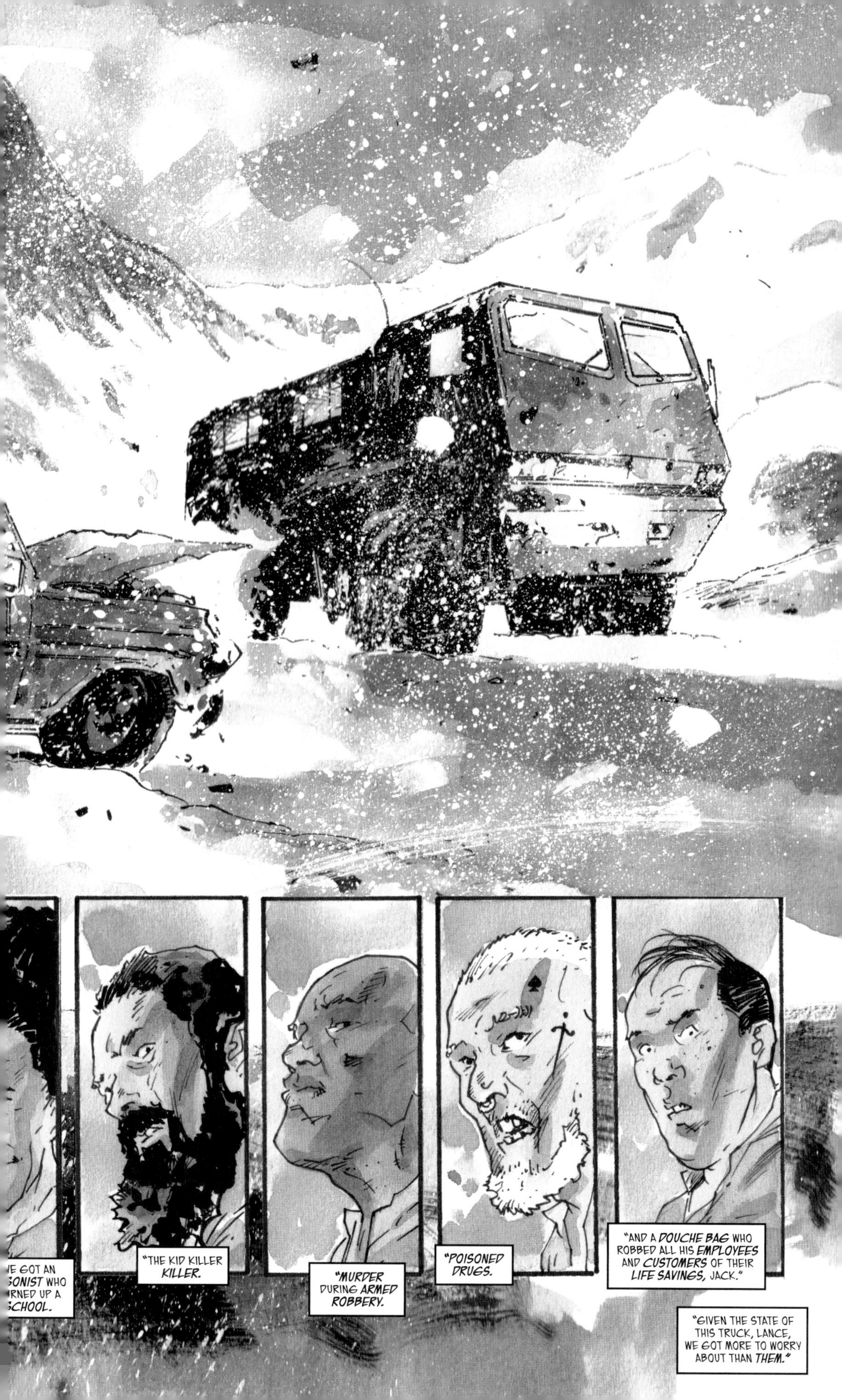
E GOT AN SONIST WHO RNED UP A SCHOOL.
"THE KID KILLER KILLER.
"MURDER DURING ARMED ROBBERY.
"POISONED DRUGS.
"AND A DOUCHE BAG WHO ROBBED ALL HIS EMPLOYEES AND CUSTOMERS OF THEIR LIFE SAVINGS, JACK."
"GIVEN THE STATE OF THIS TRUCK, LANCE, WE GOT MORE TO WORRY ABOUT THAN THEM."

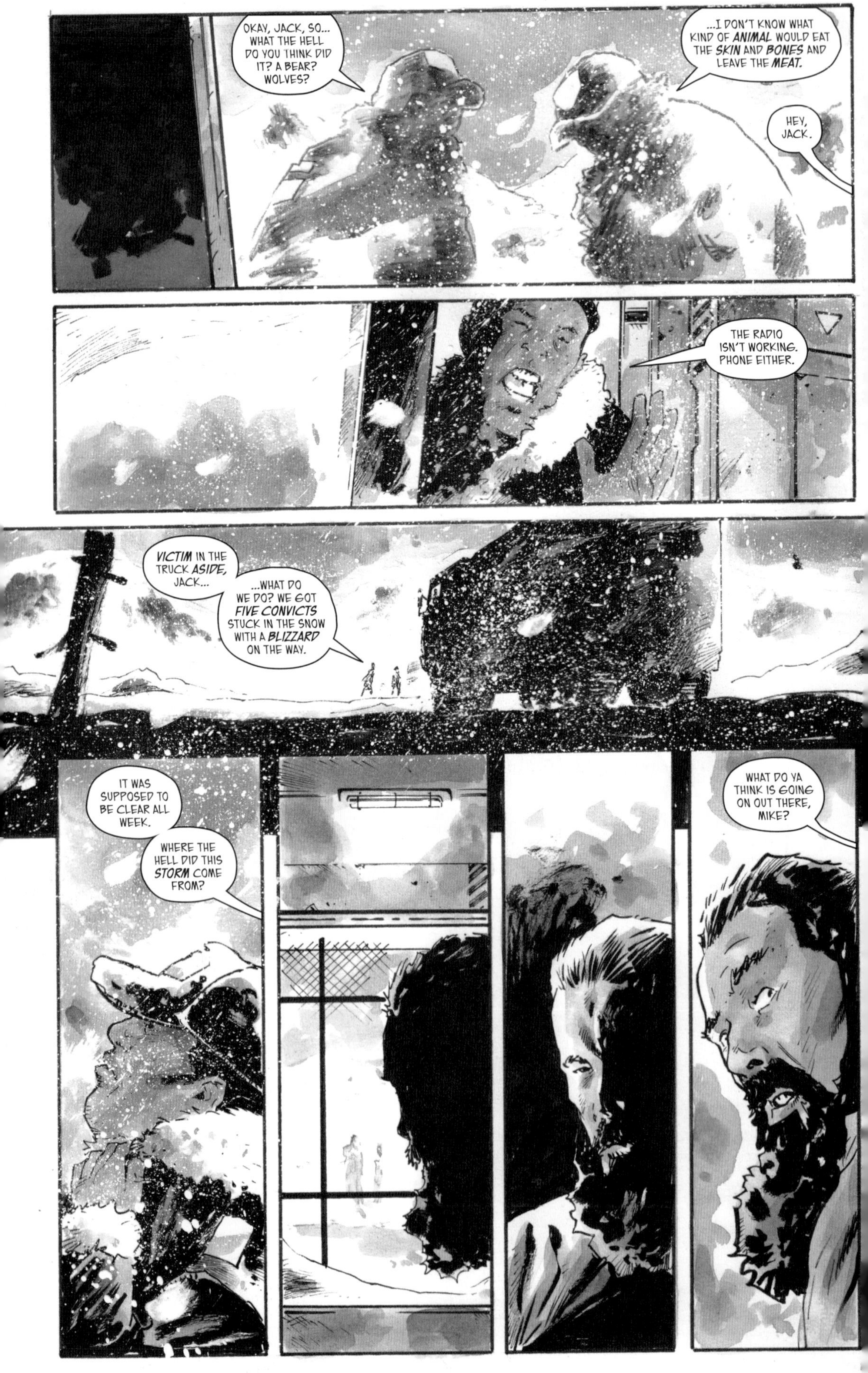
OKAY, JACK, SO... WHAT THE HELL DO YOU THINK DID IT? A BEAR? WOLVES?
...I DON'T KNOW WHAT KIND OF ANIMAL WOULD EAT THE SKIN AND BONES AND LEAVE THE MEAT.
HEY, JACK.
THE RADIO ISN'T WORKING. PHONE EITHER.
VICTIM IN THE TRUCK ASIDE, JACK...
...WHAT DO WE DO? WE GOT FIVE CONVICTS STUCK IN THE SNOW WITH A BLIZZARD ON THE WAY.
IT WAS SUPPOSED TO BE CLEAR ALL WEEK.
WHERE THE HELL DID THIS STORM COME FROM?
WHAT DO YA THINK IS GOING ON OUT THERE, MIKE?

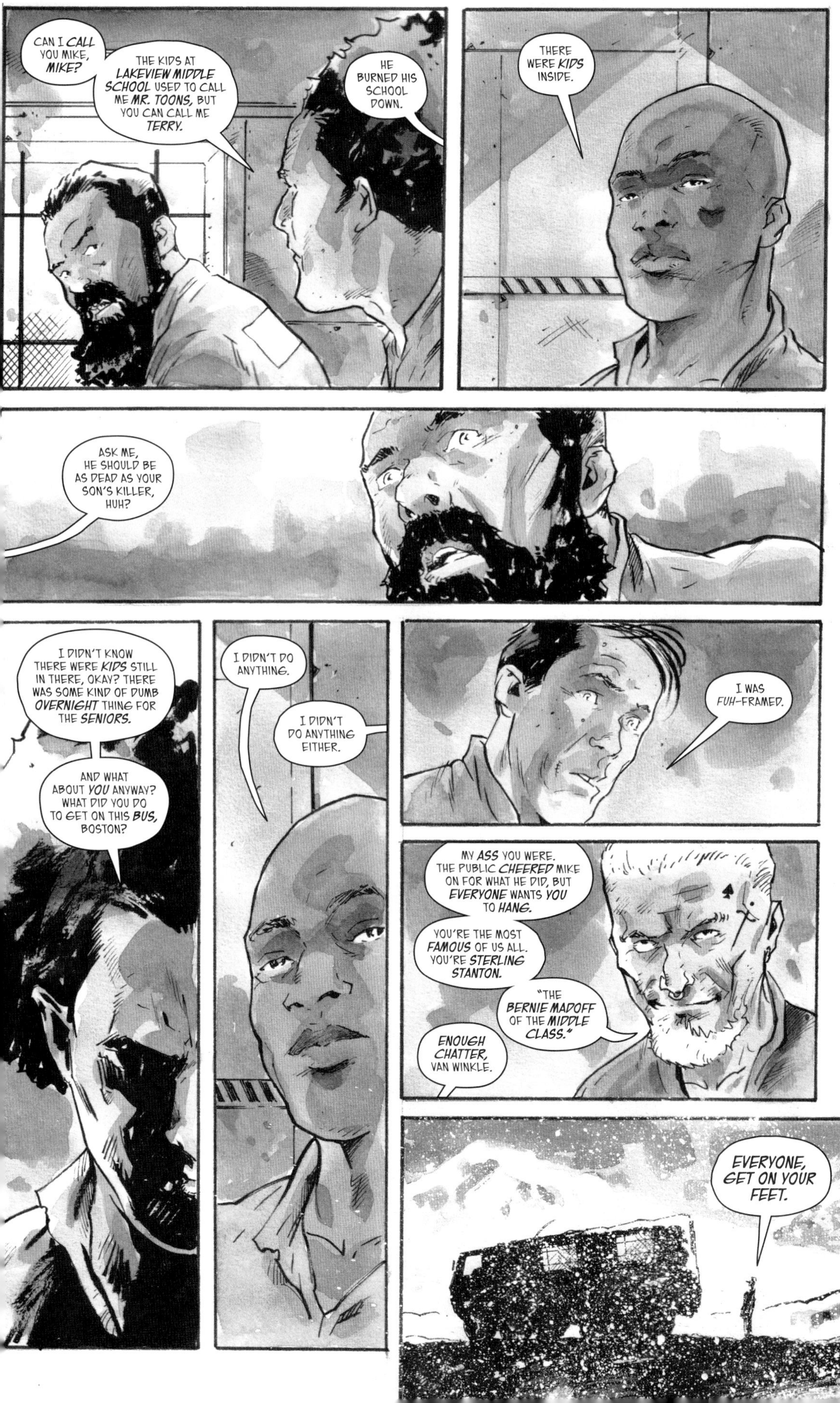
CAN I CALL YOU MIKE, MIKE?
THE KIDS AT LAKEVIEW MIDDLE SCHOOL USED TO CALL ME MR. TOONS, BUT YOU CAN CALL ME TERRY.
HE BURNED HIS SCHOOL DOWN.
THERE WERE KIDS INSIDE.
ASK ME, HE SHOULD BE AS DEAD AS YOUR SON'S KILLER, HUH?
I DIDN'T KNOW THERE WERE KIDS STILL IN THERE, OKAY? THERE WAS SOME KIND OF DUMB OVERNIGHT THING FOR THE SENIORS.
AND WHAT ABOUT YOU ANYWAY? WHAT DID YOU DO TO GET ON THIS BUS, BOSTON?
I DIDN'T DO ANYTHING.
I DIDN'T DO ANYTHING EITHER.
I WAS FUH-FRAMED.
MY ASS YOU WERE. THE PUBLIC CHEERED MIKE ON FOR WHAT HE DID, BUT EVERYONE WANTS YOU TO HANG.
YOU'RE THE MOST FAMOUS OF US ALL. YOU'RE STERLING STANTON.
"THE BERNIE MADOFF OF THE MIDDLE CLASS."
ENOUGH CHATTER, VAN WINKLE.
EVERYONE, GET ON YOUR FEET.

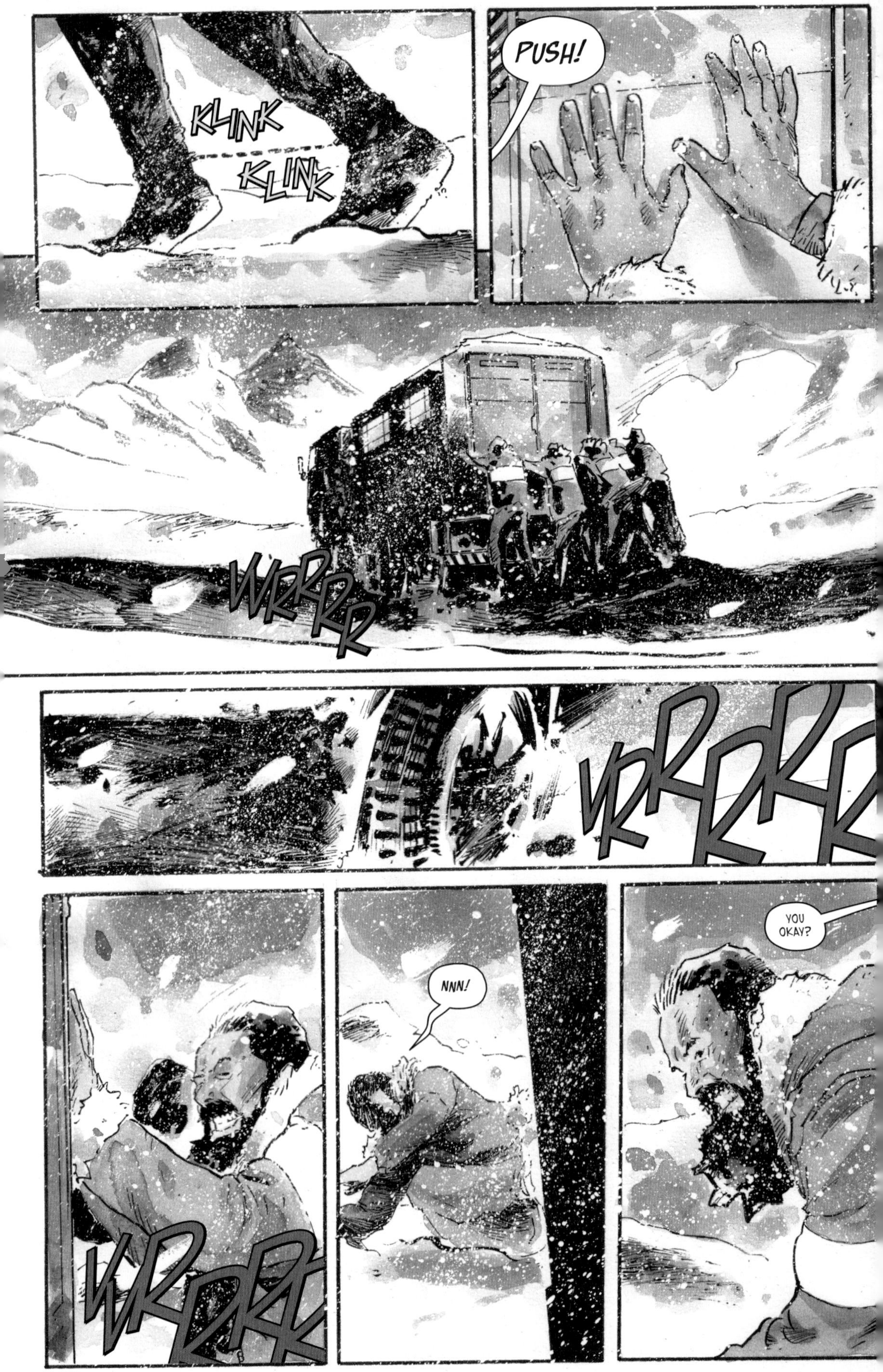
KLINK
KLINK
PUSH!
VRRRRR
VRRRRRR
VRRRRR
NNN!
YOU OKAY?

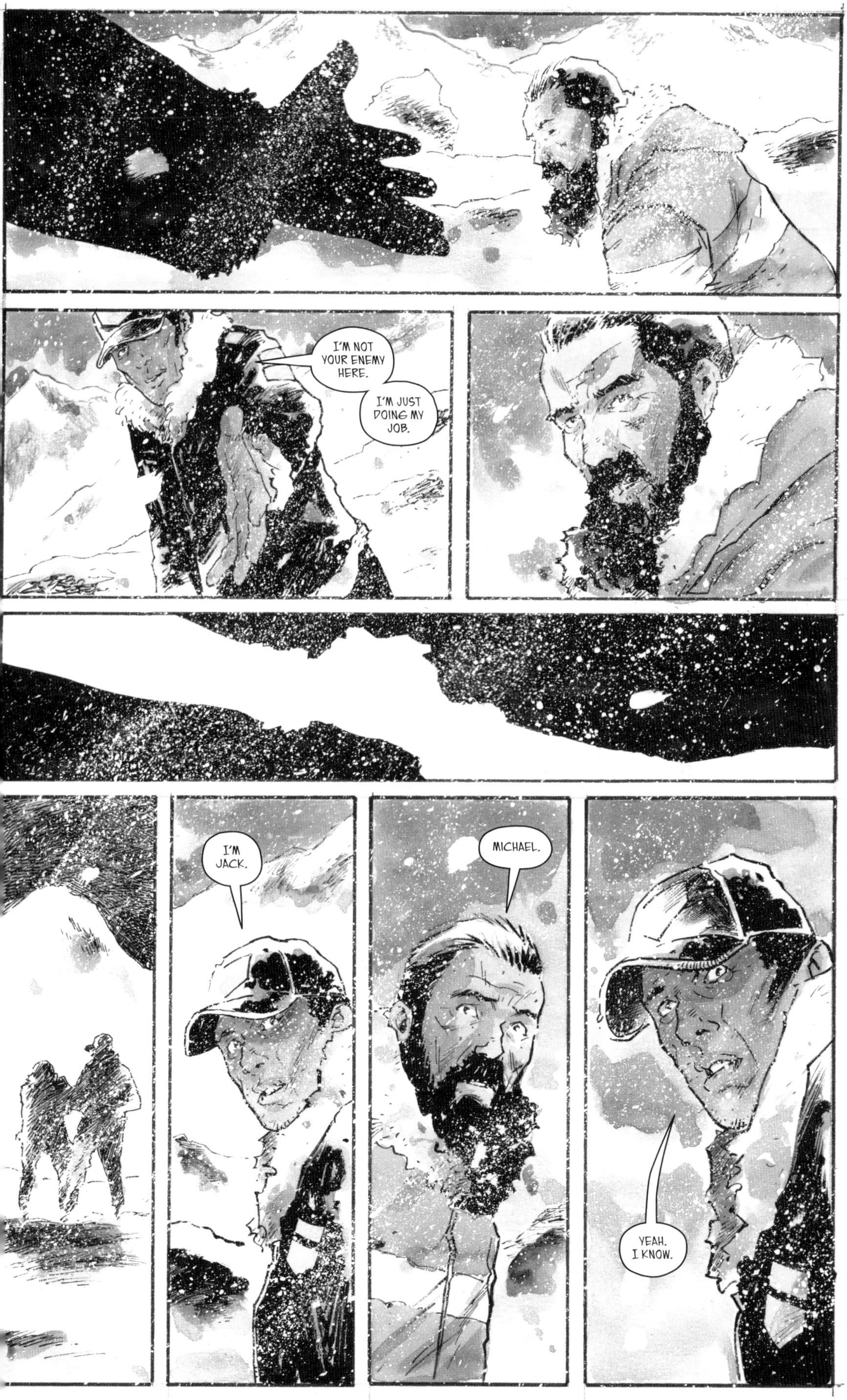
I'M NOT YOUR ENEMY HERE.
I'M JUST DOING MY JOB.
I'M JACK.
MICHAEL.
YEAH. I KNOW.

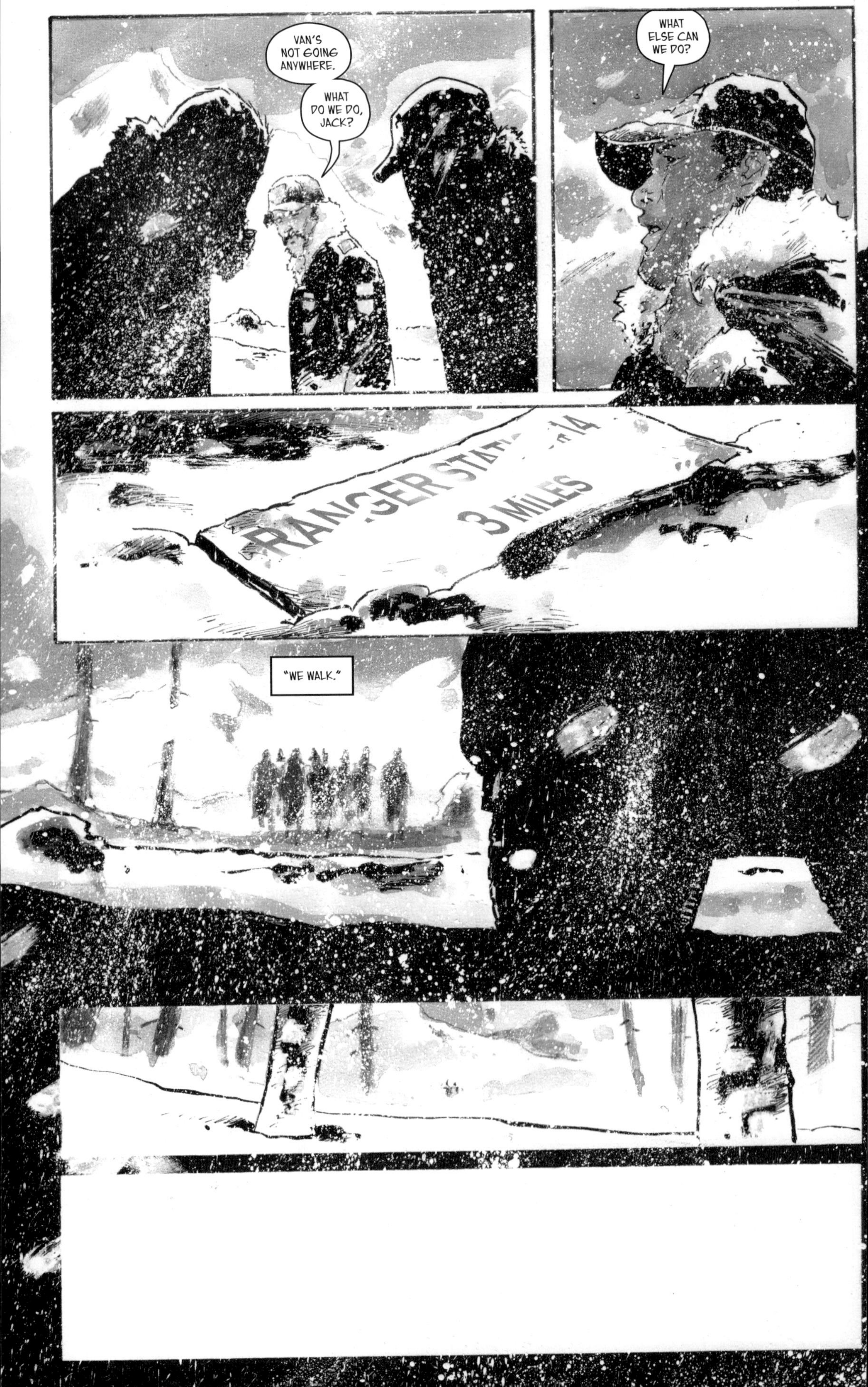
VAN'S NOT GOING ANYWHERE.
WHAT DO WE DO, JACK?
WHAT ELSE CAN WE DO?
RANGER STAT 14
3 MILES
"WE WALK."

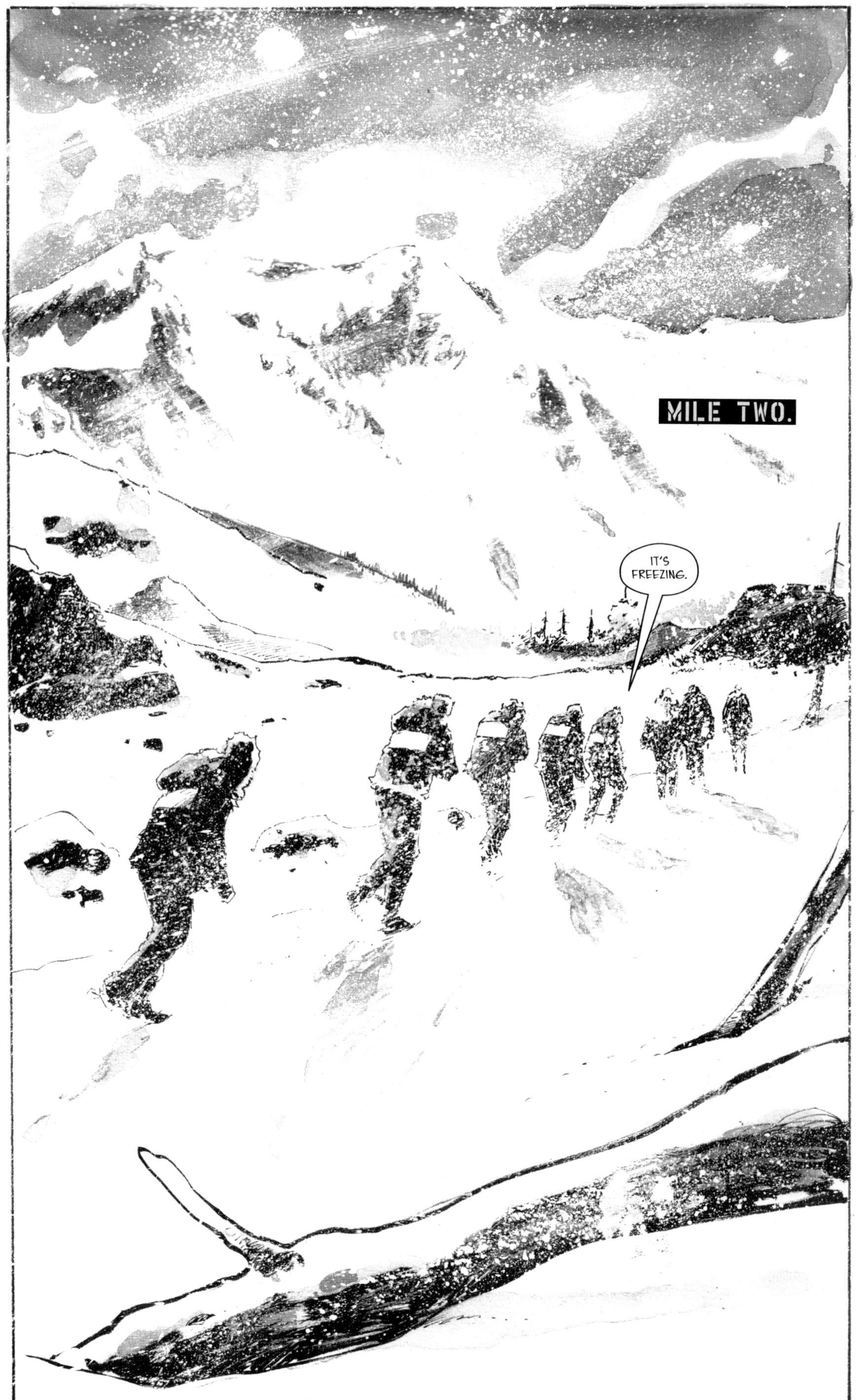
MILE TWO.
IT'S FREEZING.

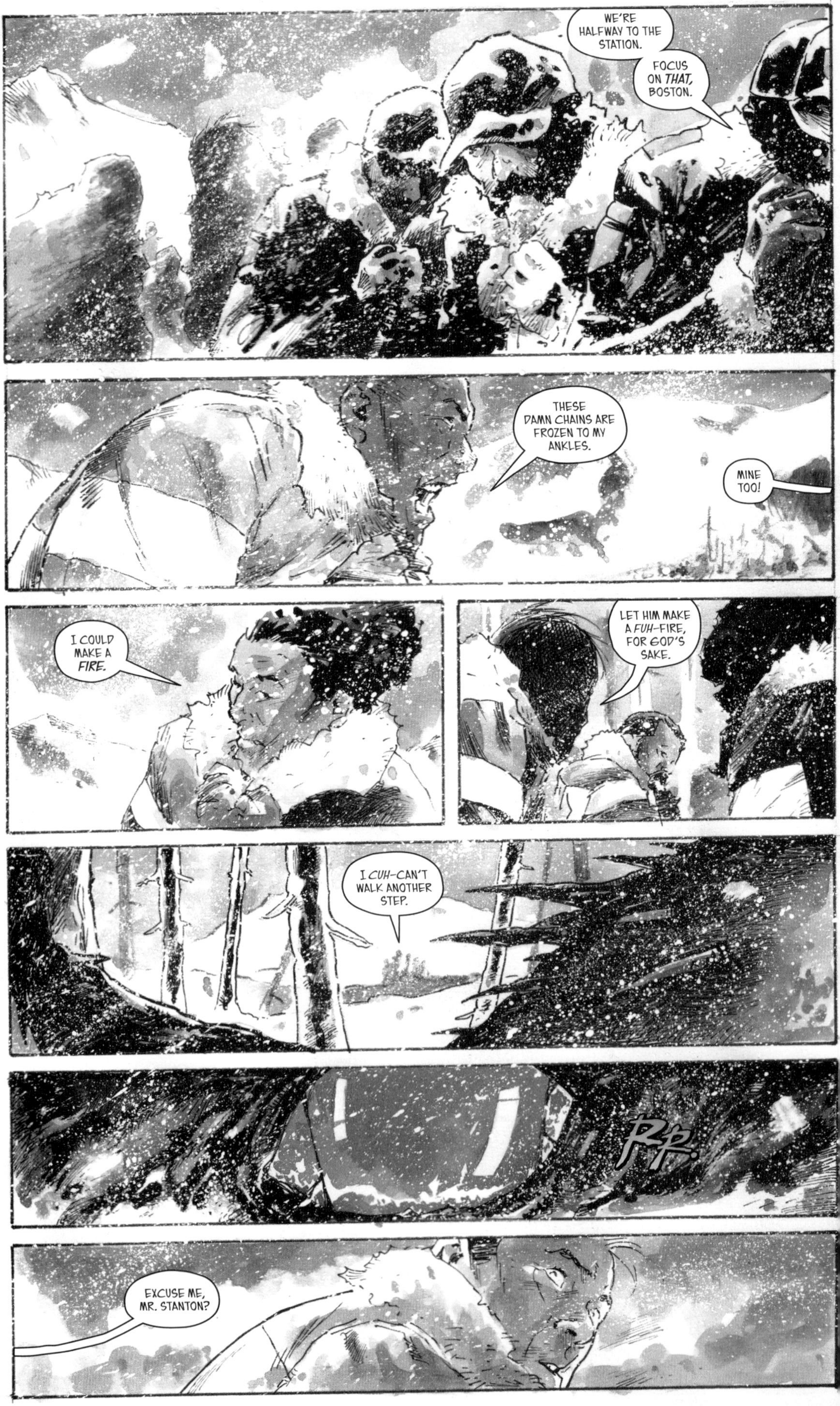
WE'RE HALFWAY TO THE STATION.
FOCUS ON *THAT,* BOSTON.
THESE DAMN CHAINS ARE FROZEN TO MY ANKLES.
MINE TOO!
I COULD MAKE A *FIRE.*
LET HIM MAKE A *FUH*-FIRE, FOR GOD'S SAKE.
I *CUH*-CAN'T WALK ANOTHER STEP.
RR.
EXCUSE ME, MR. STANTON?

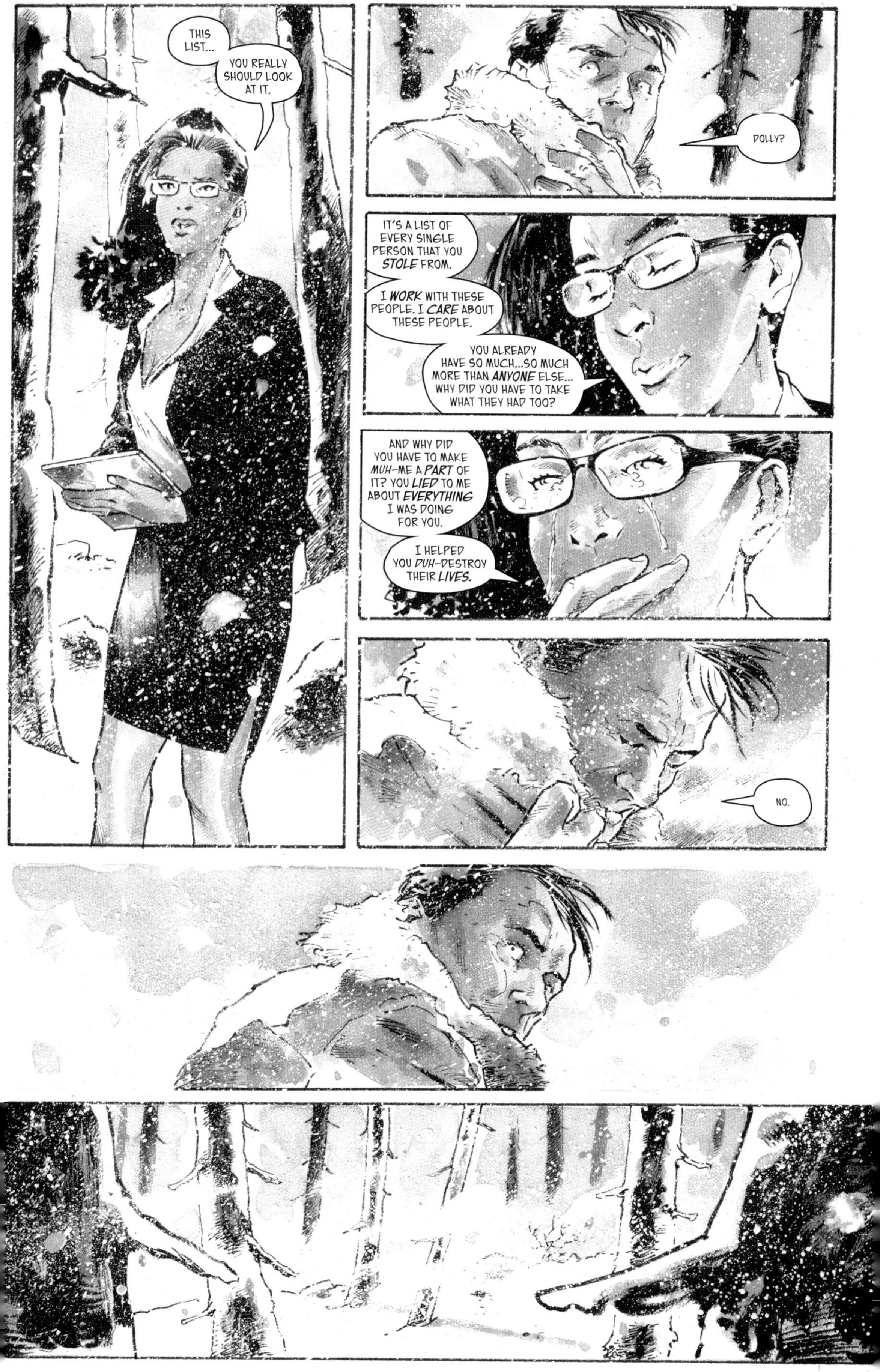
THIS LIST...
YOU REALLY SHOULD LOOK AT IT.
DOLLY?
IT'S A LIST OF EVERY SINGLE PERSON THAT YOU STOLE FROM.
I WORK WITH THESE PEOPLE. I CARE ABOUT THESE PEOPLE.
YOU ALREADY HAVE SO MUCH...SO MUCH MORE THAN ANYONE ELSE... WHY DID YOU HAVE TO TAKE WHAT THEY HAD TOO?
AND WHY DID YOU HAVE TO MAKE MUH-ME A PART OF IT? YOU LIED TO ME ABOUT EVERYTHING I WAS DOING FOR YOU.
I HELPED YOU DUH-DESTROY THEIR LIVES.
NO.

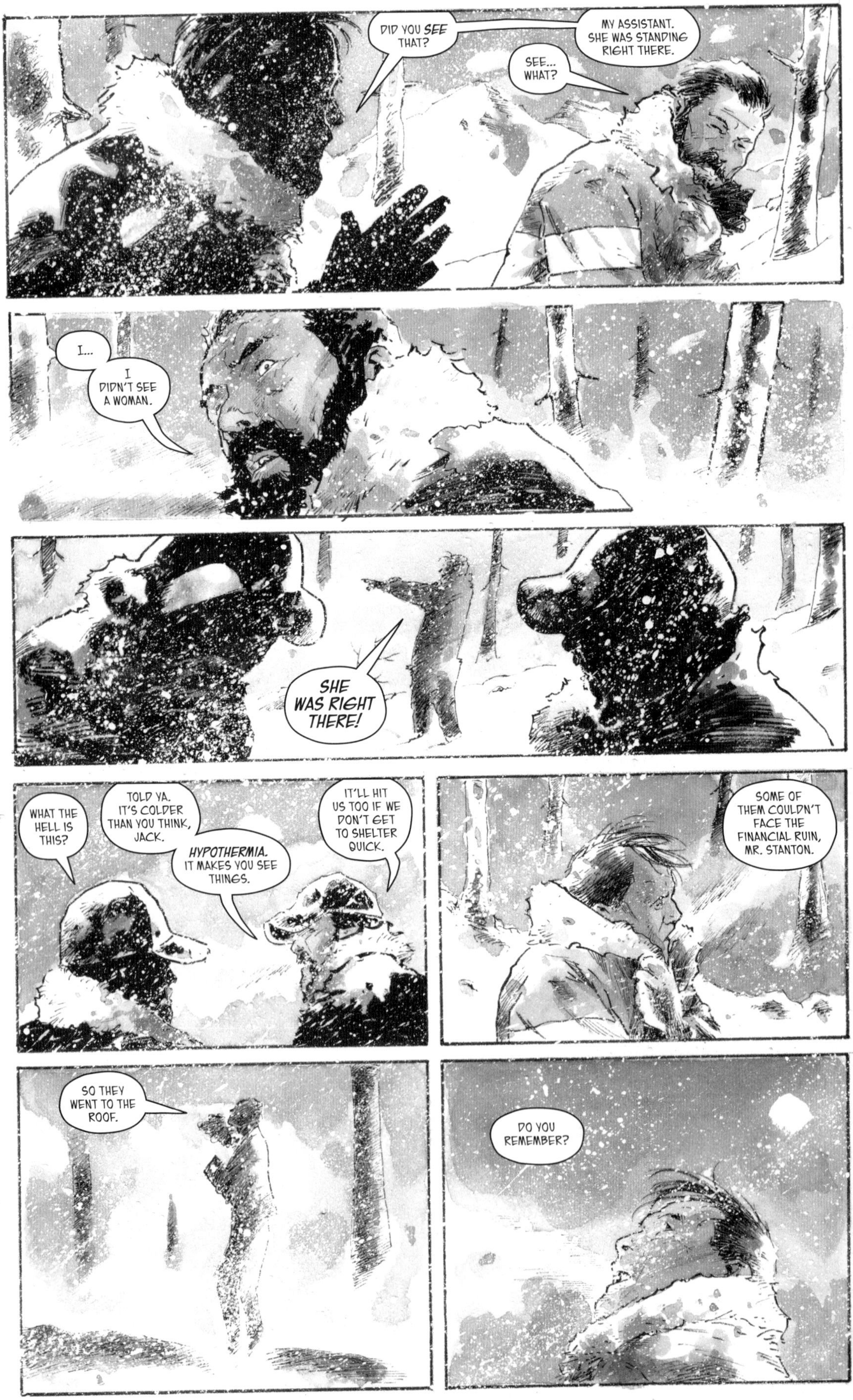
DID YOU SEE THAT?
SEE... WHAT?
MY ASSISTANT. SHE WAS STANDING RIGHT THERE.
I...
I DIDN'T SEE A WOMAN.
SHE WAS RIGHT THERE!
WHAT THE HELL IS THIS?
TOLD YA. IT'S COLDER THAN YOU THINK, JACK.
HYPOTHERMIA. IT MAKES YOU SEE THINGS.
IT'LL HIT US TOO IF WE DON'T GET TO SHELTER QUICK.
SOME OF THEM COULDN'T FACE THE FINANCIAL RUIN, MR. STANTON.
SO THEY WENT TO THE ROOF.
DO YOU REMEMBER?

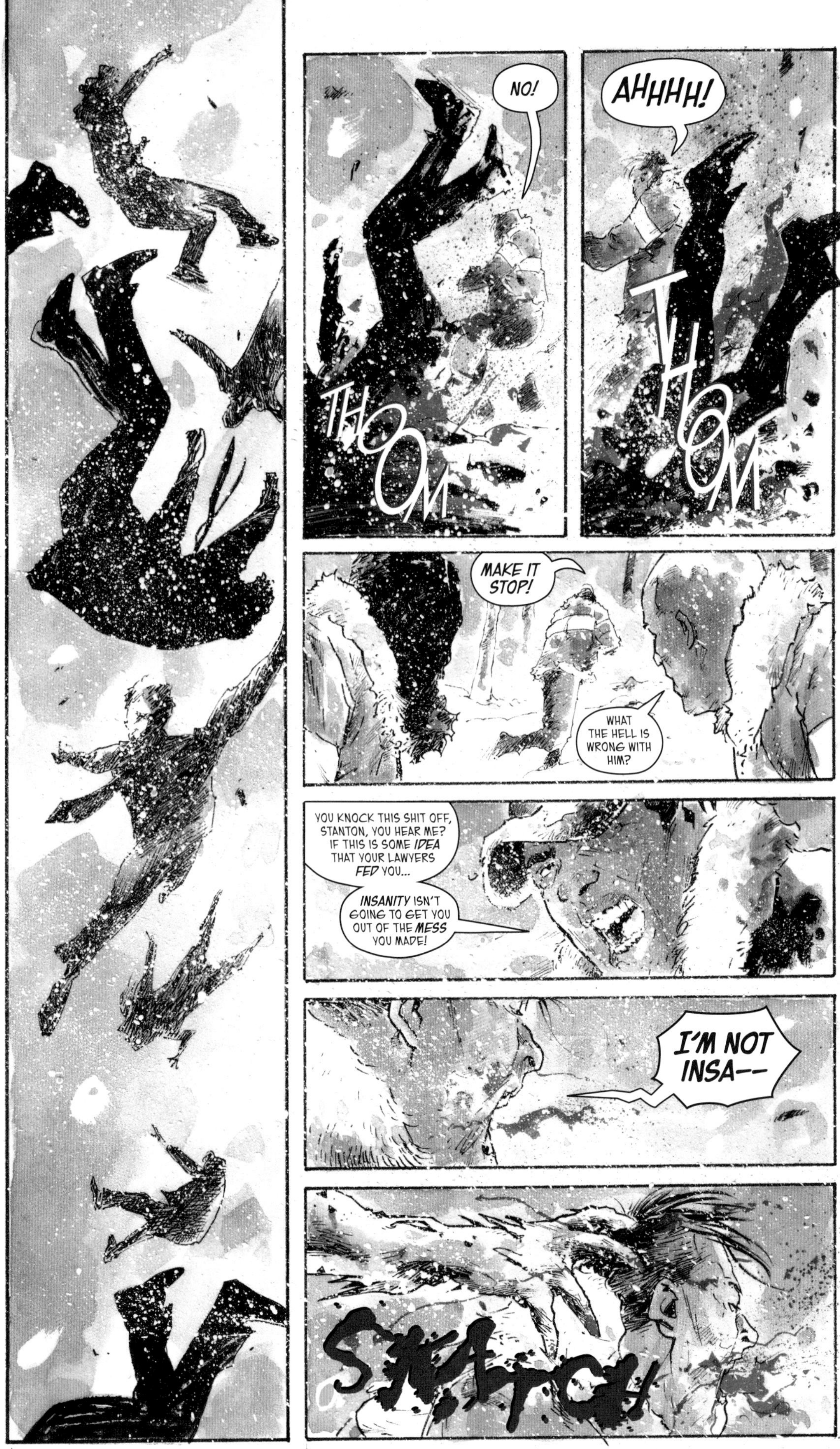
NO!
THOOM
AHHHH!
THOOM
MAKE IT STOP!
WHAT THE HELL IS WRONG WITH HIM?
YOU KNOCK THIS SHIT OFF, STANTON, YOU HEAR ME? IF THIS IS SOME IDEA THAT YOUR LAWYERS FED YOU...
INSANITY ISN'T GOING TO GET YOU OUT OF THE MESS YOU MADE!
I'M NOT INSA--
SMATCH!

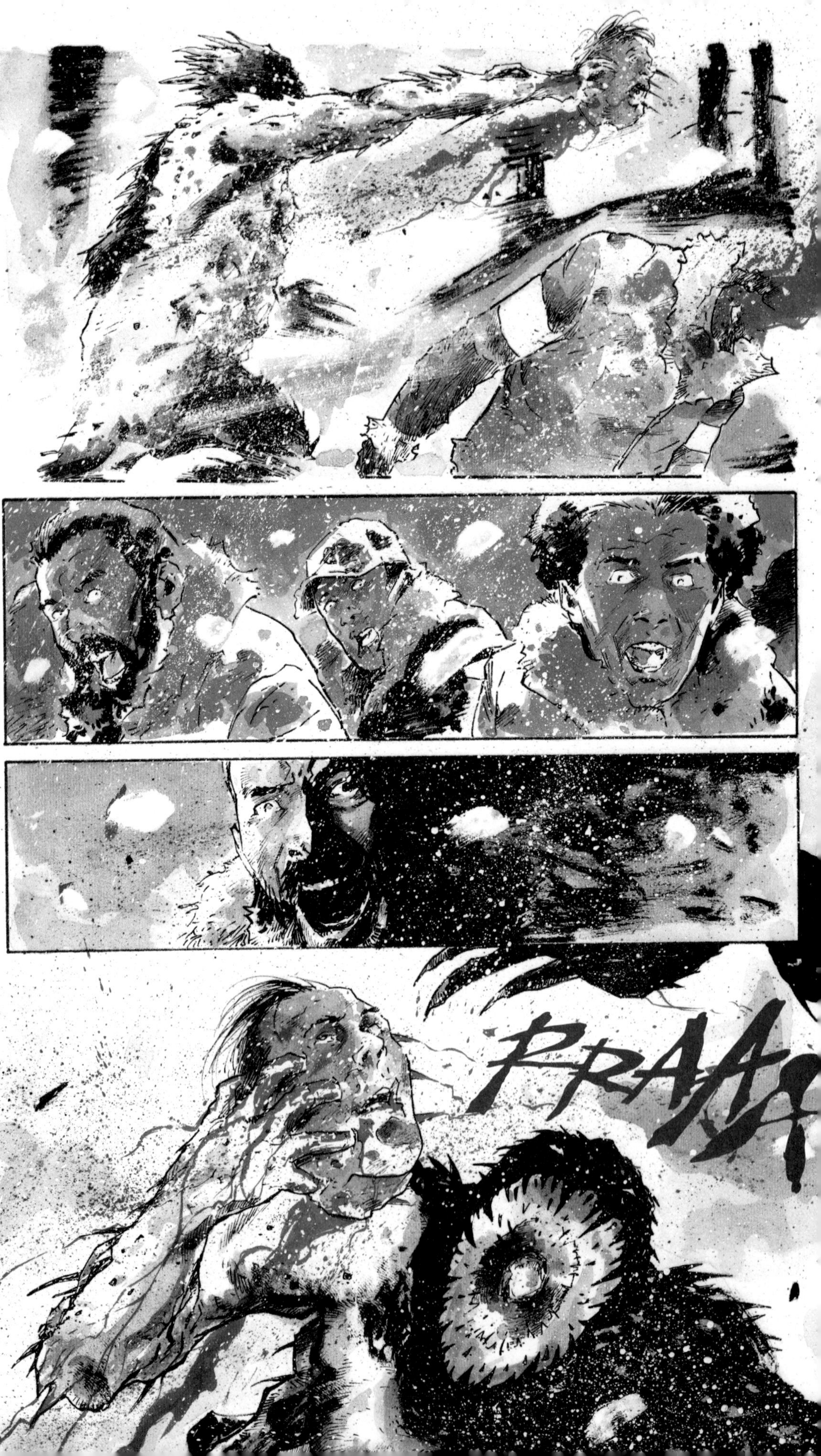
PRAA

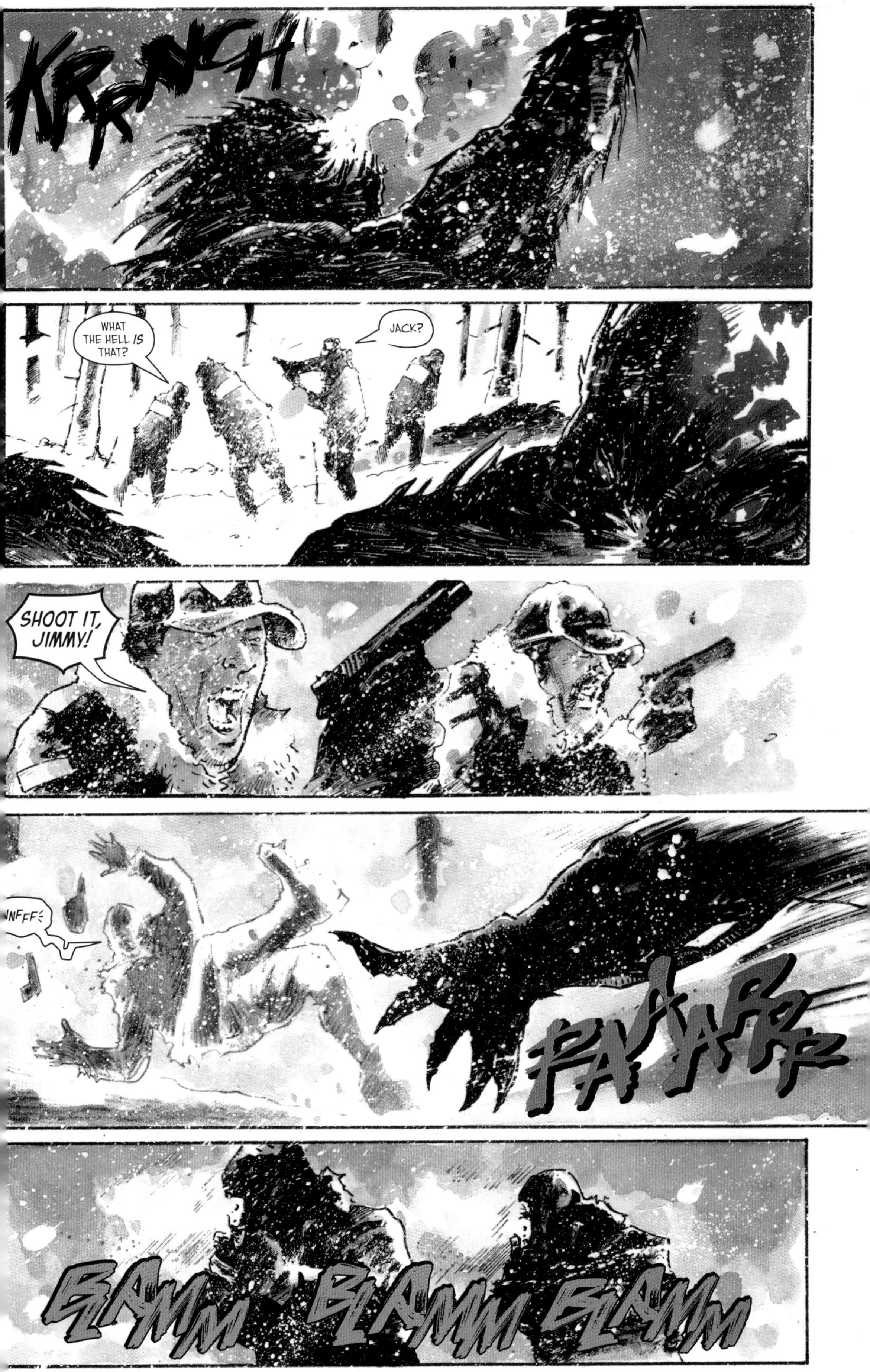
KRRRNCH
WHAT THE HELL IS THAT?
JACK?
SHOOT IT, JIMMY!
NFFF
RAAARRR
BLAMM BLAMM BLAMM

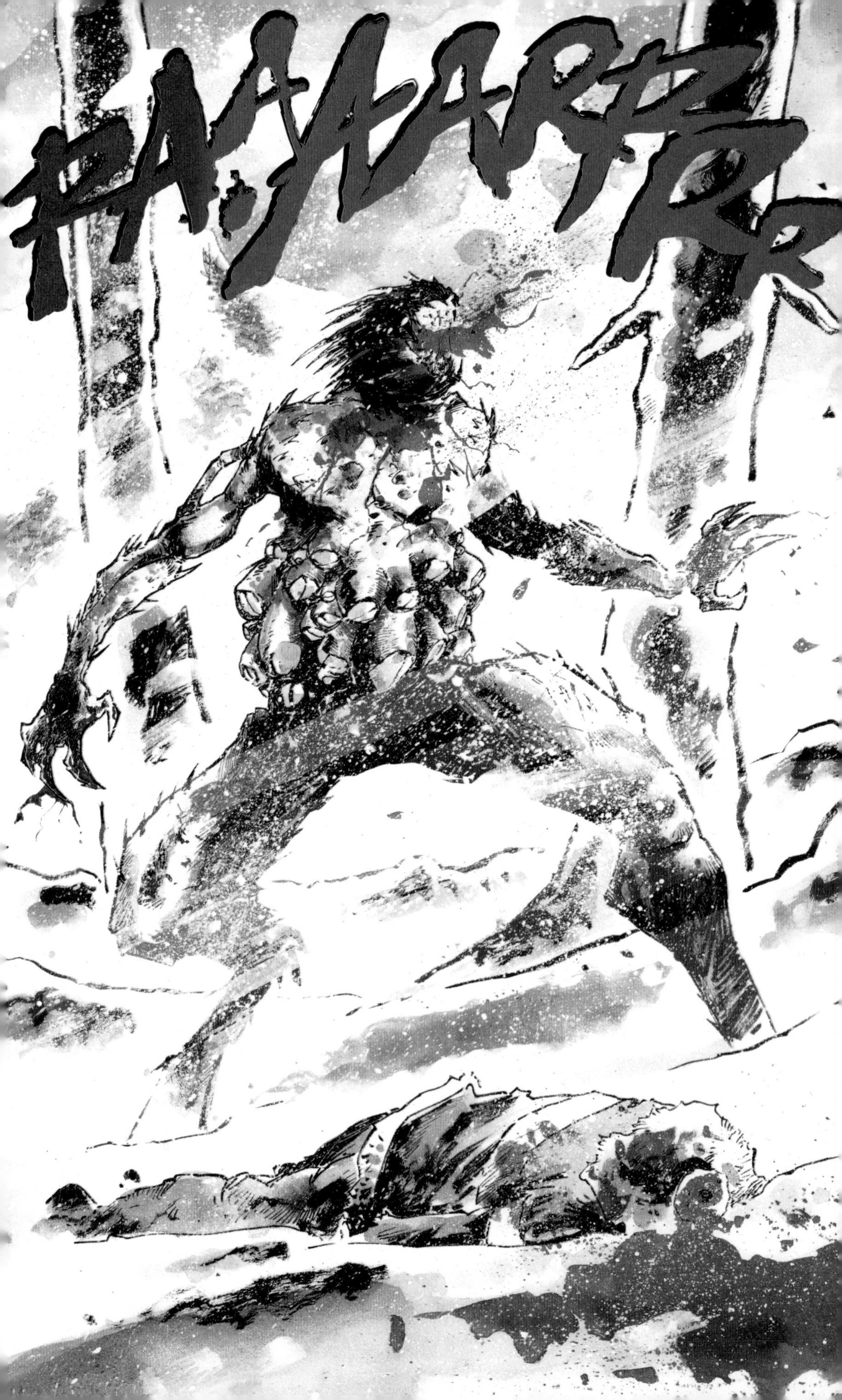
RAAARRRR

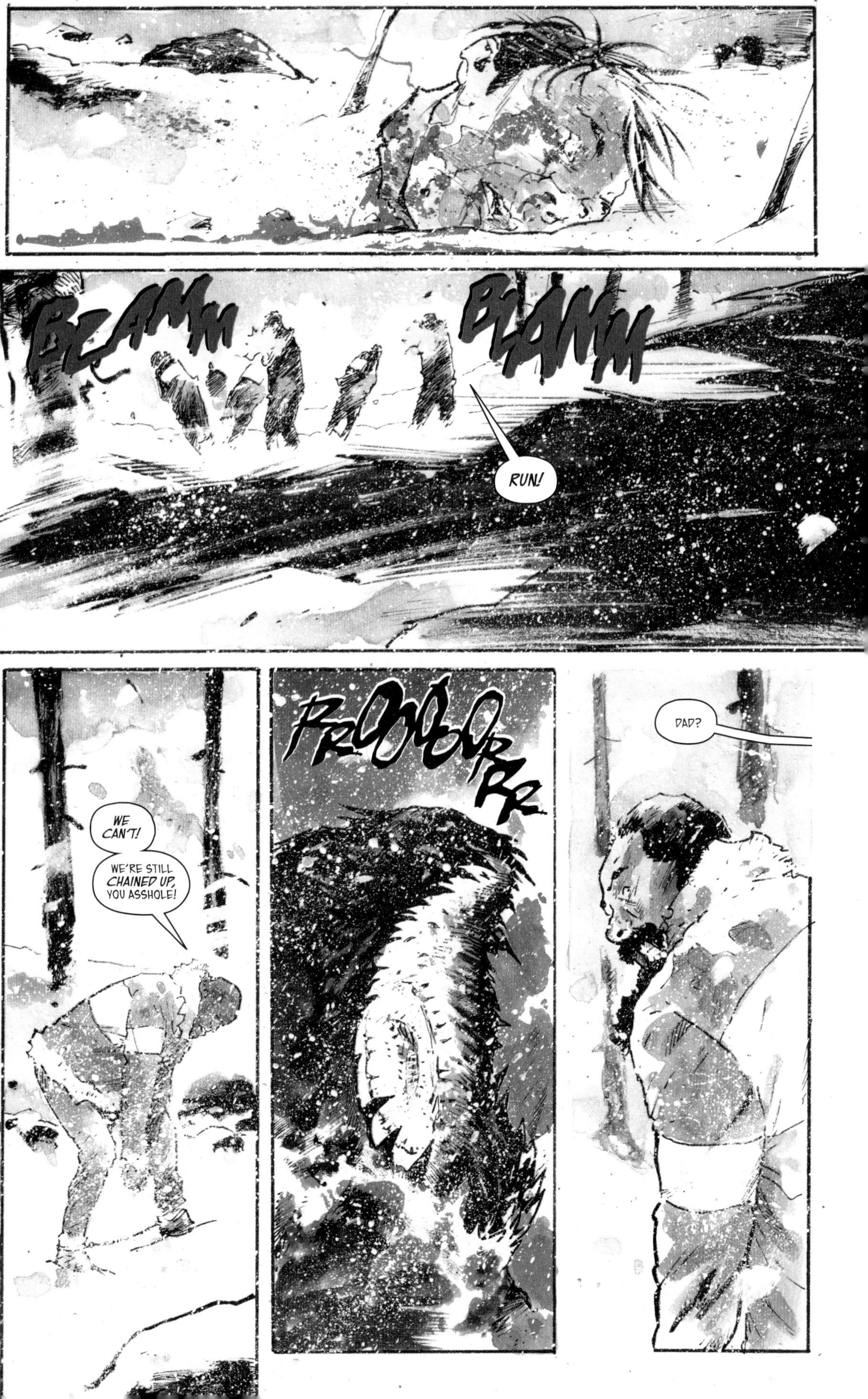
BLAMM
BLAMM
RUN!
WE CAN'T!
WE'RE STILL CHAINED UP, YOU ASSHOLE!
PROOOOORRR
DAD?

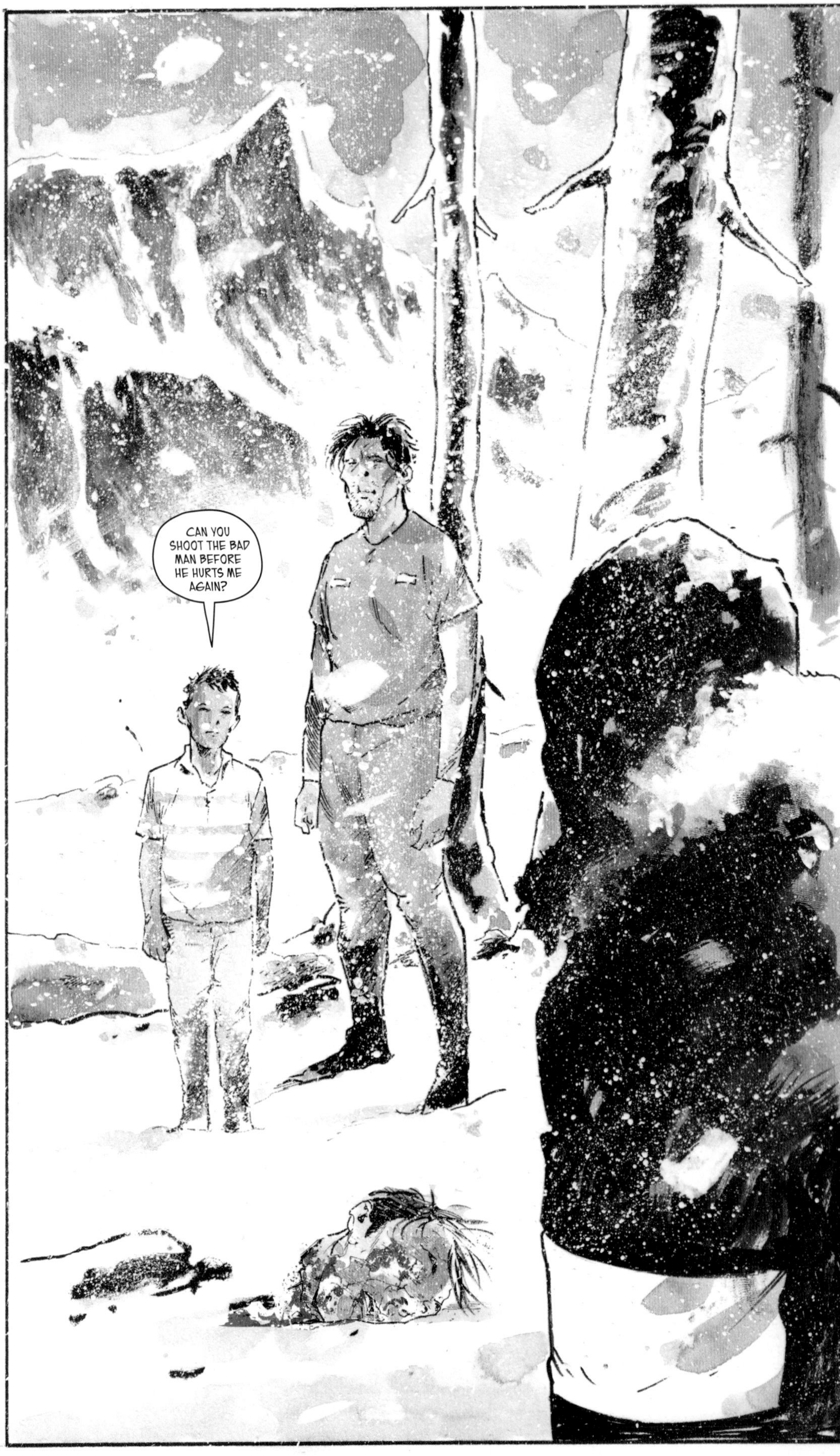
CAN YOU SHOOT THE BAD MAN BEFORE HE HURTS ME AGAIN?

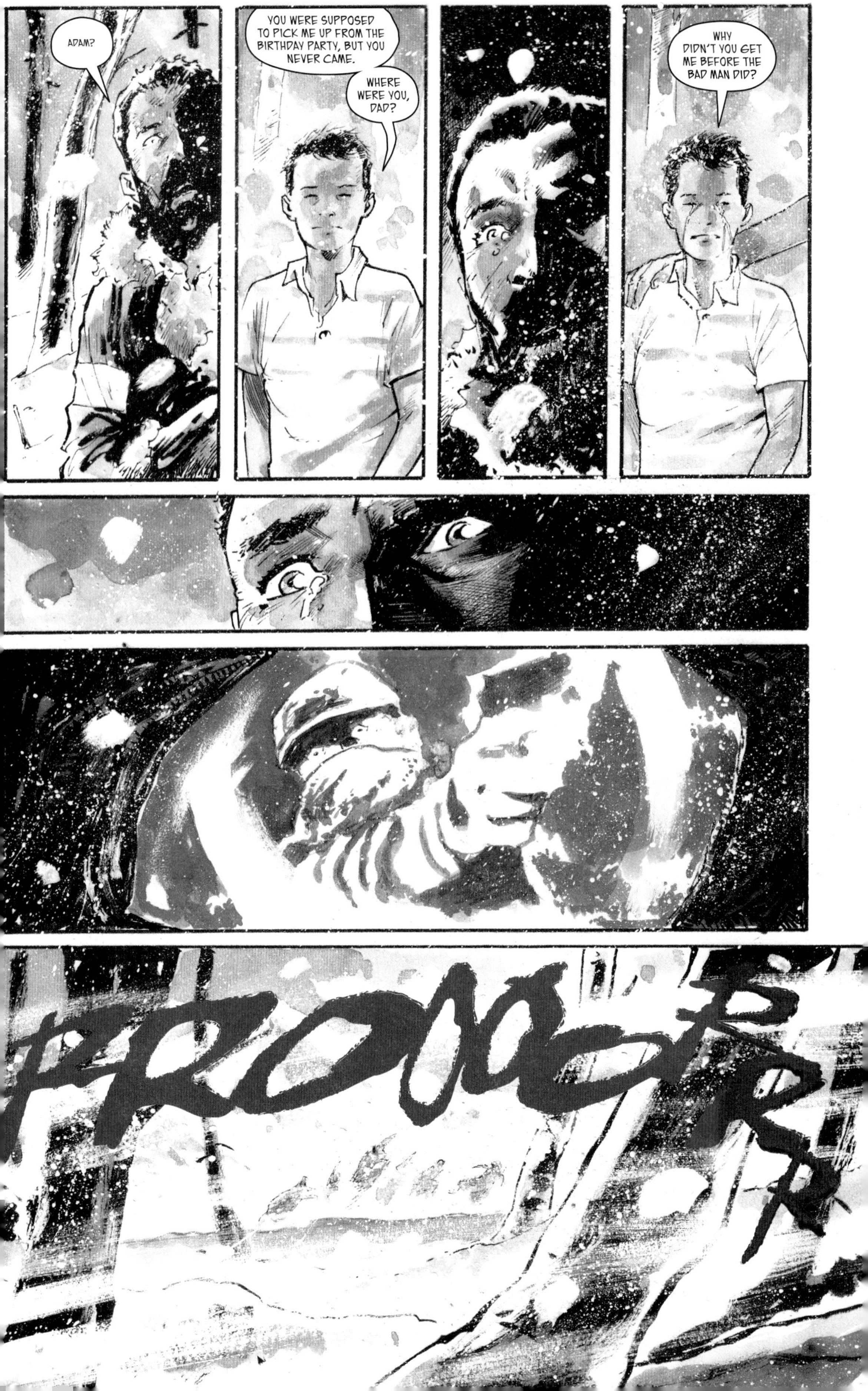
ADAM?
YOU WERE SUPPOSED TO PICK ME UP FROM THE BIRTHDAY PARTY, BUT YOU NEVER CAME.
WHERE WERE YOU, DAD?
WHY DIDN'T YOU GET ME BEFORE THE BAD MAN DID?
BROOOOR

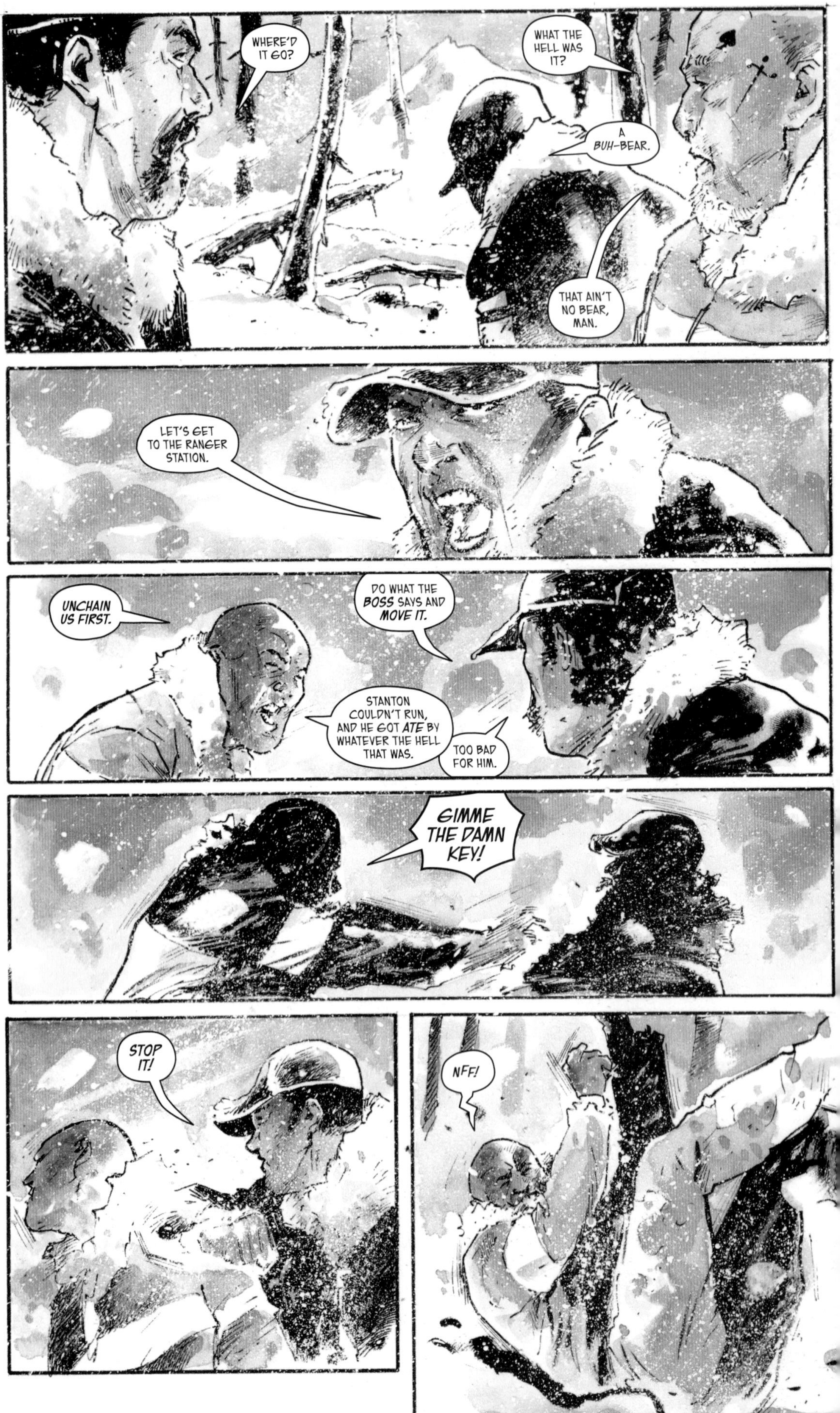
WHERE'D IT GO?
WHAT THE HELL WAS IT?
A BUH-BEAR.
THAT AIN'T NO BEAR, MAN.
LET'S GET TO THE RANGER STATION.
UNCHAIN US FIRST.
DO WHAT THE BOSS SAYS AND MOVE IT.
STANTON COULDN'T RUN, AND HE GOT ATE BY WHATEVER THE HELL THAT WAS.
TOO BAD FOR HIM.
GIMME THE DAMN KEY!
STOP IT!
NFF!

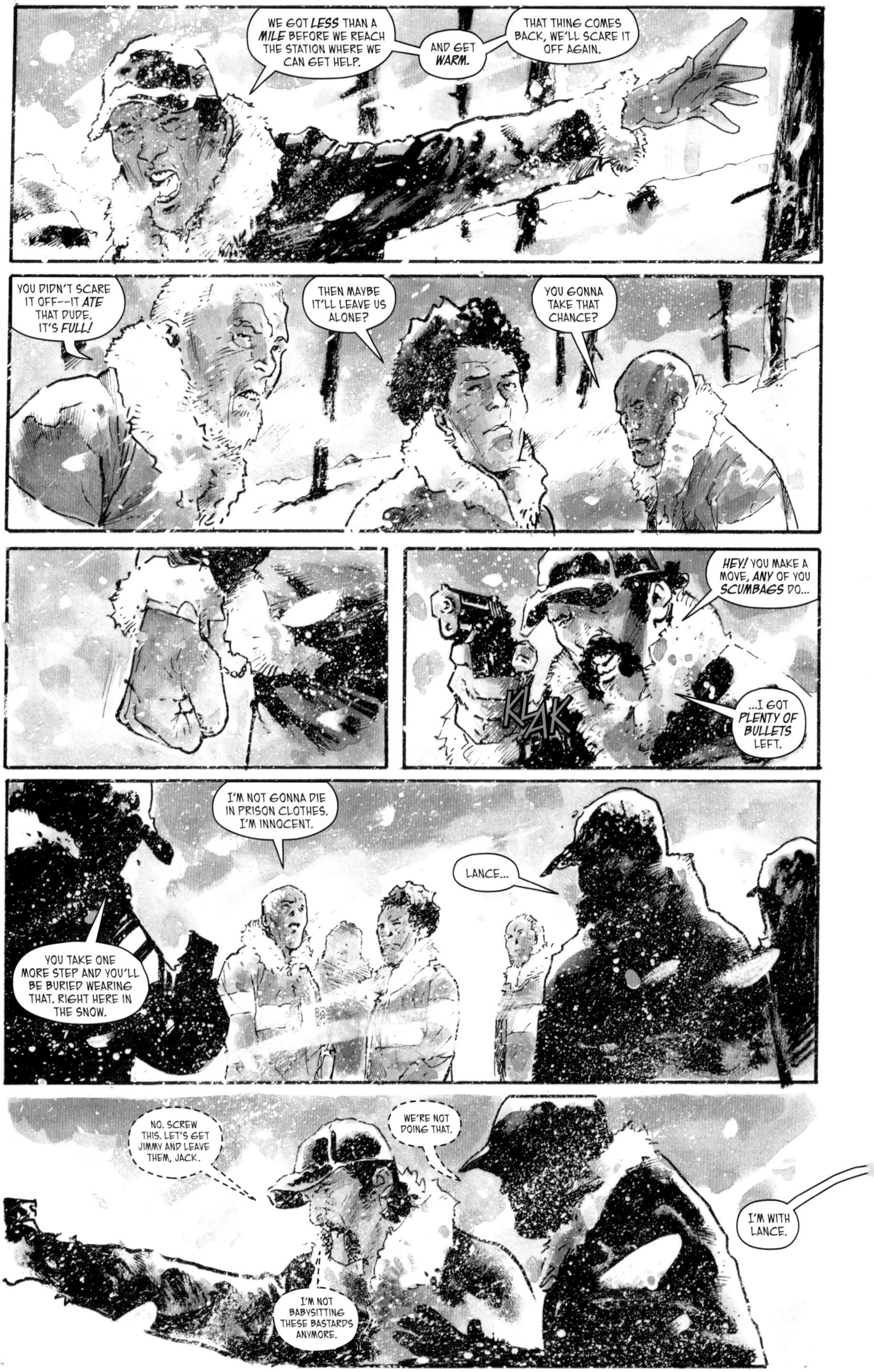
WE GOT LESS THAN A MILE BEFORE WE REACH THE STATION WHERE WE CAN GET HELP.
AND GET WARM.
THAT THING COMES BACK, WE'LL SCARE IT OFF AGAIN.
YOU DIDN'T SCARE IT OFF--IT ATE THAT DUDE. IT'S FULL!
THEN MAYBE IT'LL LEAVE US ALONE?
YOU GONNA TAKE THAT CHANCE?
HEY! YOU MAKE A MOVE, ANY OF YOU SCUMBAGS DO...
KLAK
...I GOT PLENTY OF BULLETS LEFT.
I'M NOT GONNA DIE IN PRISON CLOTHES. I'M INNOCENT.
LANCE...
YOU TAKE ONE MORE STEP AND YOU'LL BE BURIED WEARING THAT. RIGHT HERE IN THE SNOW.
NO. SCREW THIS. LET'S GET JIMMY AND LEAVE THEM, JACK.
WE'RE NOT DOING THAT.
I'M NOT BABYSITTING THESE BASTARDS ANYMORE.
I'M WITH LANCE.

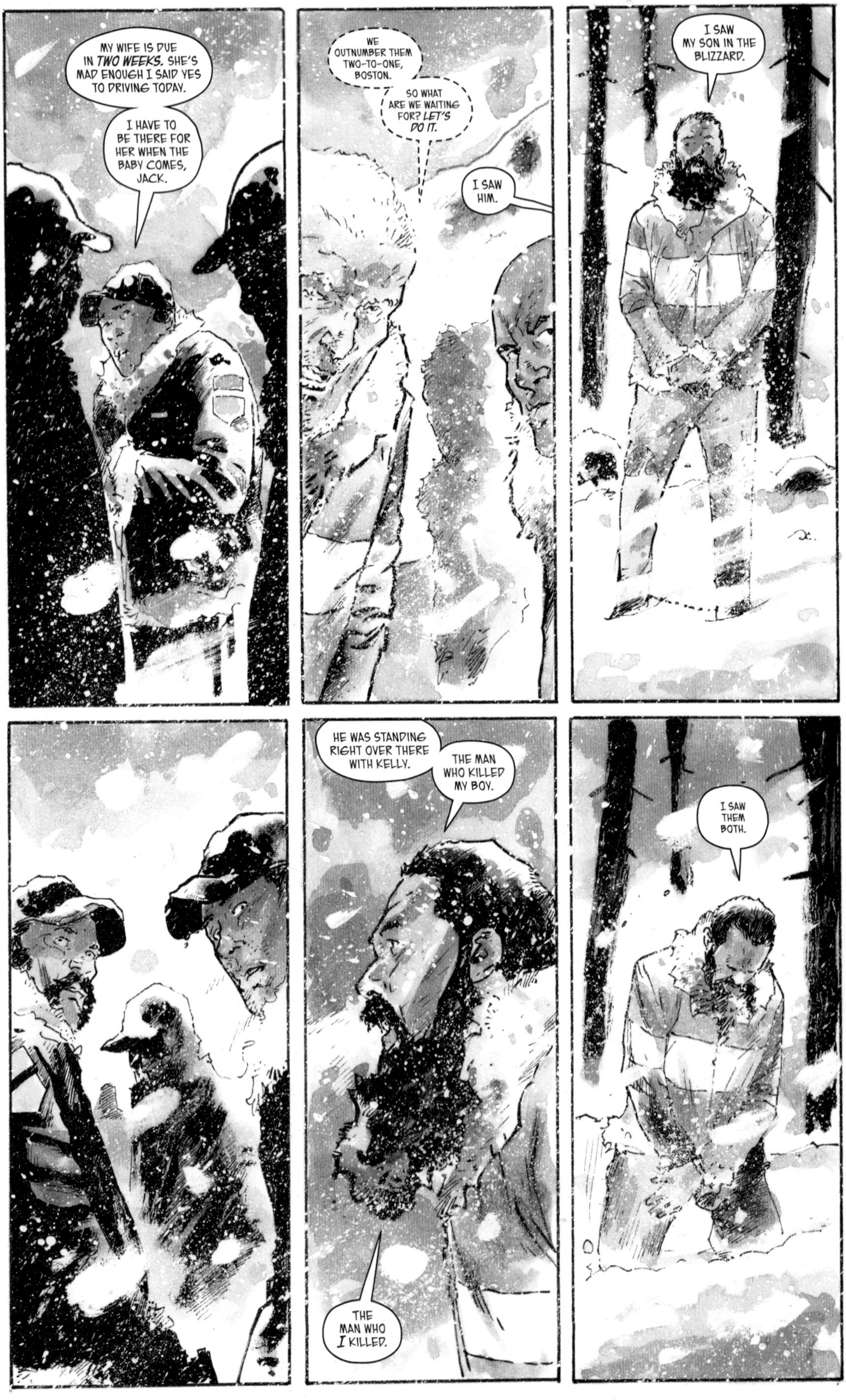
MY WIFE IS DUE IN TWO WEEKS. SHE'S MAD ENOUGH I SAID YES TO DRIVING TODAY.
I HAVE TO BE THERE FOR HER WHEN THE BABY COMES, JACK.
WE OUTNUMBER THEM TWO-TO-ONE, BOSTON.
SO WHAT ARE WE WAITING FOR? LET'S DO IT.
I SAW HIM.
I SAW MY SON IN THE BLIZZARD.
HE WAS STANDING RIGHT OVER THERE WITH KELLY.
THE MAN WHO KILLED MY BOY.
THE MAN WHO I KILLED.
I SAW THEM BOTH.

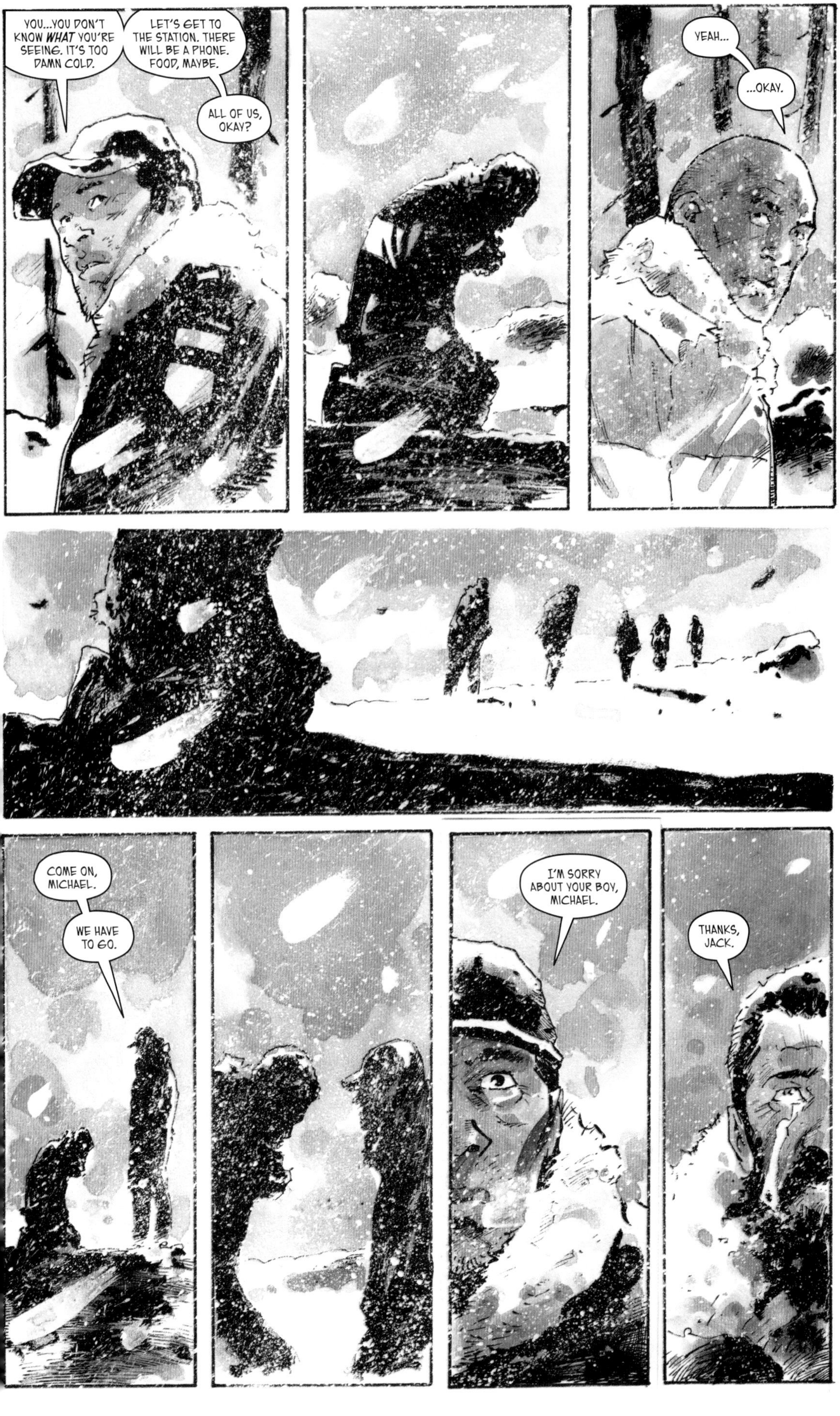
YOU...YOU DON'T KNOW *WHAT* YOU'RE SEEING. IT'S TOO DAMN COLD.
LET'S GET TO THE STATION. THERE WILL BE A PHONE. FOOD, MAYBE.
ALL OF US, OKAY?
YEAH...
...OKAY.
COME ON, MICHAEL.
WE HAVE TO GO.
I'M SORRY ABOUT YOUR BOY, MICHAEL.
THANKS, JACK.

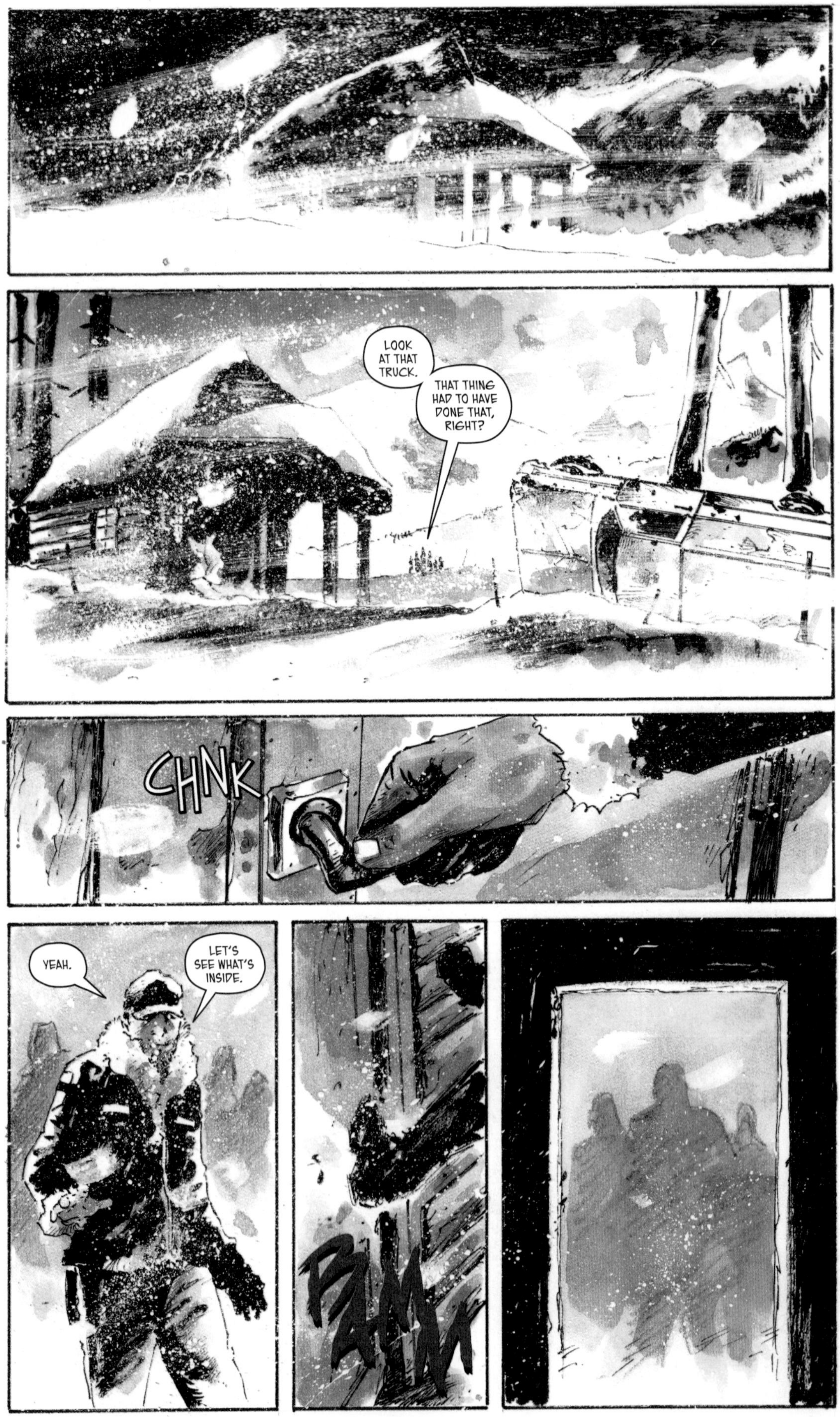
LOOK AT THAT TRUCK.
THAT THING HAD TO HAVE DONE THAT, RIGHT?
CHNK
YEAH.
LET'S SEE WHAT'S INSIDE.
BAM

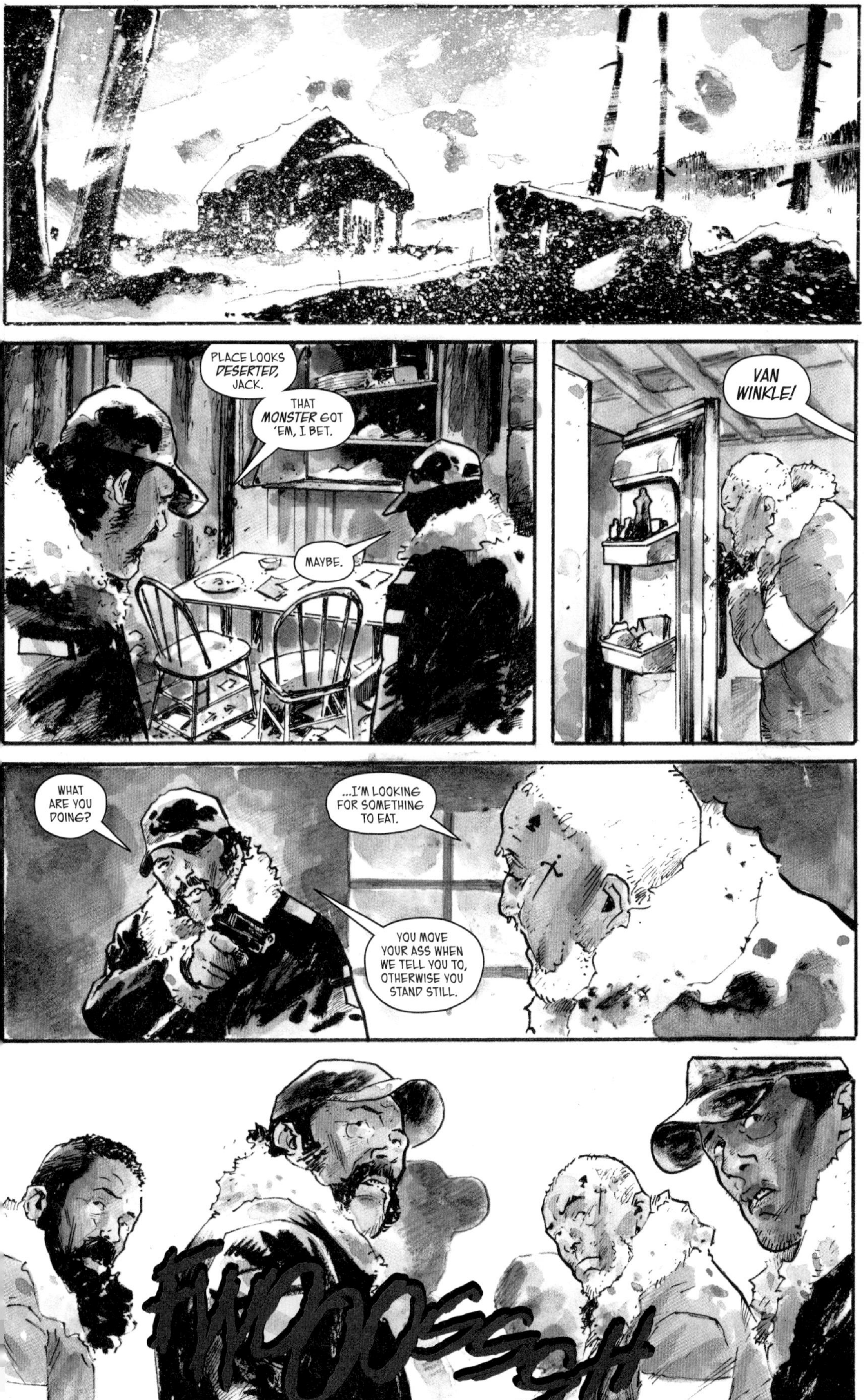
PLACE LOOKS DESERTED, JACK.
THAT MONSTER GOT 'EM, I BET.
MAYBE.
VAN WINKLE!
WHAT ARE YOU DOING?
...I'M LOOKING FOR SOMETHING TO EAT.
YOU MOVE YOUR ASS WHEN WE TELL YOU TO, OTHERWISE YOU STAND STILL.
FWOOOSSSH

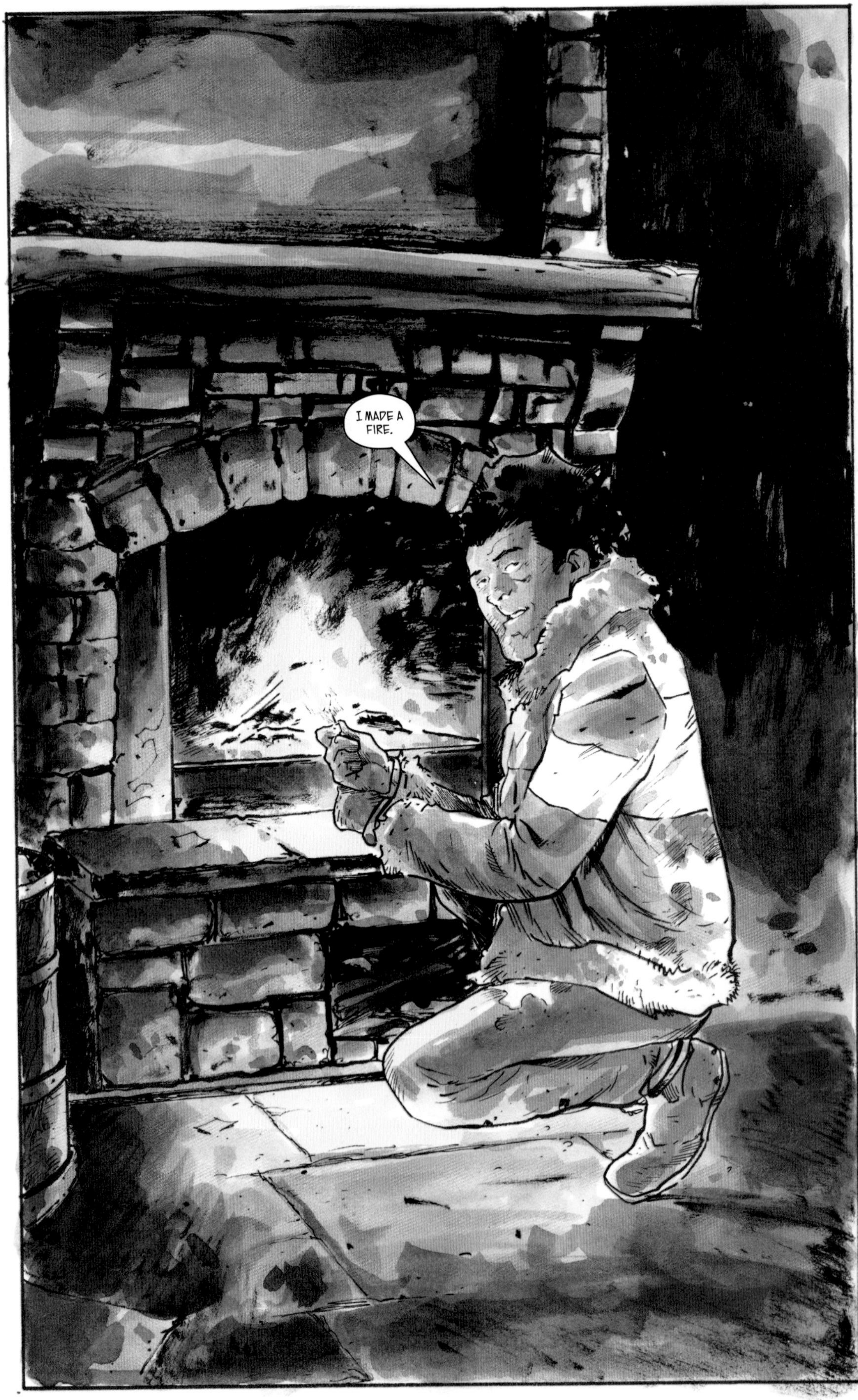
I MADE A FIRE.

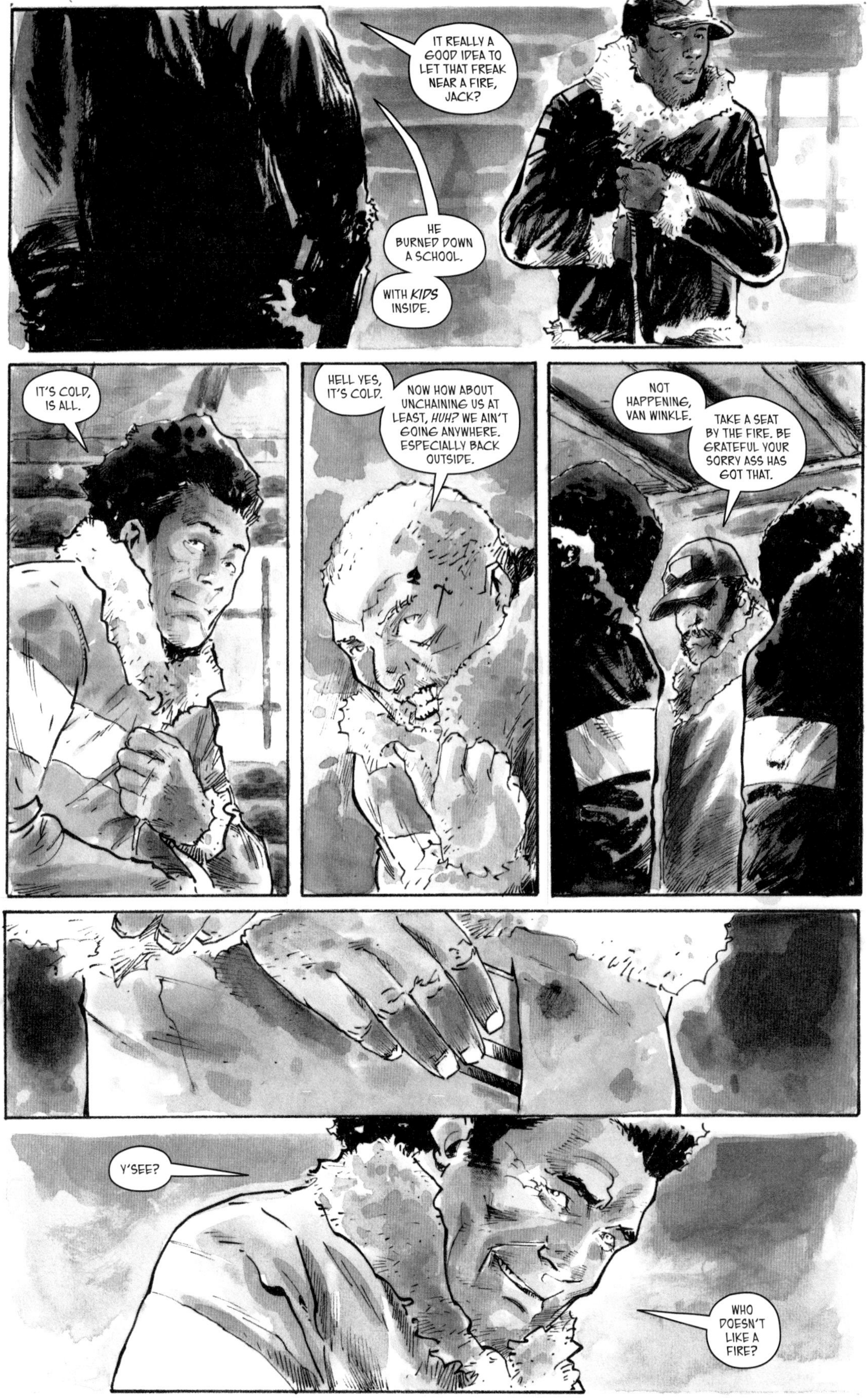
IT REALLY A GOOD IDEA TO LET THAT FREAK NEAR A FIRE, JACK?
HE BURNED DOWN A SCHOOL.
WITH KIDS INSIDE.
IT'S COLD, IS ALL.
HELL YES, IT'S COLD.
NOW HOW ABOUT UNCHAINING US AT LEAST, HUH? WE AIN'T GOING ANYWHERE. ESPECIALLY BACK OUTSIDE.
NOT HAPPENING, VAN WINKLE.
TAKE A SEAT BY THE FIRE. BE GRATEFUL YOUR SORRY ASS HAS GOT THAT.
Y'SEE?
WHO DOESN'T LIKE A FIRE?

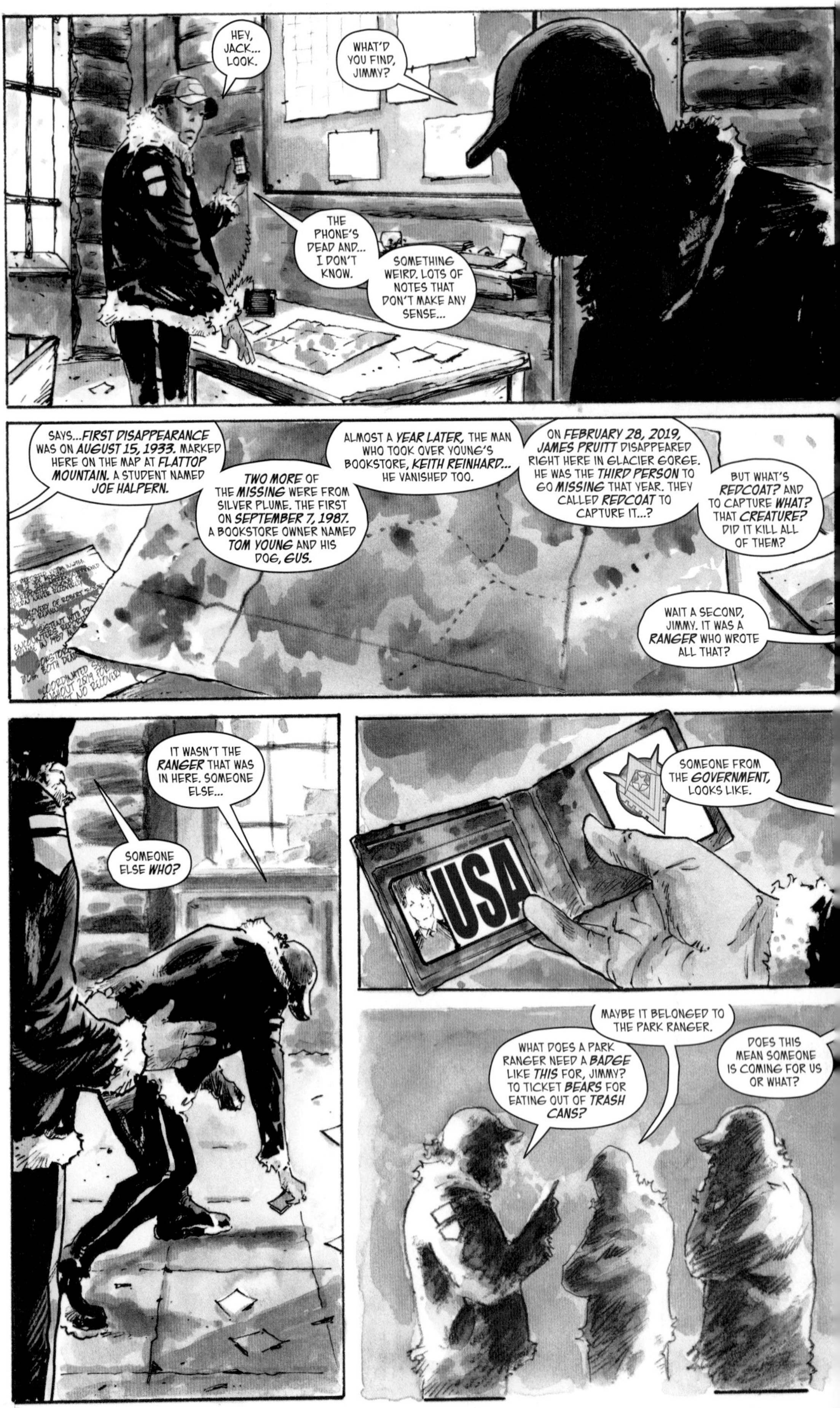

HEY, JACK... LOOK.
WHAT'D YOU FIND, JIMMY?
THE PHONE'S DEAD AND... I DON'T KNOW.
SOMETHING WEIRD. LOTS OF NOTES THAT DON'T MAKE ANY SENSE...
SAYS...FIRST DISAPPEARANCE WAS ON AUGUST 15, 1933. MARKED HERE ON THE MAP AT FLATTOP MOUNTAIN. A STUDENT NAMED JOE HALPERN.
TWO MORE OF THE MISSING WERE FROM SILVER PLUME. THE FIRST ON SEPTEMBER 7, 1987. A BOOKSTORE OWNER NAMED TOM YOUNG AND HIS DOG, GUS.
ALMOST A YEAR LATER, THE MAN WHO TOOK OVER YOUNG'S BOOKSTORE, KEITH REINHARD... HE VANISHED TOO.
ON FEBRUARY 28, 2019, JAMES PRUITT DISAPPEARED RIGHT HERE IN GLACIER GORGE. HE WAS THE THIRD PERSON TO GO MISSING THAT YEAR. THEY CALLED REDCOAT TO CAPTURE IT...?
BUT WHAT'S REDCOAT? AND TO CAPTURE WHAT? THAT CREATURE? DID IT KILL ALL OF THEM?
WAIT A SECOND, JIMMY. IT WAS A RANGER WHO WROTE ALL THAT?
IT WASN'T THE RANGER THAT WAS IN HERE. SOMEONE ELSE...
SOMEONE ELSE WHO?
USA
SOMEONE FROM THE GOVERNMENT, LOOKS LIKE.
MAYBE IT BELONGED TO THE PARK RANGER.
WHAT DOES A PARK RANGER NEED A BADGE LIKE THIS FOR, JIMMY? TO TICKET BEARS FOR EATING OUT OF TRASH CANS?
DOES THIS MEAN SOMEONE IS COMING FOR US OR WHAT?

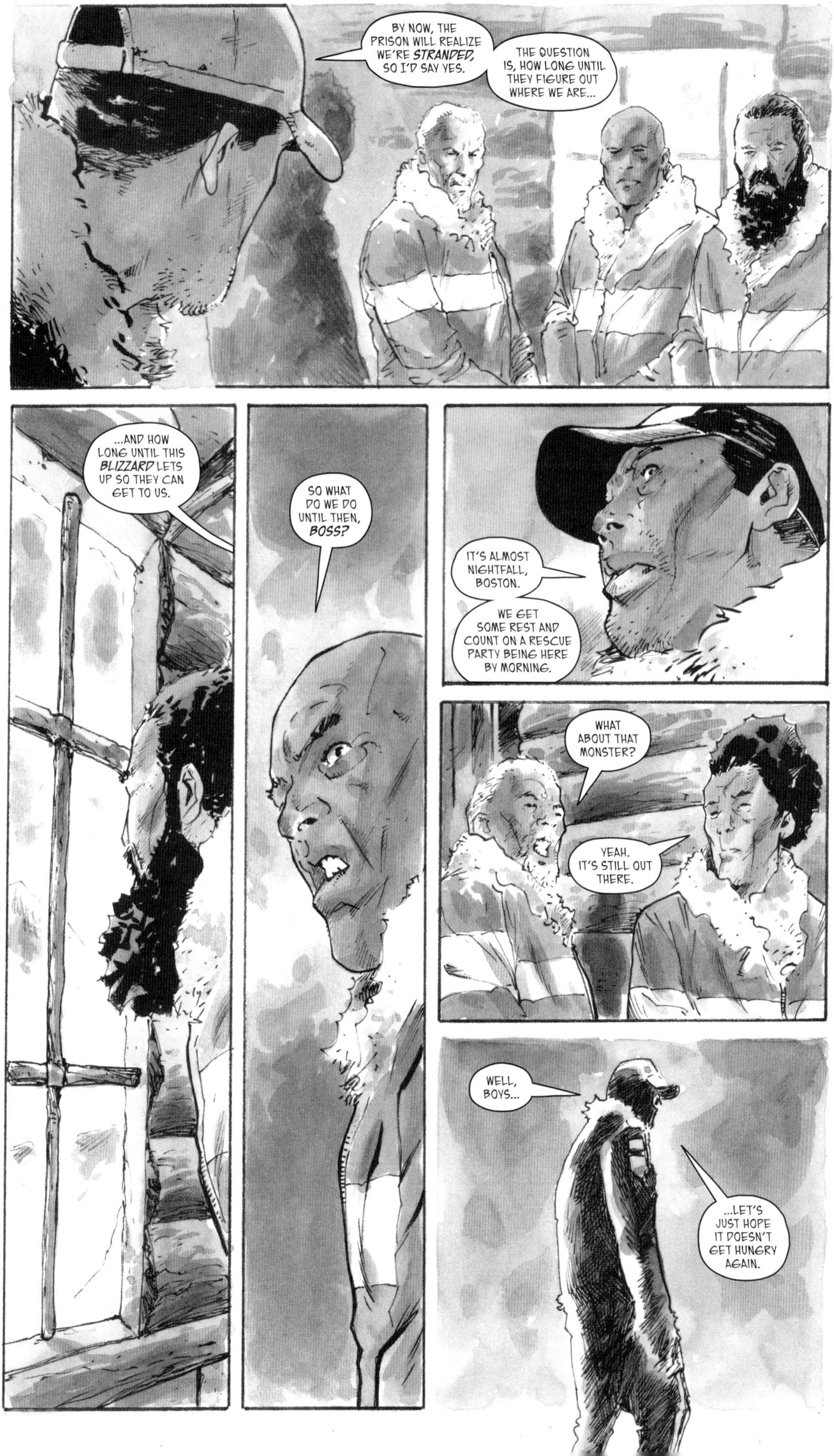
BY NOW, THE PRISON WILL REALIZE WE'RE STRANDED, SO I'D SAY YES.
THE QUESTION IS, HOW LONG UNTIL THEY FIGURE OUT WHERE WE ARE...
...AND HOW LONG UNTIL THIS BLIZZARD LETS UP SO THEY CAN GET TO US.
SO WHAT DO WE DO UNTIL THEN, BOSS?
IT'S ALMOST NIGHTFALL, BOSTON.
WE GET SOME REST AND COUNT ON A RESCUE PARTY BEING HERE BY MORNING.
WHAT ABOUT THAT MONSTER?
YEAH. IT'S STILL OUT THERE.
WELL, BOYS...
...LET'S JUST HOPE IT DOESN'T GET HUNGRY AGAIN.

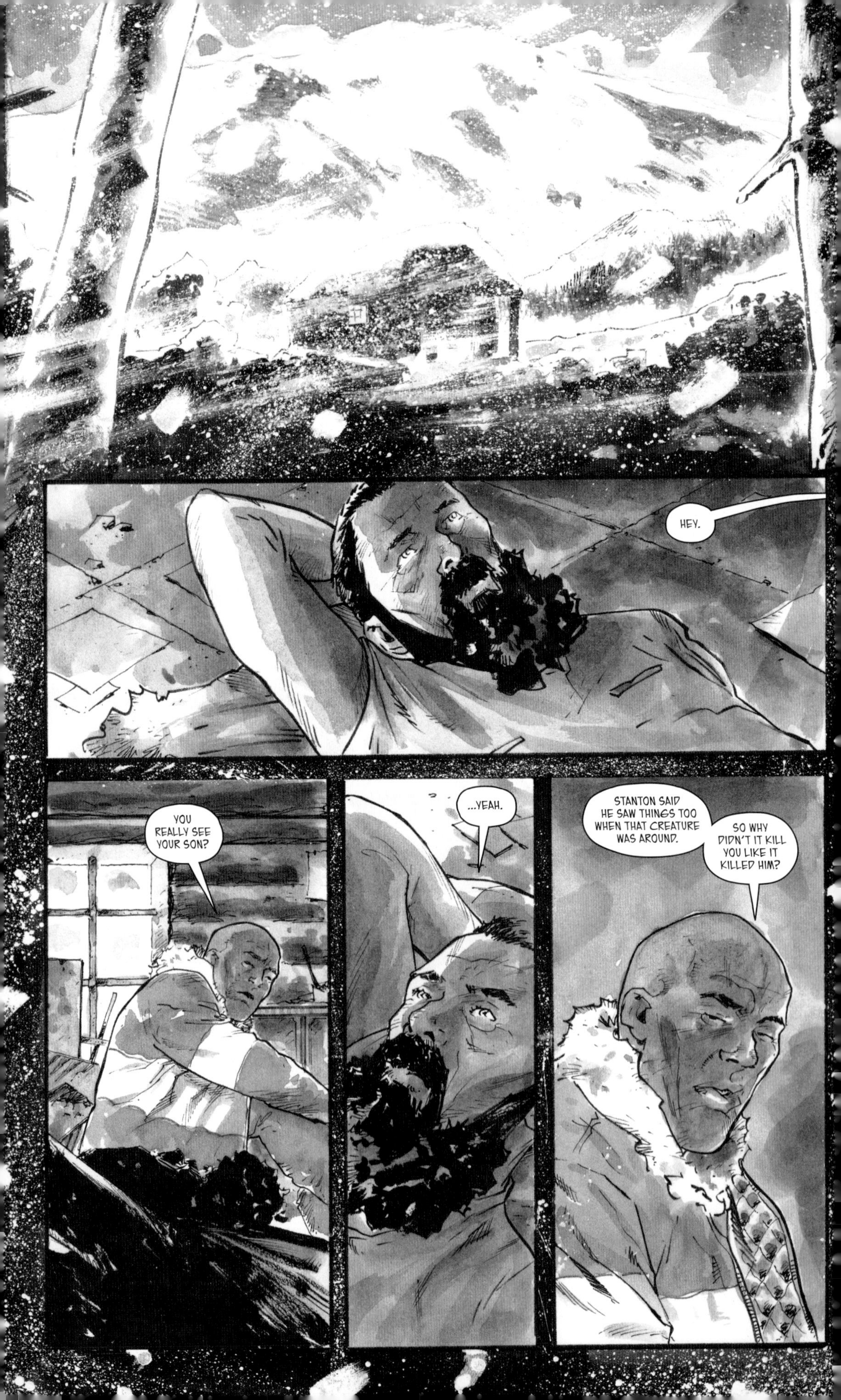
HEY.
YOU REALLY SEE YOUR SON?
...YEAH.
STANTON SAID HE SAW THINGS TOO WHEN THAT CREATURE WAS AROUND.
SO WHY DIDN'T IT KILL YOU LIKE IT KILLED HIM?

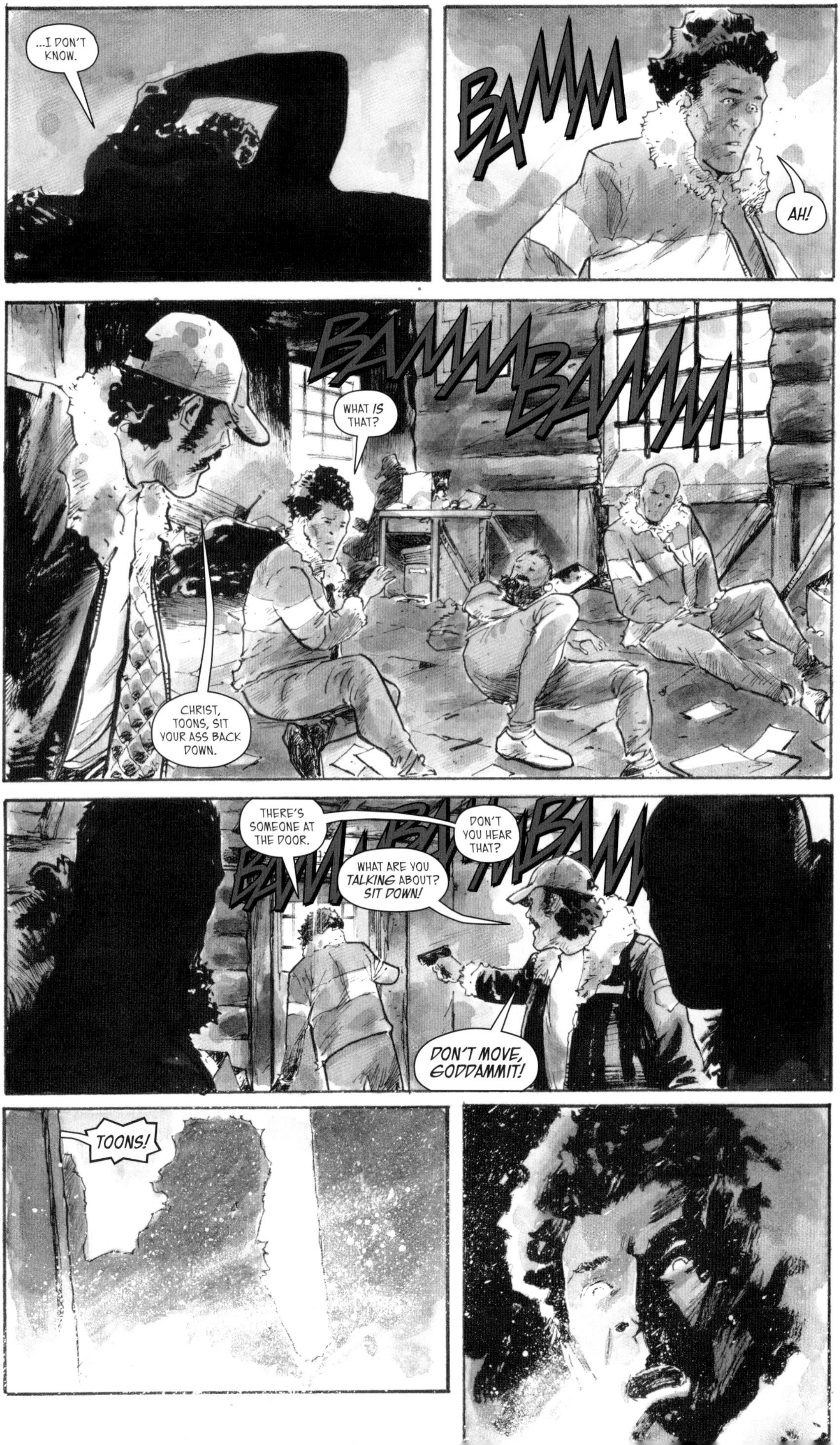
...I DON'T KNOW.
BAMM
AH!
BAMM BAMM
WHAT *IS* THAT?
CHRIST, TOONS, SIT YOUR ASS BACK DOWN.
THERE'S SOMEONE AT THE DOOR.
DON'T YOU HEAR THAT?
WHAT ARE YOU *TALKING* ABOUT? SIT DOWN!
DON'T MOVE, GODDAMMIT!
TOONS!

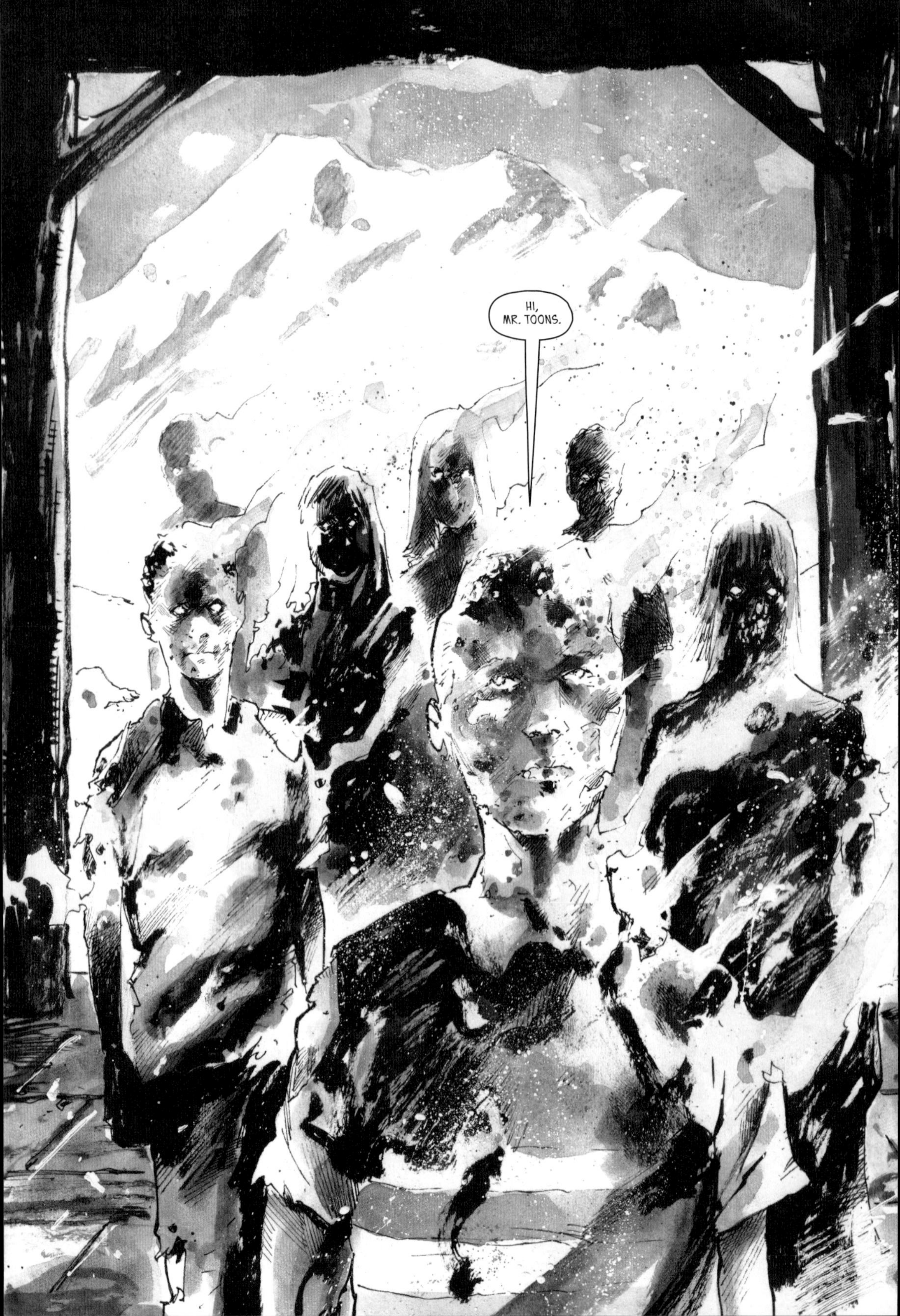
HI, MR. TOONS.

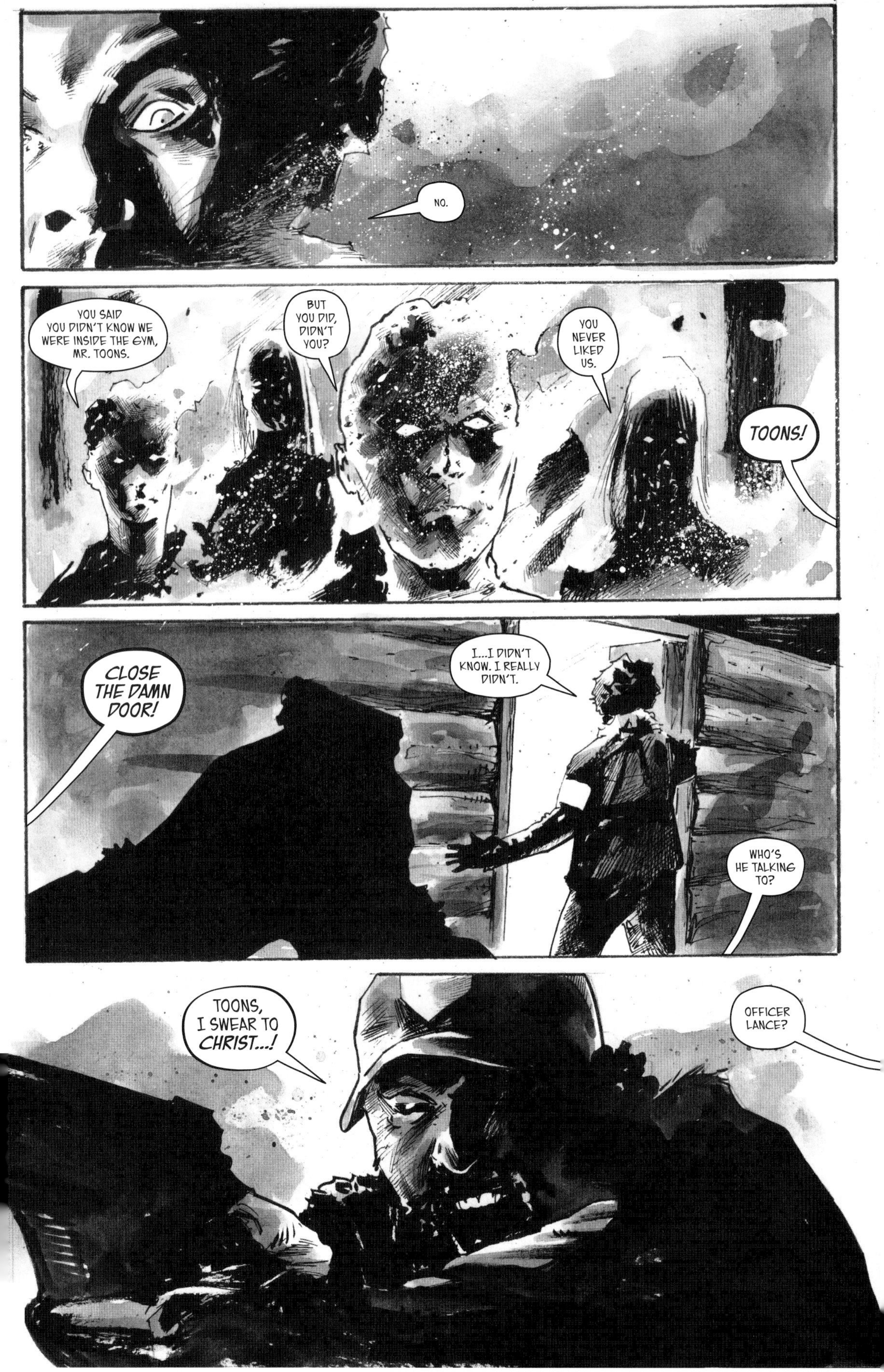
NO.
YOU SAID YOU DIDN'T KNOW WE WERE INSIDE THE GYM, MR. TOONS.
BUT YOU DID, DIDN'T YOU?
YOU NEVER LIKED US.
TOONS!
CLOSE THE DAMN DOOR!
I...I DIDN'T KNOW. I REALLY DIDN'T.
WHO'S HE TALKING TO?
TOONS, I SWEAR TO CHRIST...!
OFFICER LANCE?

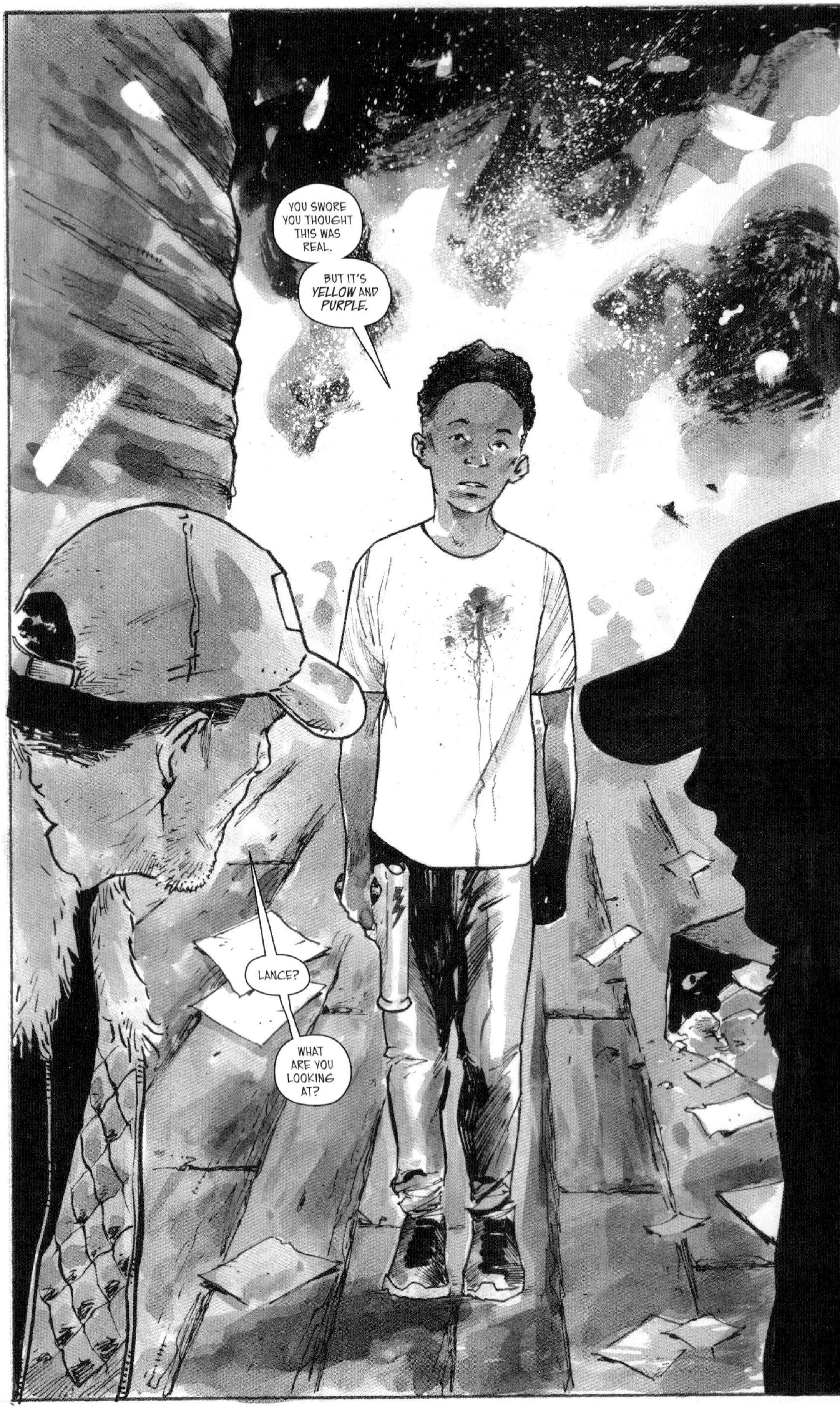
YOU SWORE YOU THOUGHT THIS WAS REAL.
BUT IT'S *YELLOW* AND *PURPLE.*
LANCE?
WHAT ARE YOU LOOKING AT?

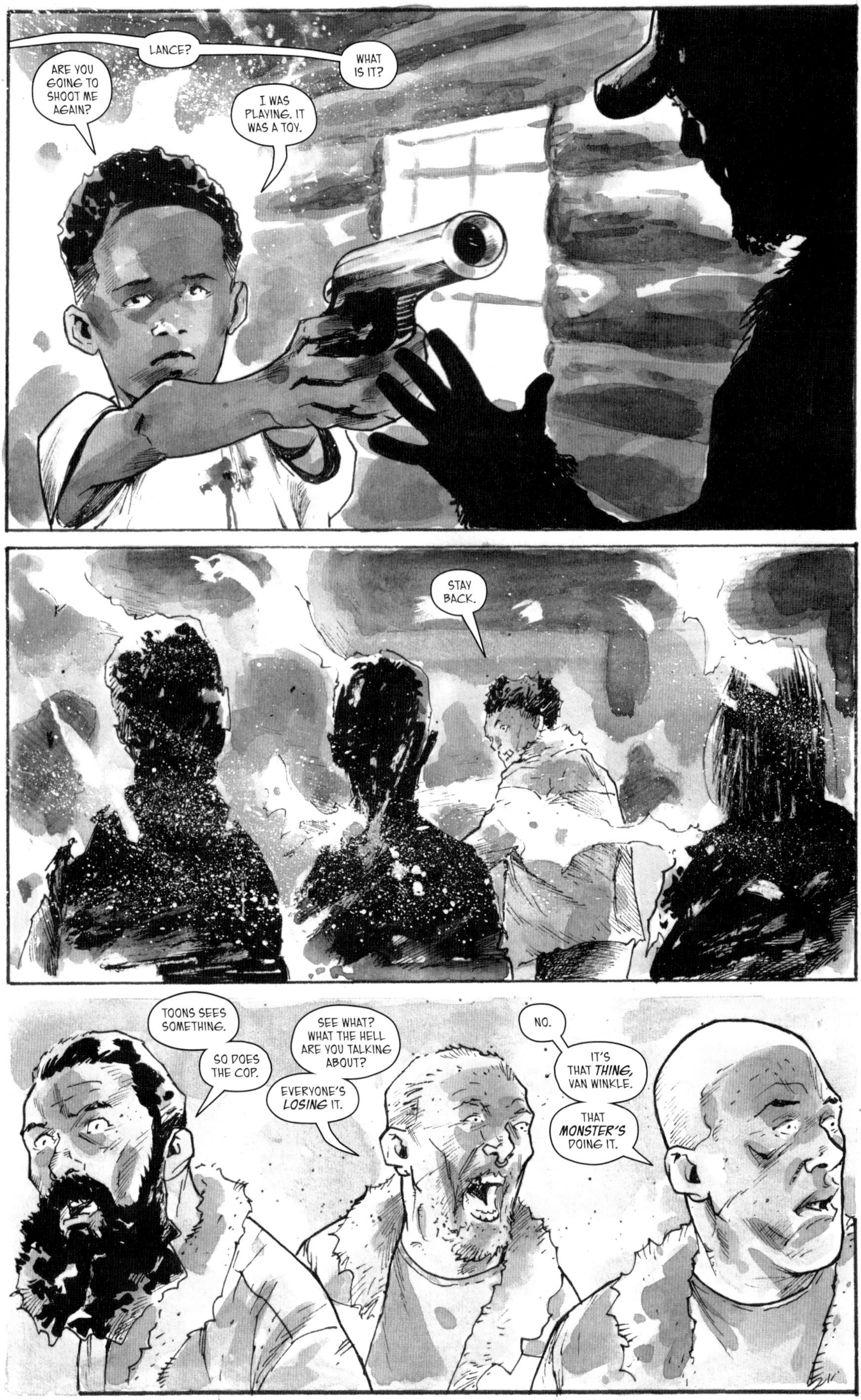
ARE YOU GOING TO SHOOT ME AGAIN?
LANCE?
I WAS PLAYING. IT WAS A TOY.
WHAT IS IT?
STAY BACK.
TOONS SEES SOMETHING.
SO DOES THE COP.
SEE WHAT? WHAT THE HELL ARE YOU TALKING ABOUT?
EVERYONE'S *LOSING* IT.
NO.
IT'S THAT *THING,* VAN WINKLE.
THAT *MONSTER'S* DOING IT.

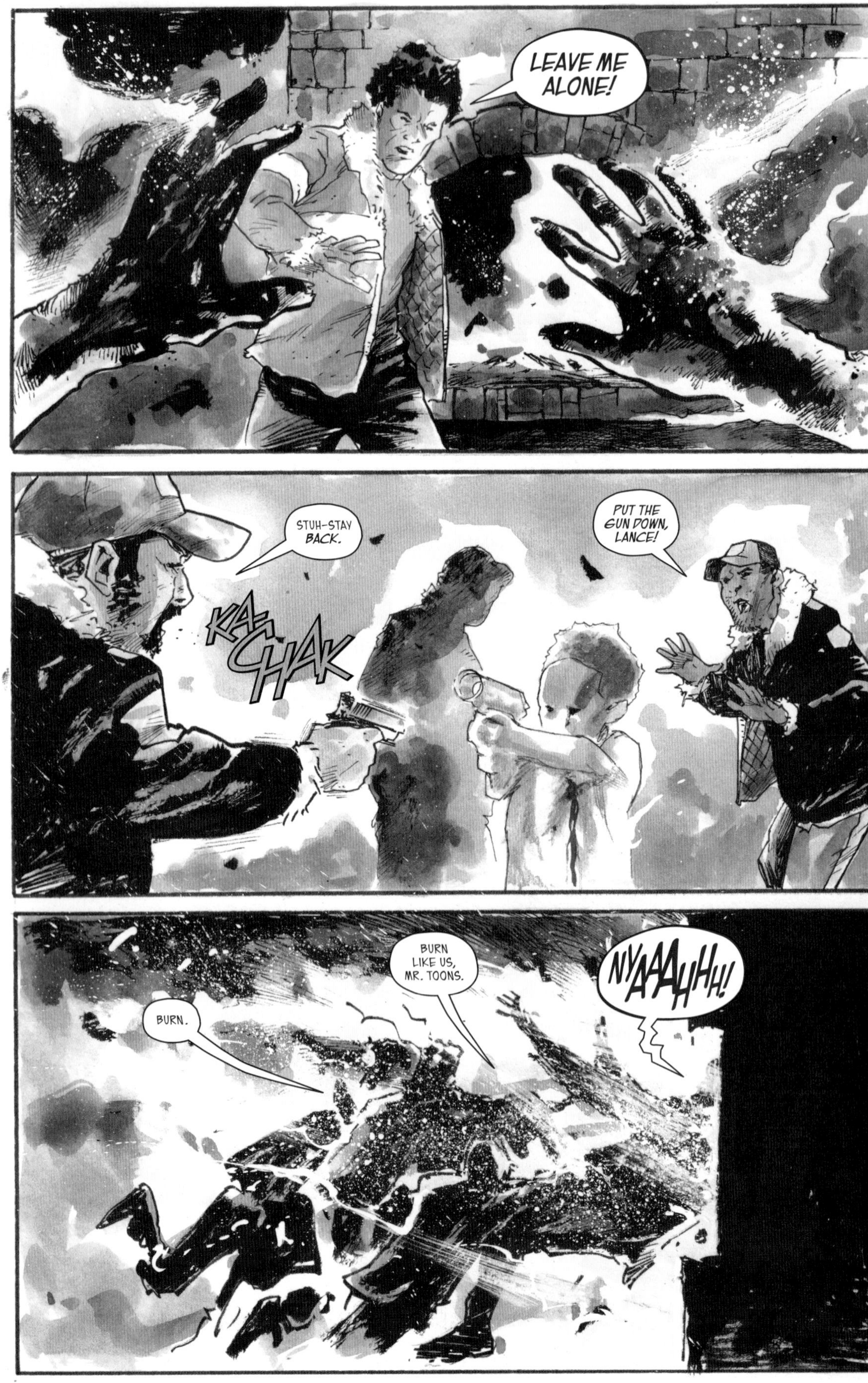
LEAVE ME ALONE!
STUH-STAY BACK.
KA-CHAK
PUT THE GUN DOWN, LANCE!
BURN.
BURN LIKE US, MR. TOONS.
NYAAAHHH!

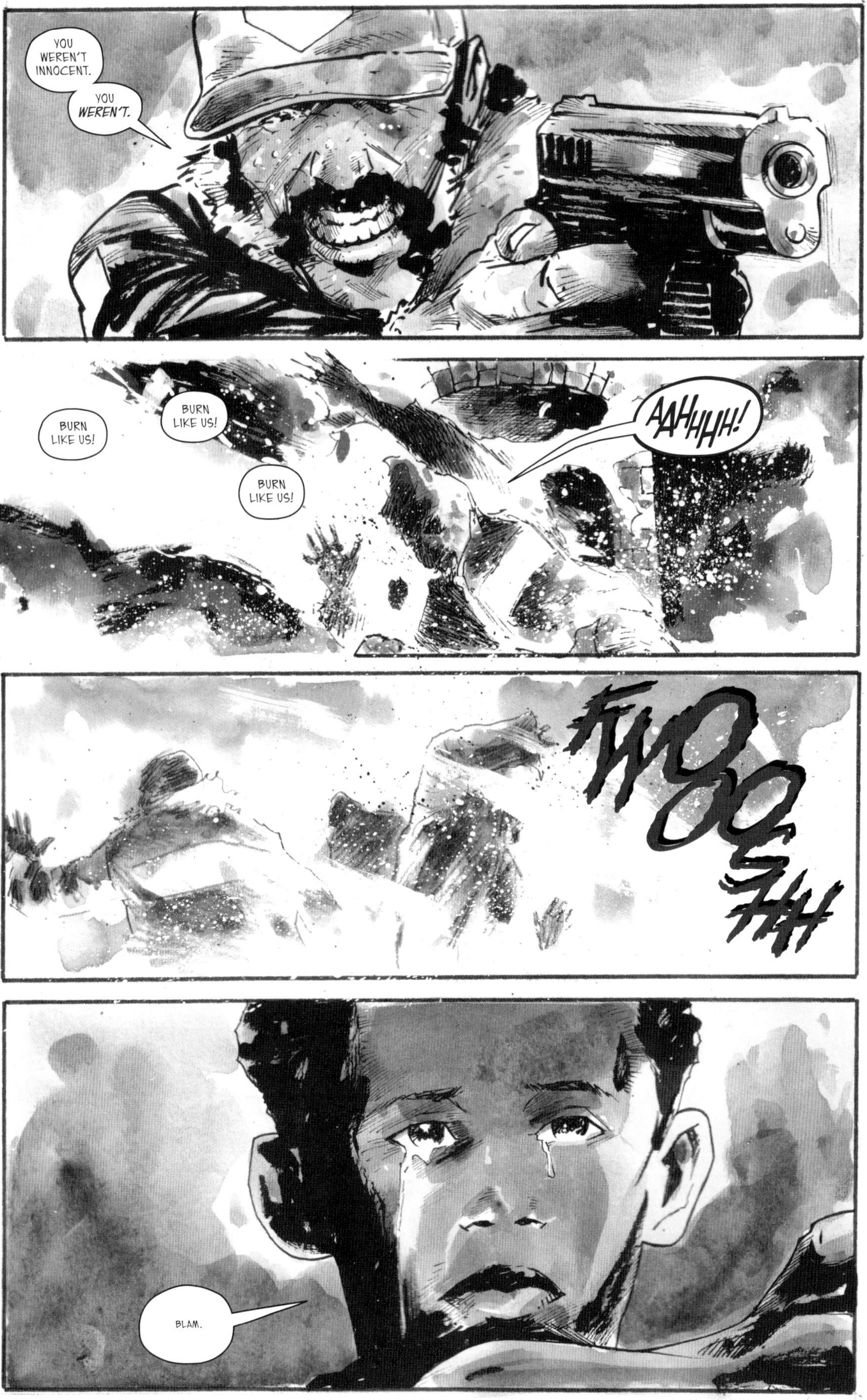
YOU WEREN'T INNOCENT.
YOU WEREN'T.
BURN LIKE US!
BURN LIKE US!
BURN LIKE US!
AAHHHH!
FWOOSHH
BLAM.

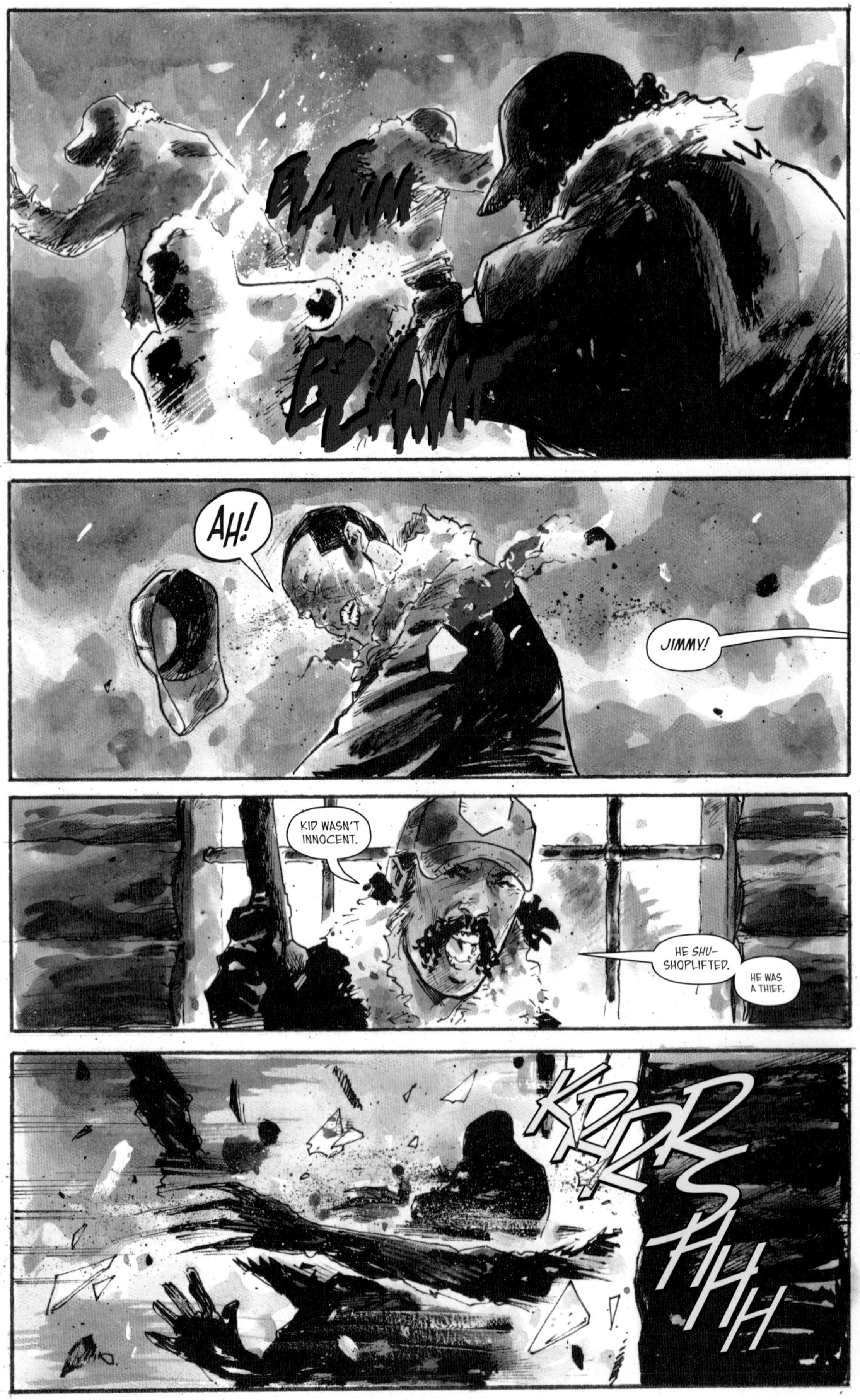
BLAMM
BLAMM
AH!
JIMMY!
KID WASN'T INNOCENT.
HE SHU-SHOPLIFTED.
HE WAS A THIEF.
KRRRSHHH

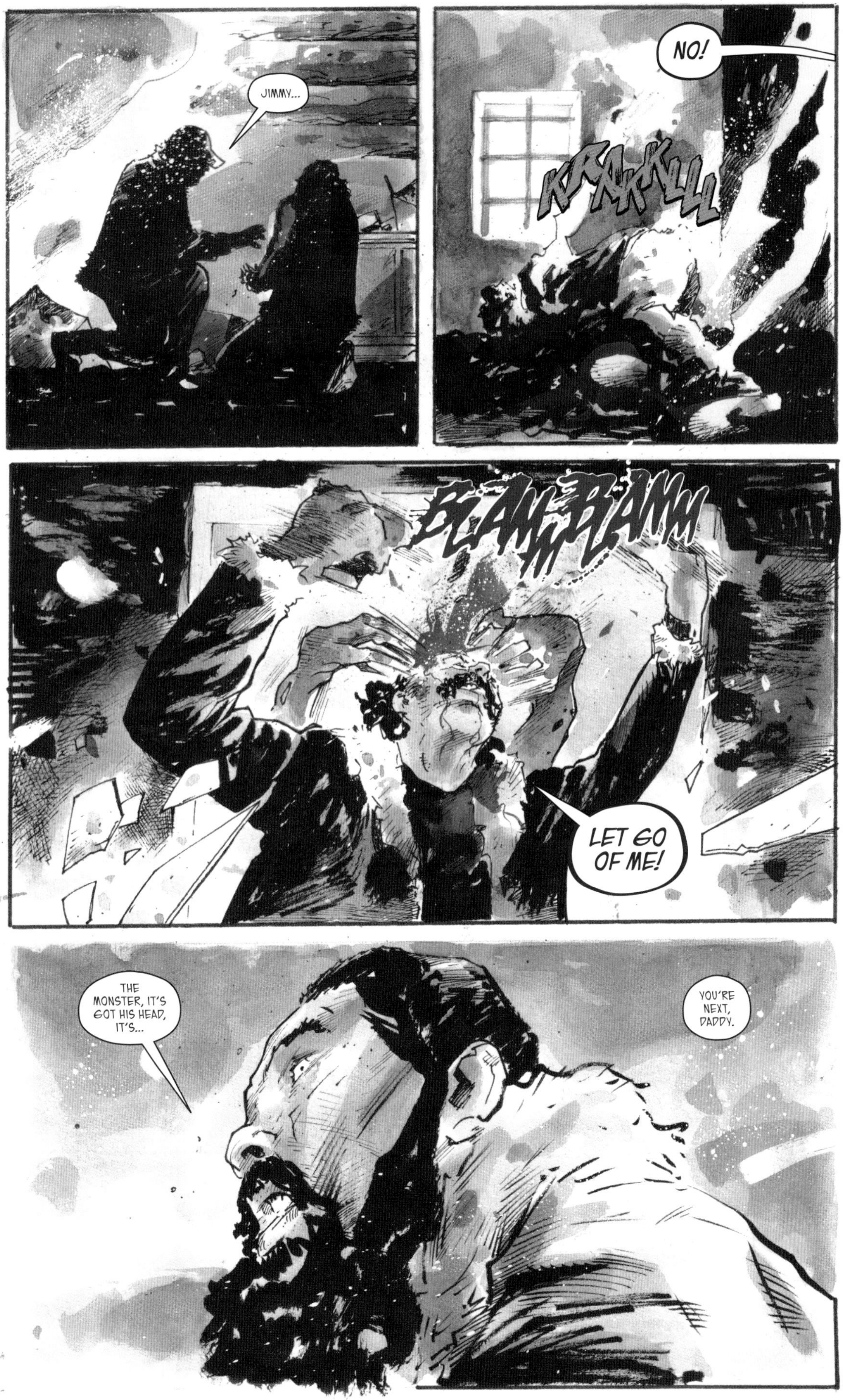
JIMMY...
NO!
KRAKKLLL
BLAMM BLAMM
LET GO OF ME!
THE MONSTER, IT'S GOT HIS HEAD, IT'S...
YOU'RE NEXT, DADDY.

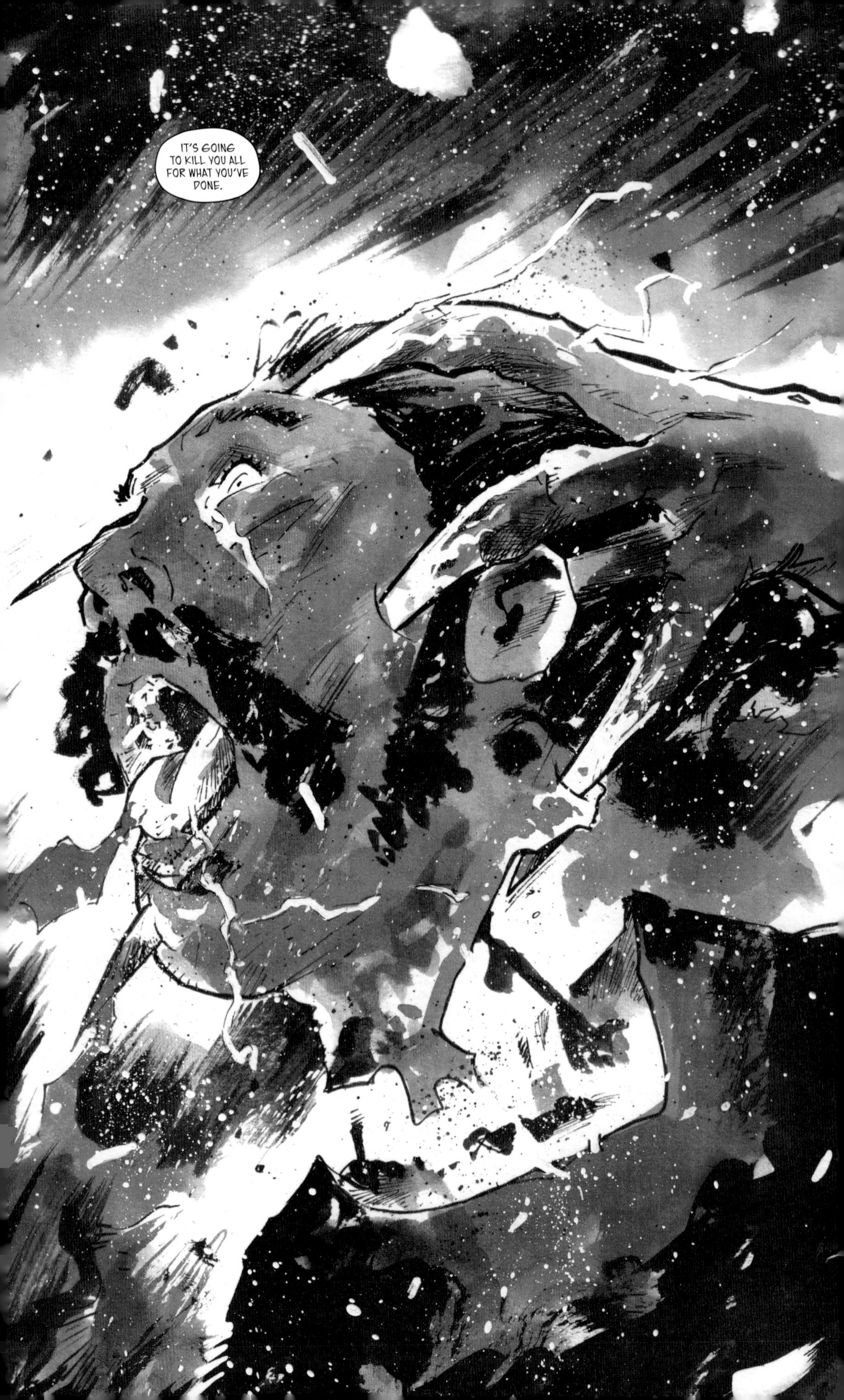
IT'S GOING TO KILL YOU ALL FOR WHAT YOU'VE DONE.

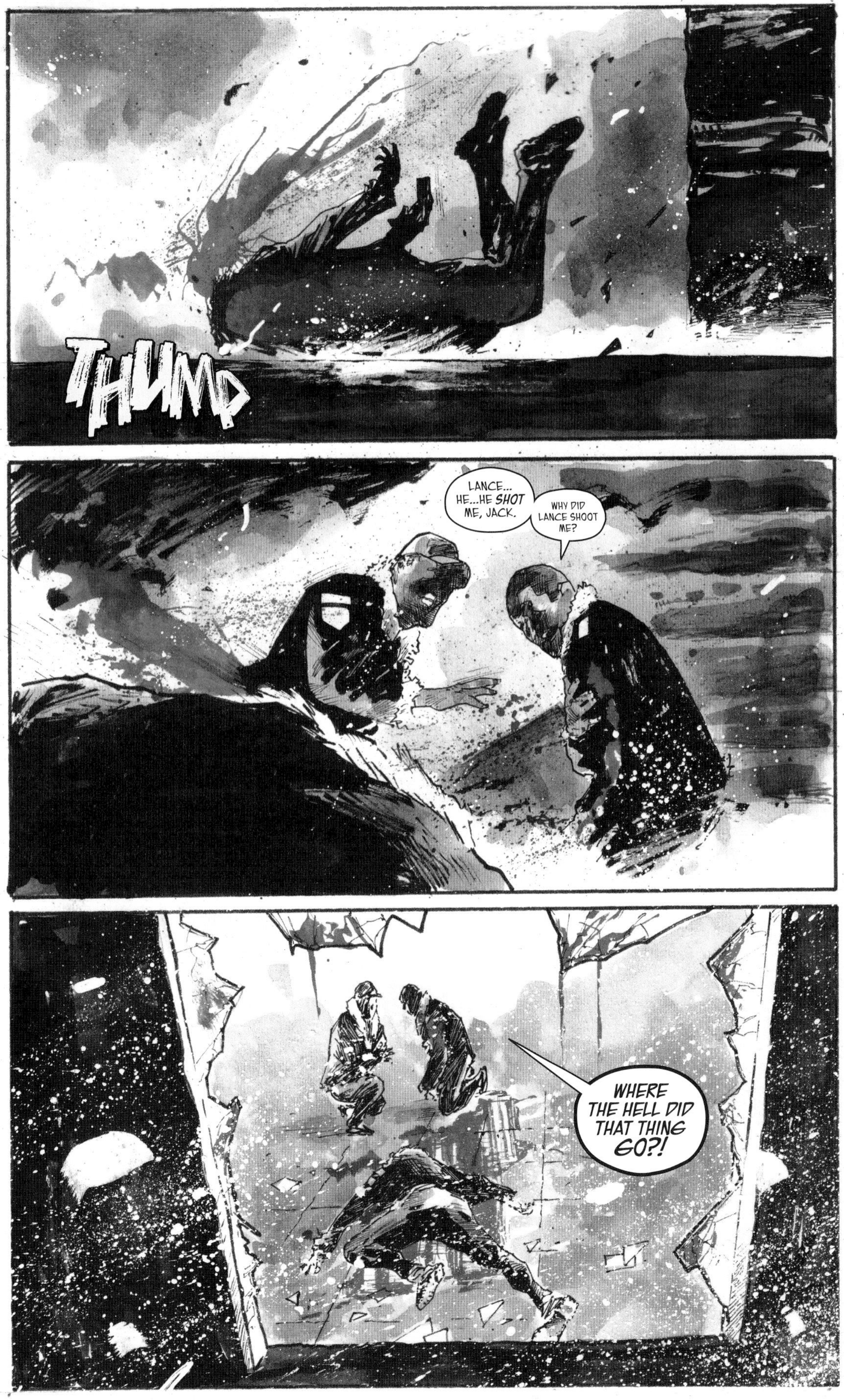
THUMP
LANCE... HE...HE SHOT ME, JACK.
WHY DID LANCE SHOOT ME?
WHERE THE HELL DID THAT THING GO?!

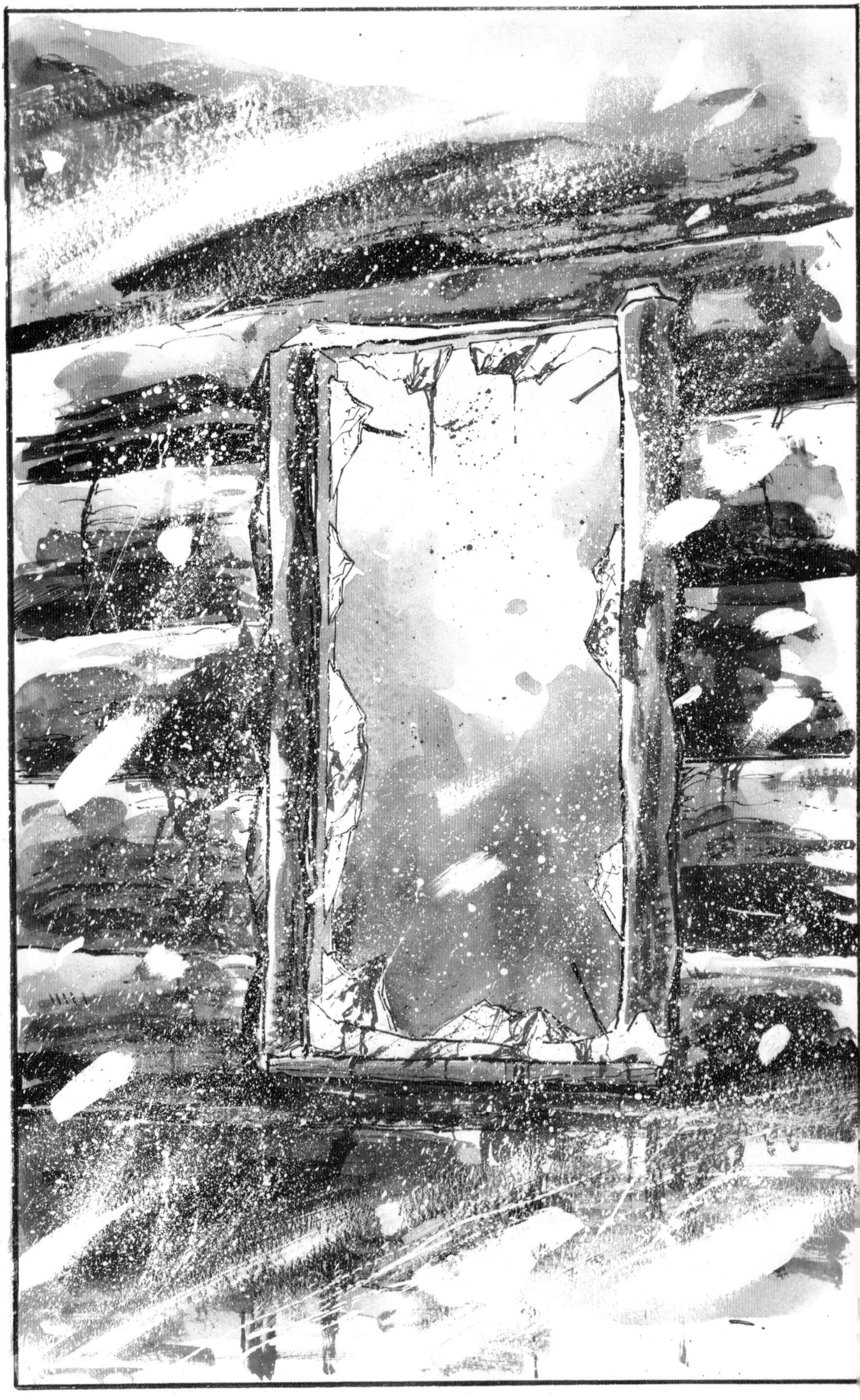

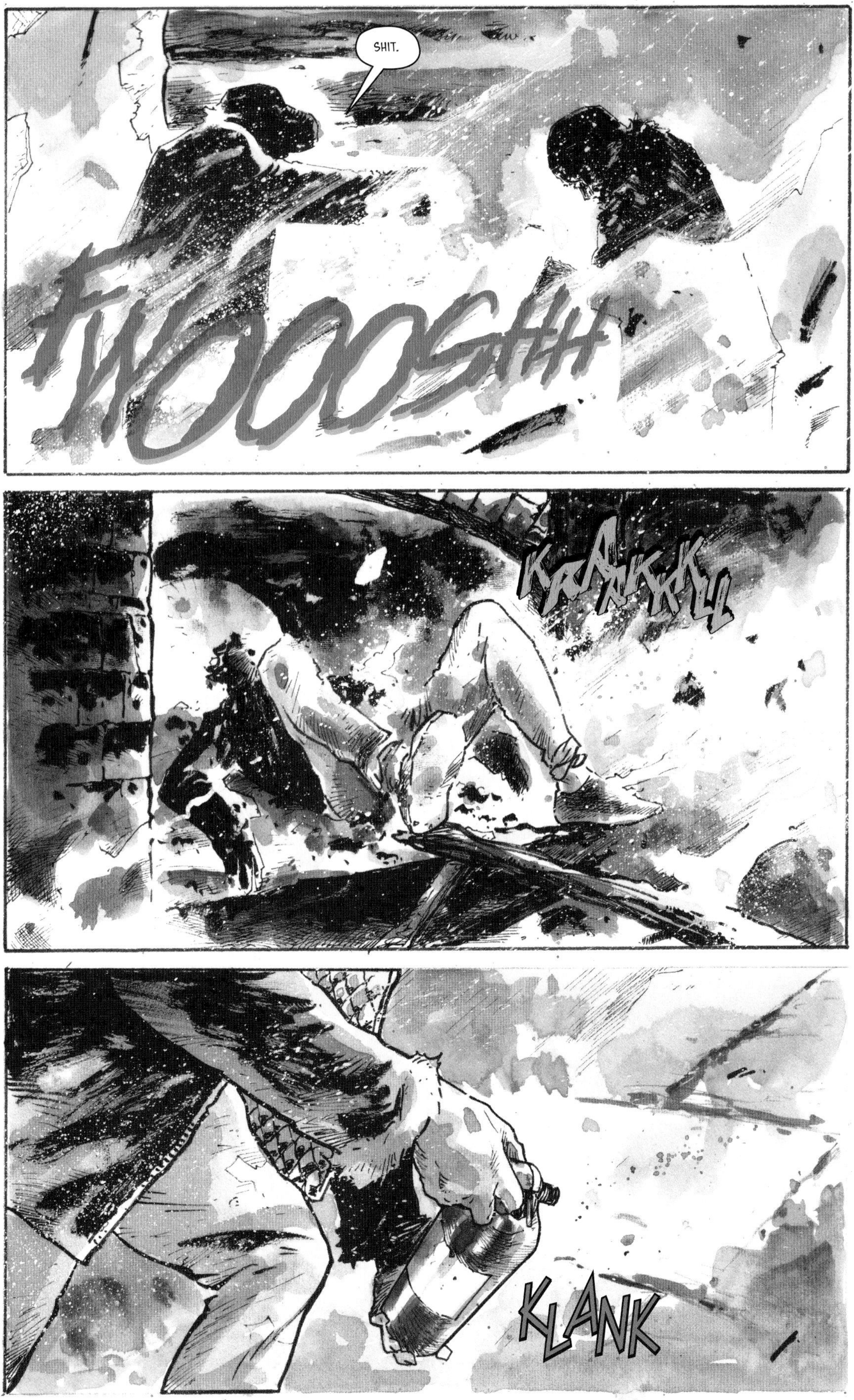
SHIT.
FWOOOSHH
KRAKKKLL
KLANK

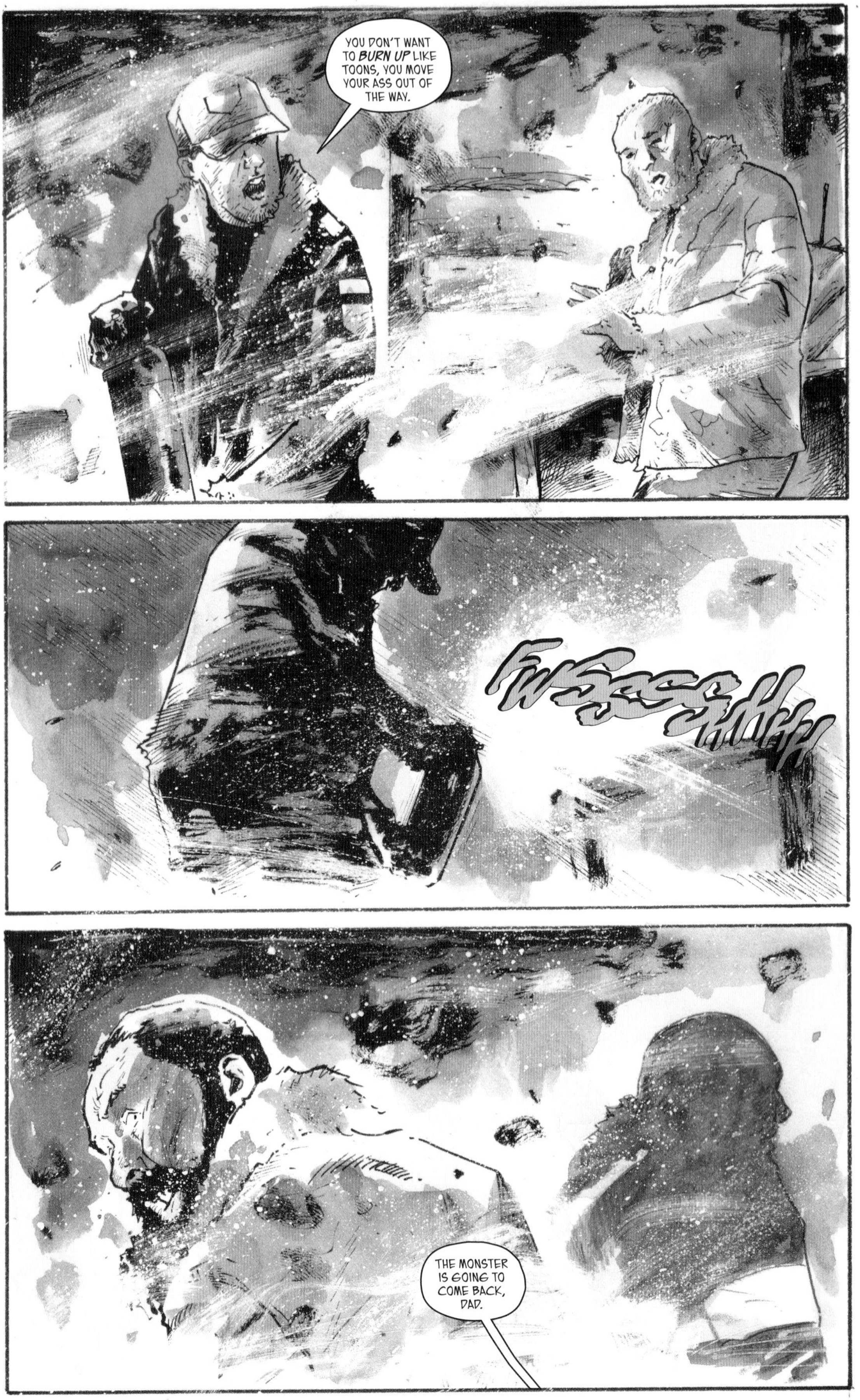
YOU DON'T WANT TO BURN UP LIKE TOONS, YOU MOVE YOUR ASS OUT OF THE WAY.
FWSSSSCHHHH
THE MONSTER IS GOING TO COME BACK, DAD.

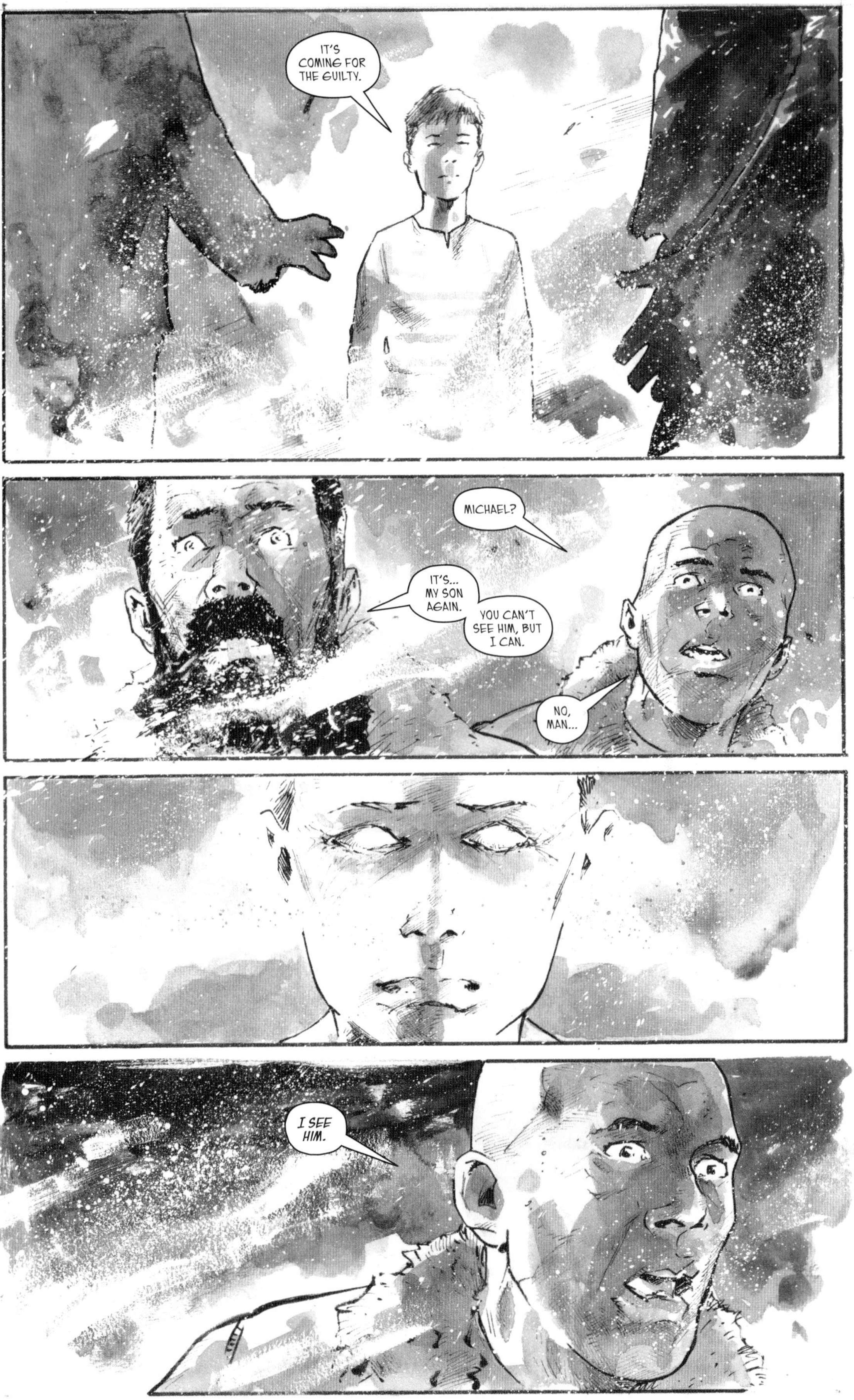
IT'S COMING FOR THE GUILTY.
MICHAEL?
IT'S... MY SON AGAIN.
YOU CAN'T SEE HIM, BUT I CAN.
NO, MAN...
I SEE HIM.

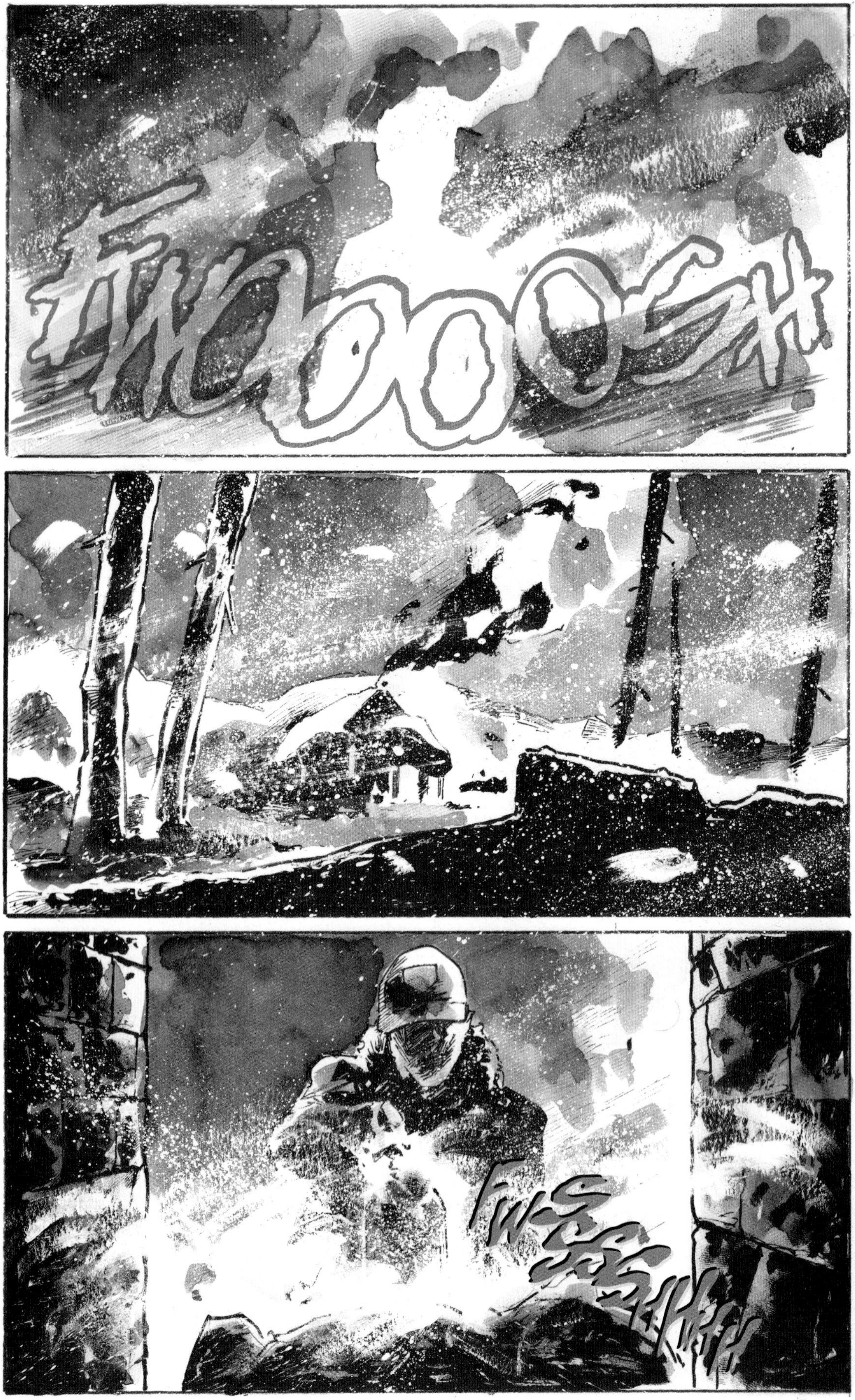
FWOOOSH
FWSSSHHH

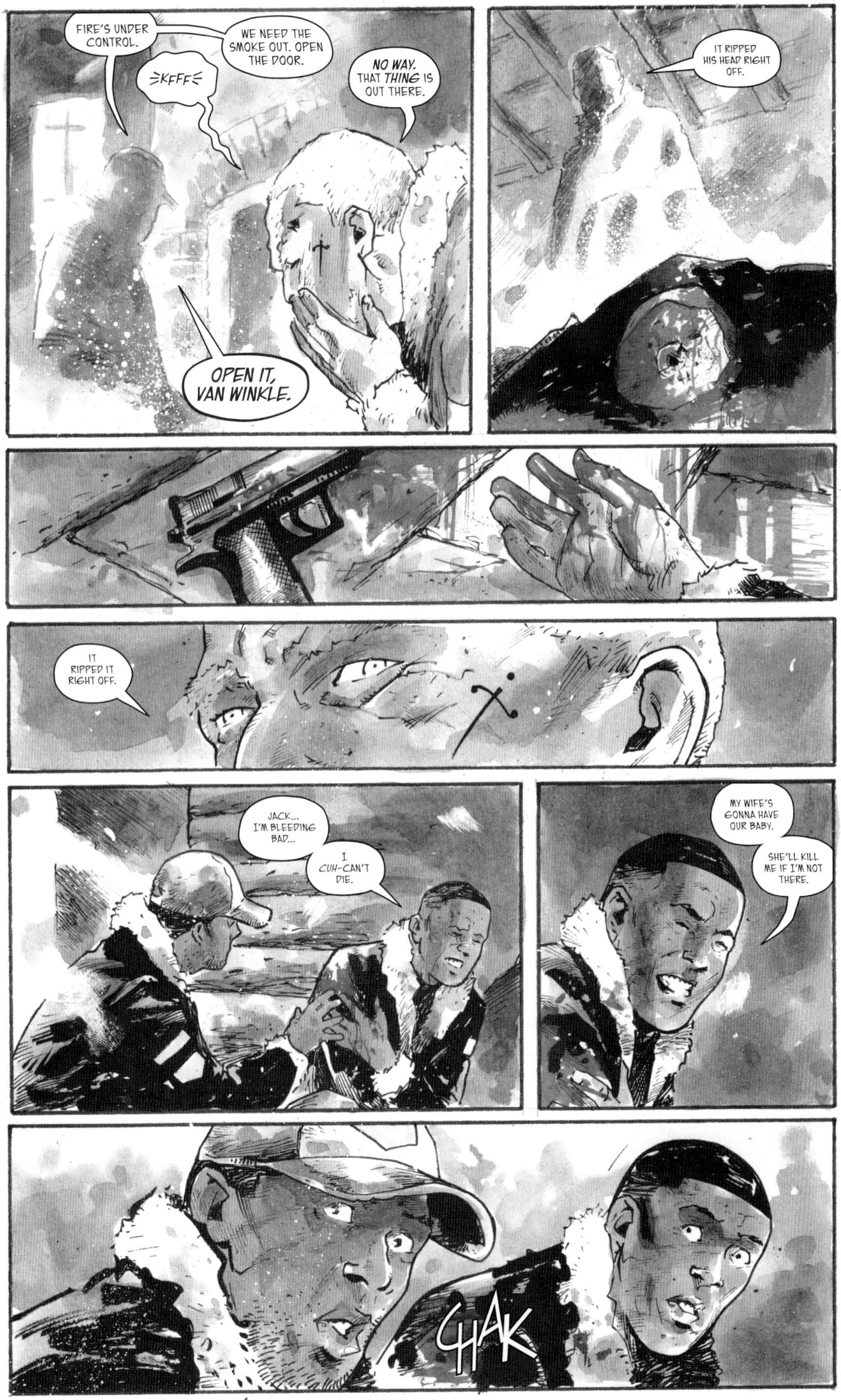
FIRE'S UNDER CONTROL.
WE NEED THE SMOKE OUT. OPEN THE DOOR.
KFFF
NO WAY. THAT THING IS OUT THERE.
OPEN IT, VAN WINKLE.
IT RIPPED HIS HEAD RIGHT OFF.
IT RIPPED IT RIGHT OFF.
JACK... I'M BLEEDING BAD...
I CUH-CAN'T DIE.
MY WIFE'S GONNA HAVE OUR BABY.
SHE'LL KILL ME IF I'M NOT THERE.
CHAK

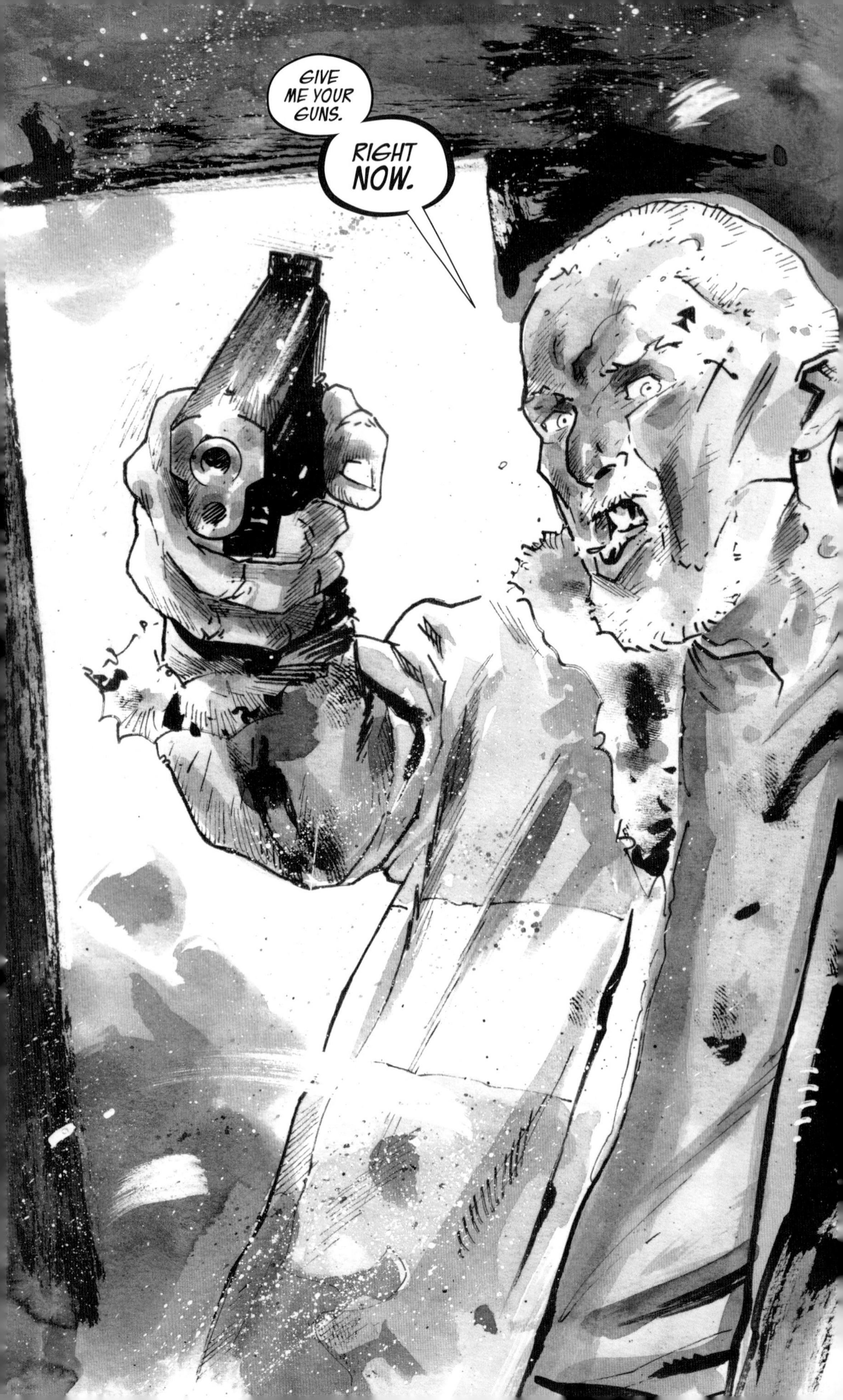
GIVE ME YOUR GUNS.
RIGHT NOW.

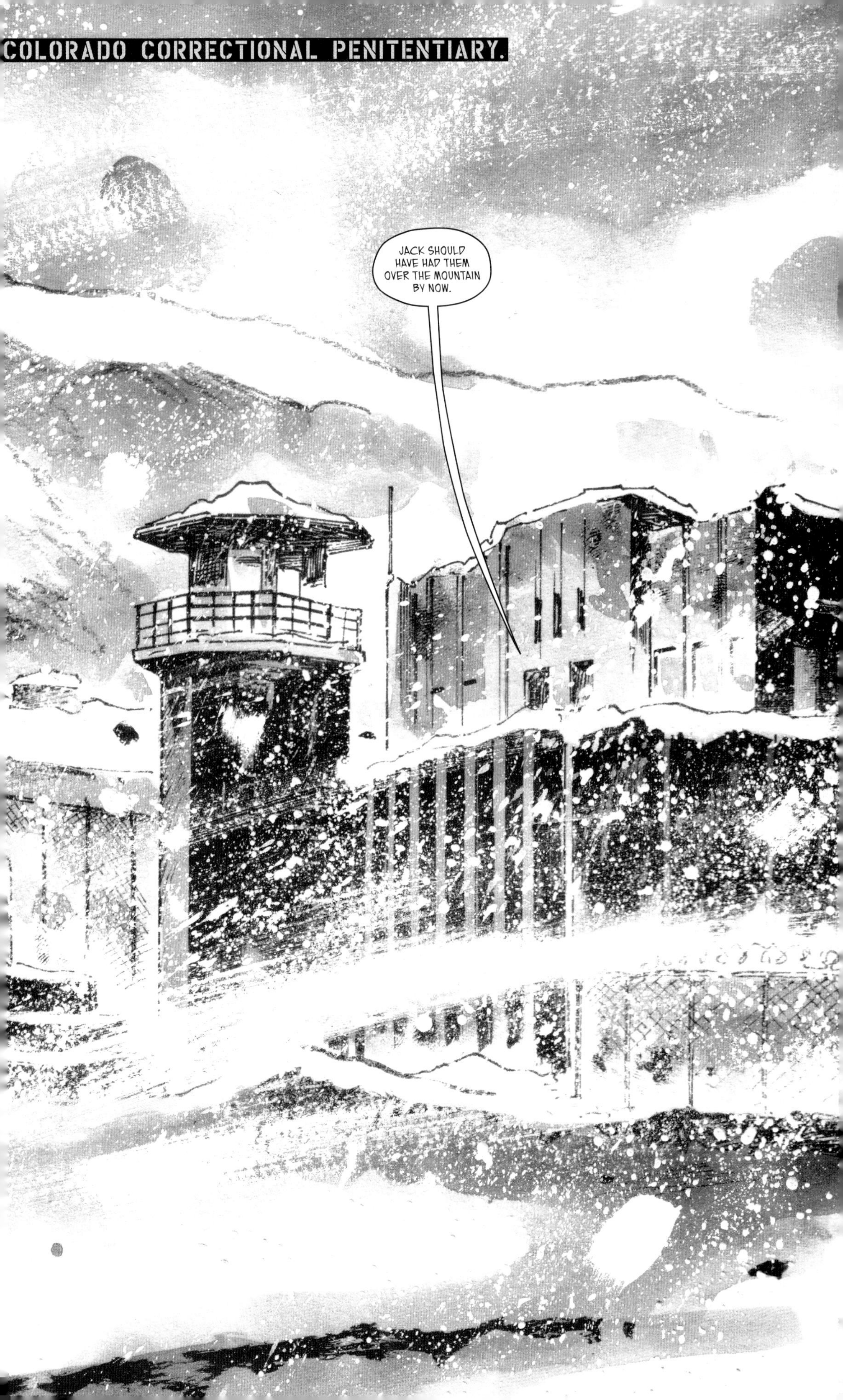
COLORADO CORRECTIONAL PENITENTIARY.
JACK SHOULD HAVE HAD THEM OVER THE MOUNTAIN BY NOW.

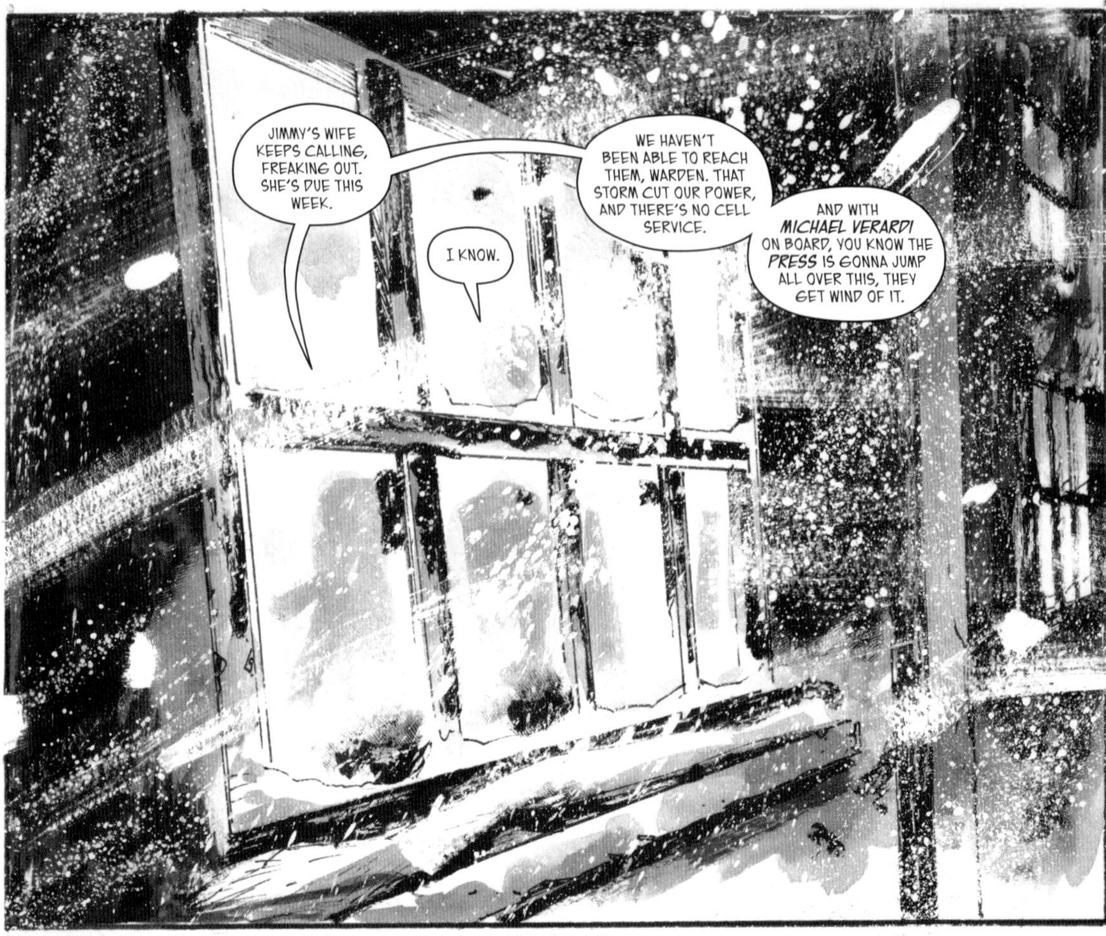
JIMMY'S WIFE KEEPS CALLING, FREAKING OUT. SHE'S DUE THIS WEEK.
WE HAVEN'T BEEN ABLE TO REACH THEM, WARDEN. THAT STORM CUT OUR POWER, AND THERE'S NO CELL SERVICE.
I KNOW.
AND WITH MICHAEL VERARDI ON BOARD, YOU KNOW THE PRESS IS GONNA JUMP ALL OVER THIS, THEY GET WIND OF IT.
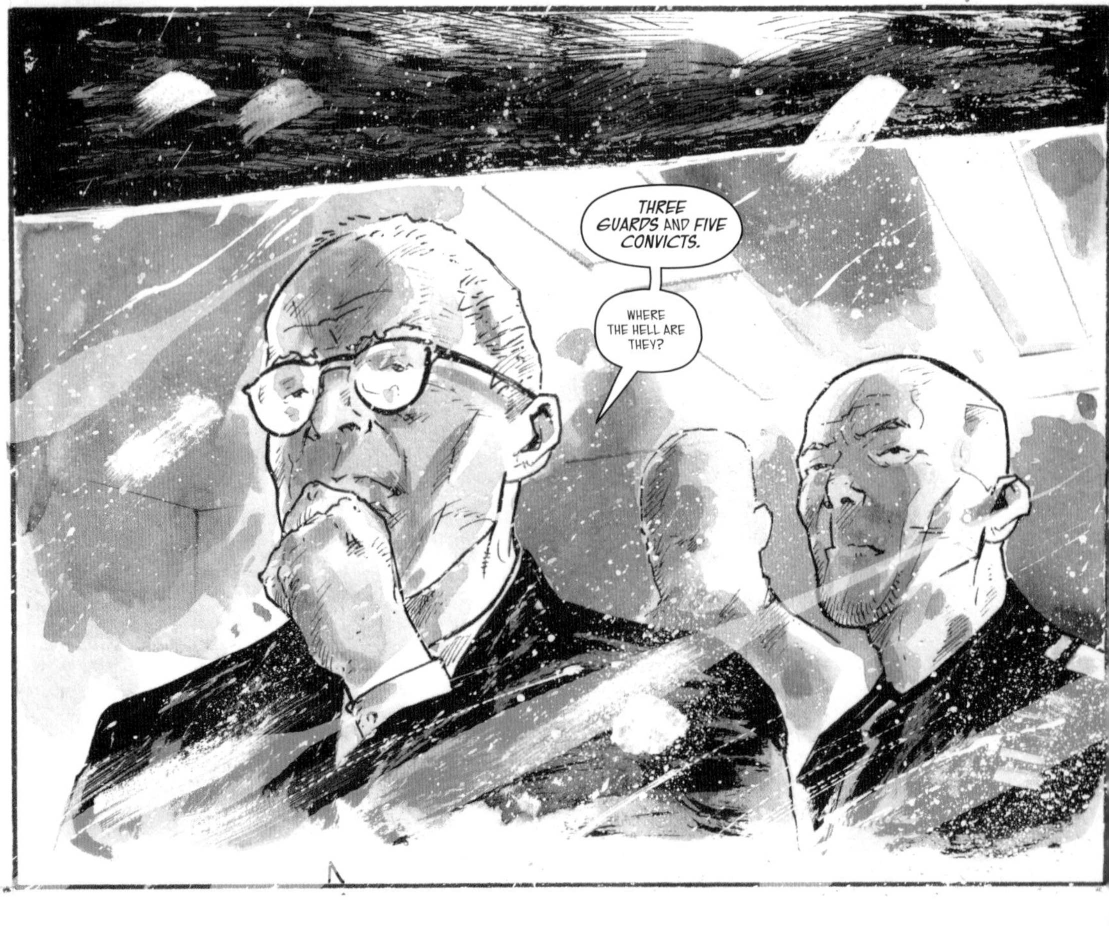
THREE GUARDS AND FIVE CONVICTS.
WHERE THE HELL ARE THEY?

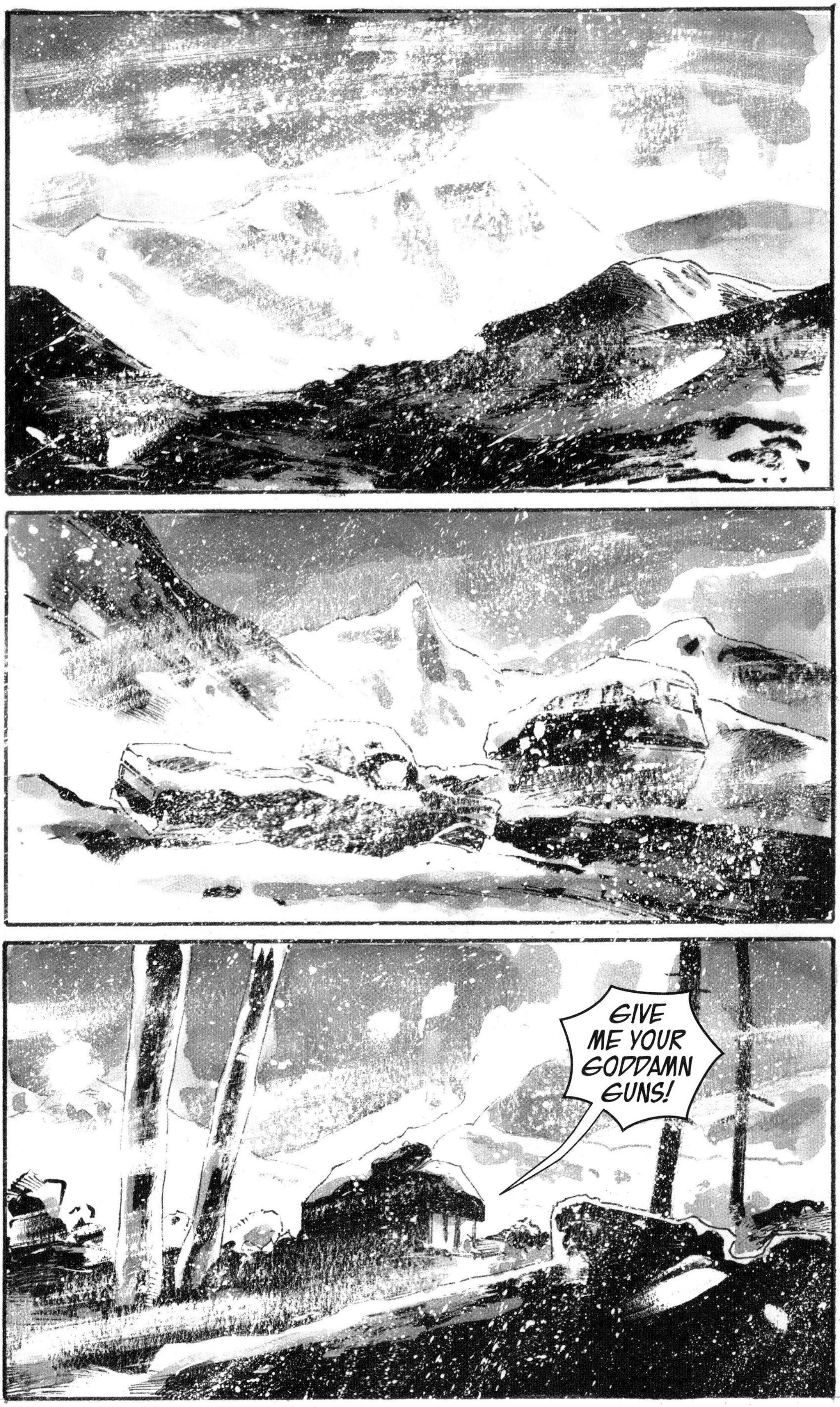
GIVE ME YOUR GODDAMN GUNS!

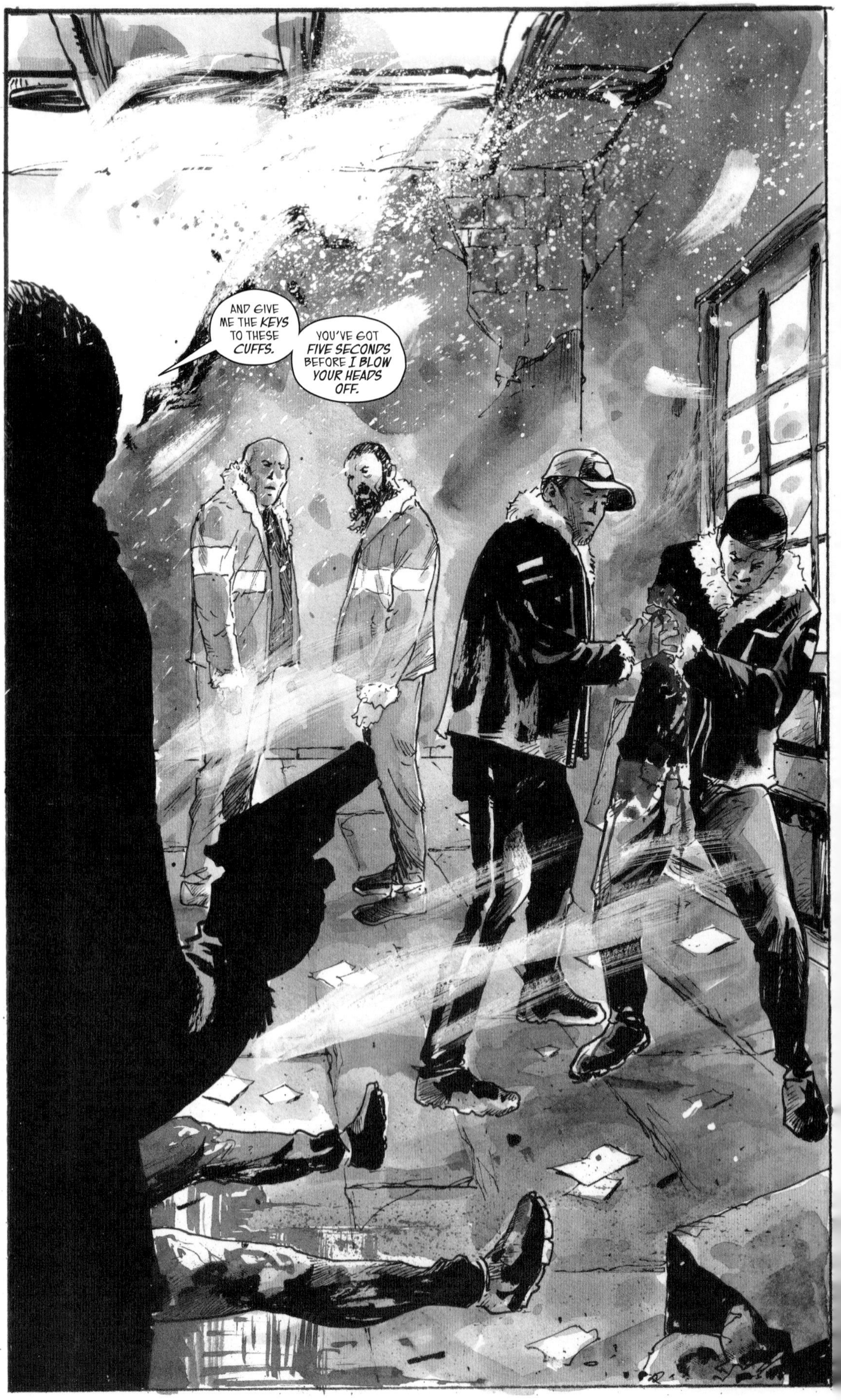
AND GIVE ME THE KEYS TO THESE CUFFS.
YOU'VE GOT FIVE SECONDS BEFORE I BLOW YOUR HEADS OFF.

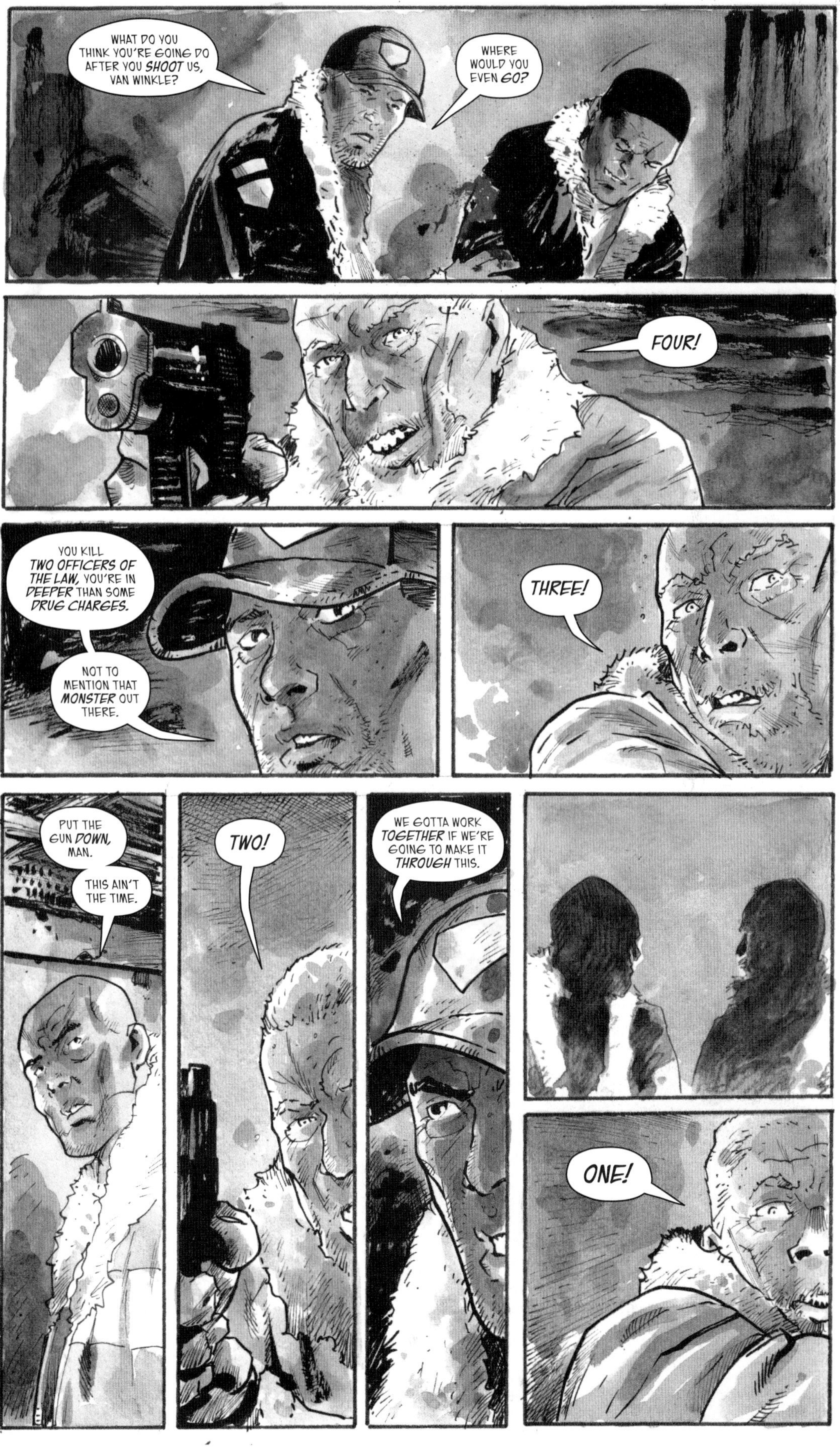
WHAT DO YOU THINK YOU'RE GOING DO AFTER YOU SHOOT US, VAN WINKLE?
WHERE WOULD YOU EVEN GO?
FOUR!
YOU KILL TWO OFFICERS OF THE LAW, YOU'RE IN DEEPER THAN SOME DRUG CHARGES.
NOT TO MENTION THAT MONSTER OUT THERE.
THREE!
PUT THE GUN DOWN, MAN.
THIS AIN'T THE TIME.
TWO!
WE GOTTA WORK TOGETHER IF WE'RE GOING TO MAKE IT THROUGH THIS.
ONE!

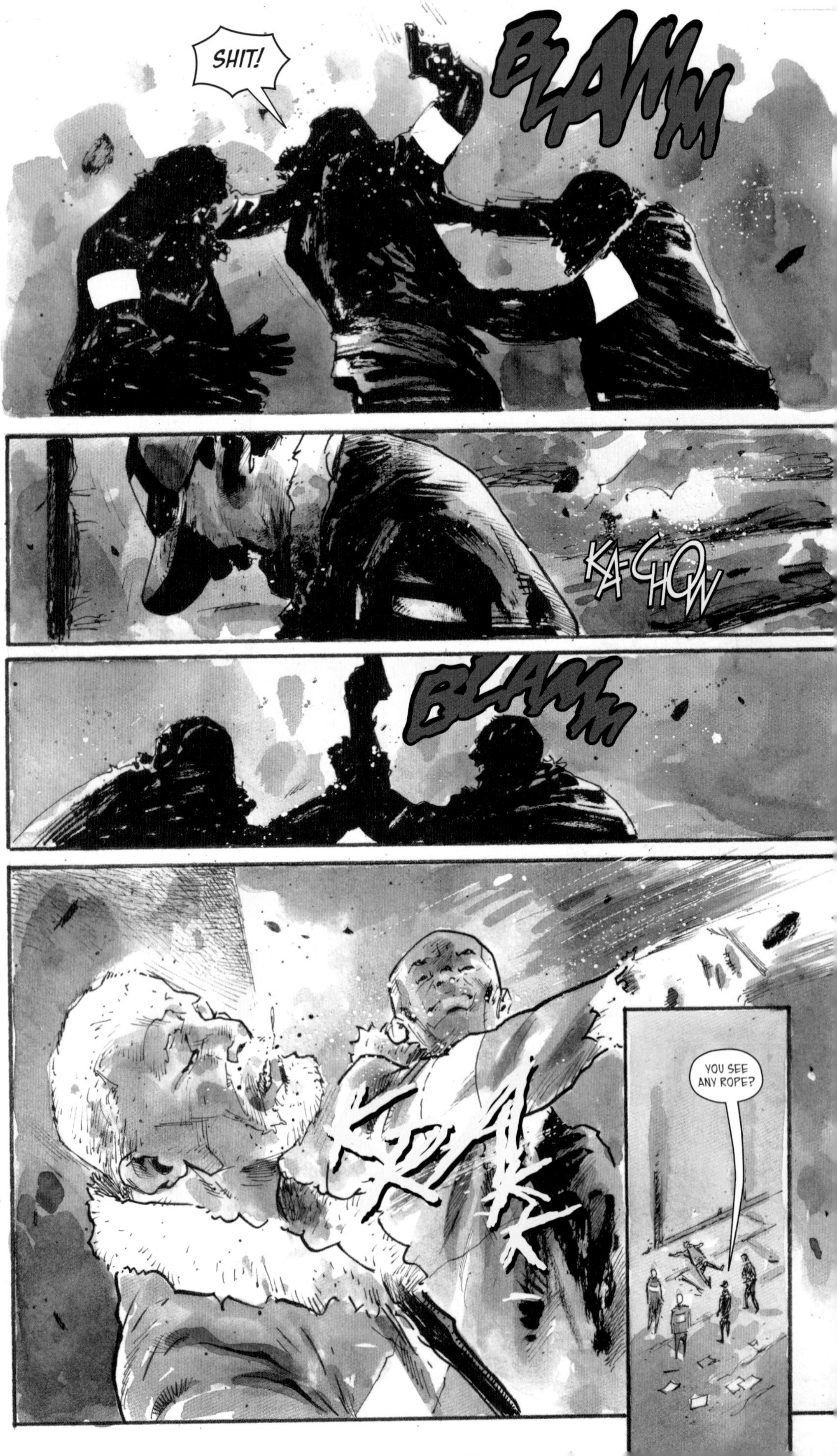
SHIT!
BLAMM
KA-CHOW
BLAMM
YOU SEE ANY ROPE?

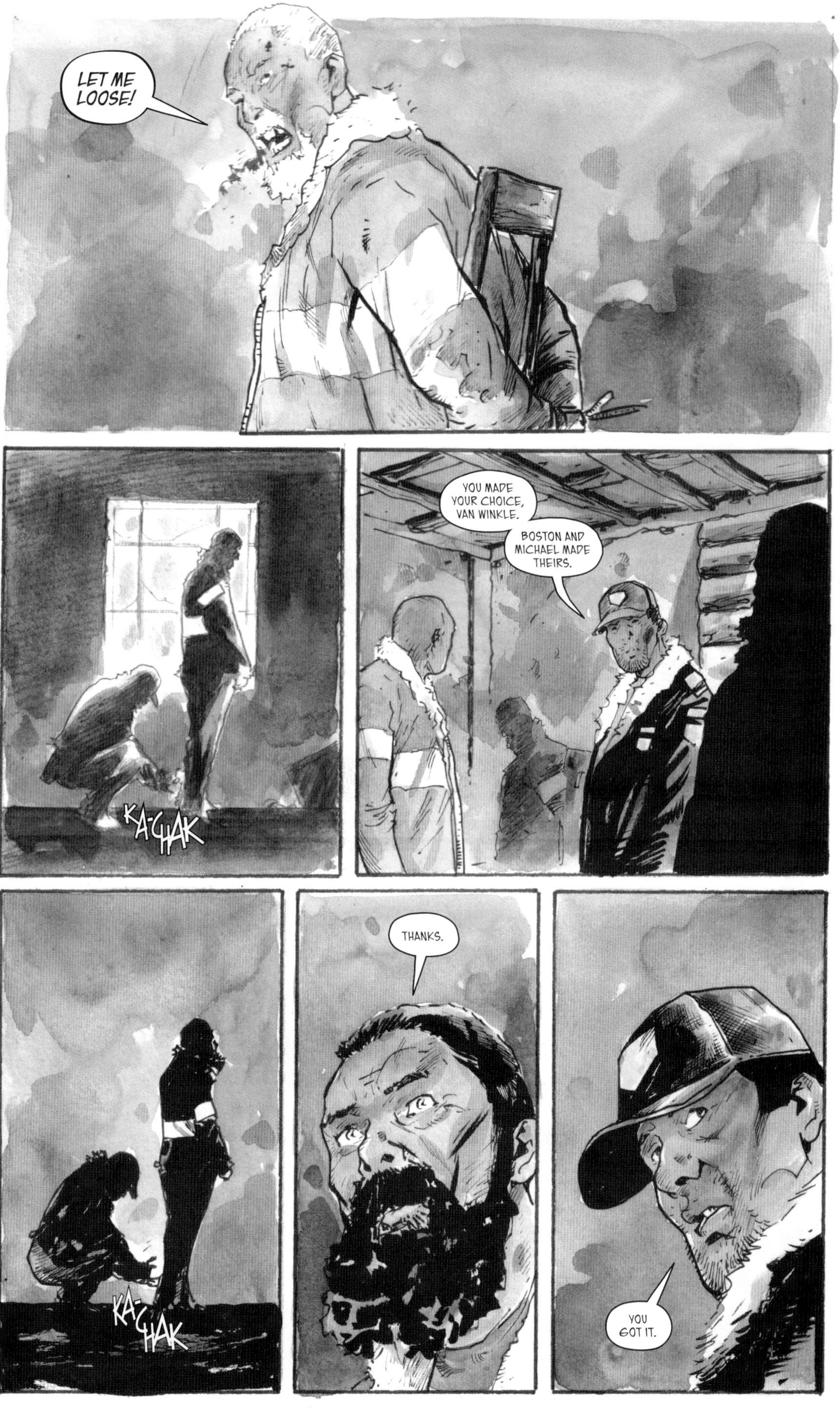

LET ME LOOSE!
KA-CHAK
YOU MADE YOUR CHOICE, VAN WINKLE.
BOSTON AND MICHAEL MADE THEIRS.
KA-CHAK
THANKS.
YOU GOT IT.

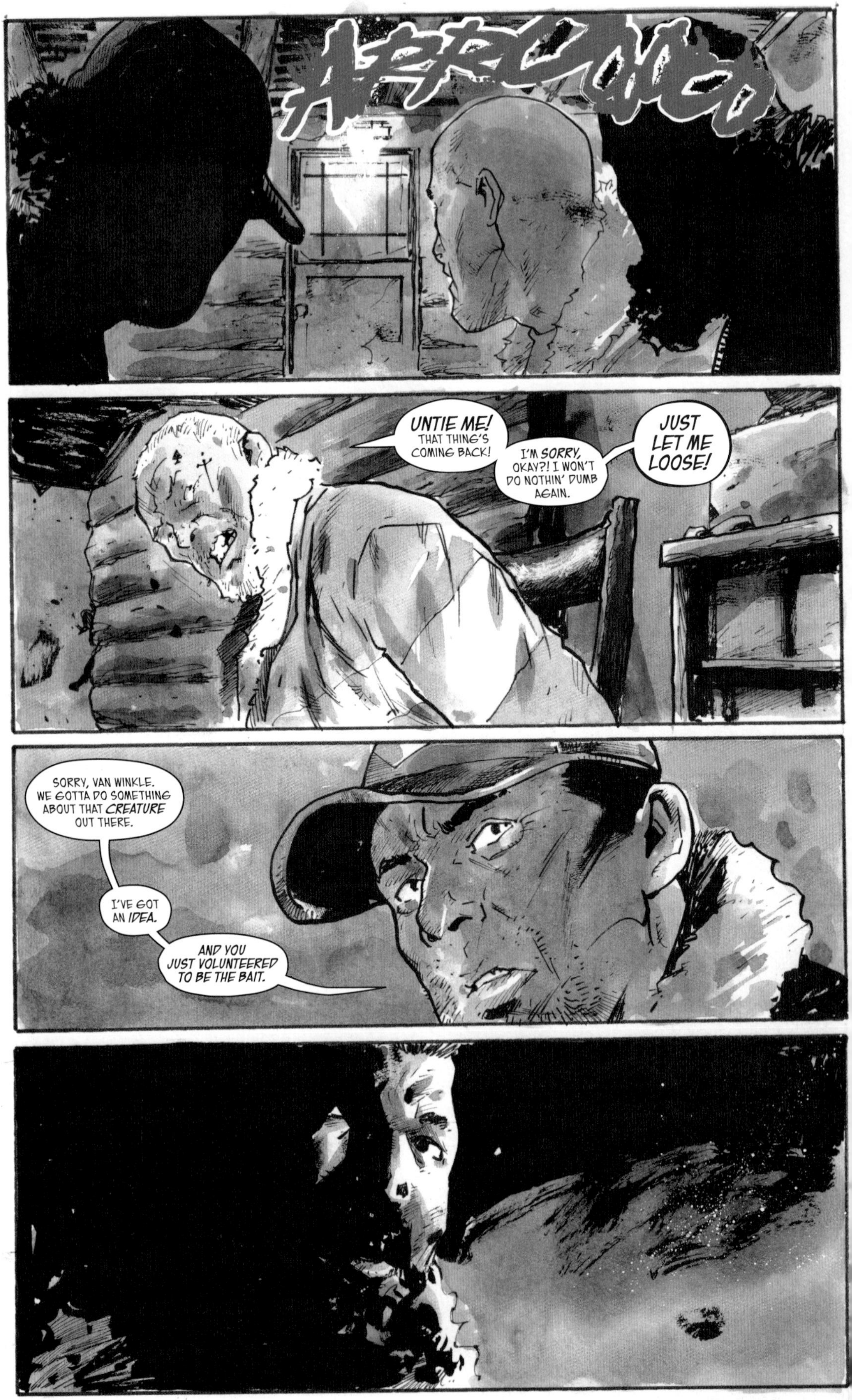
UNTIE ME! THAT THING'S COMING BACK!
I'M SORRY, OKAY?! I WON'T DO NOTHIN' DUMB AGAIN.
JUST LET ME LOOSE!
SORRY, VAN WINKLE. WE GOTTA DO SOMETHING ABOUT THAT CREATURE OUT THERE.
I'VE GOT AN IDEA.
AND YOU JUST VOLUNTEERED TO BE THE BAIT.

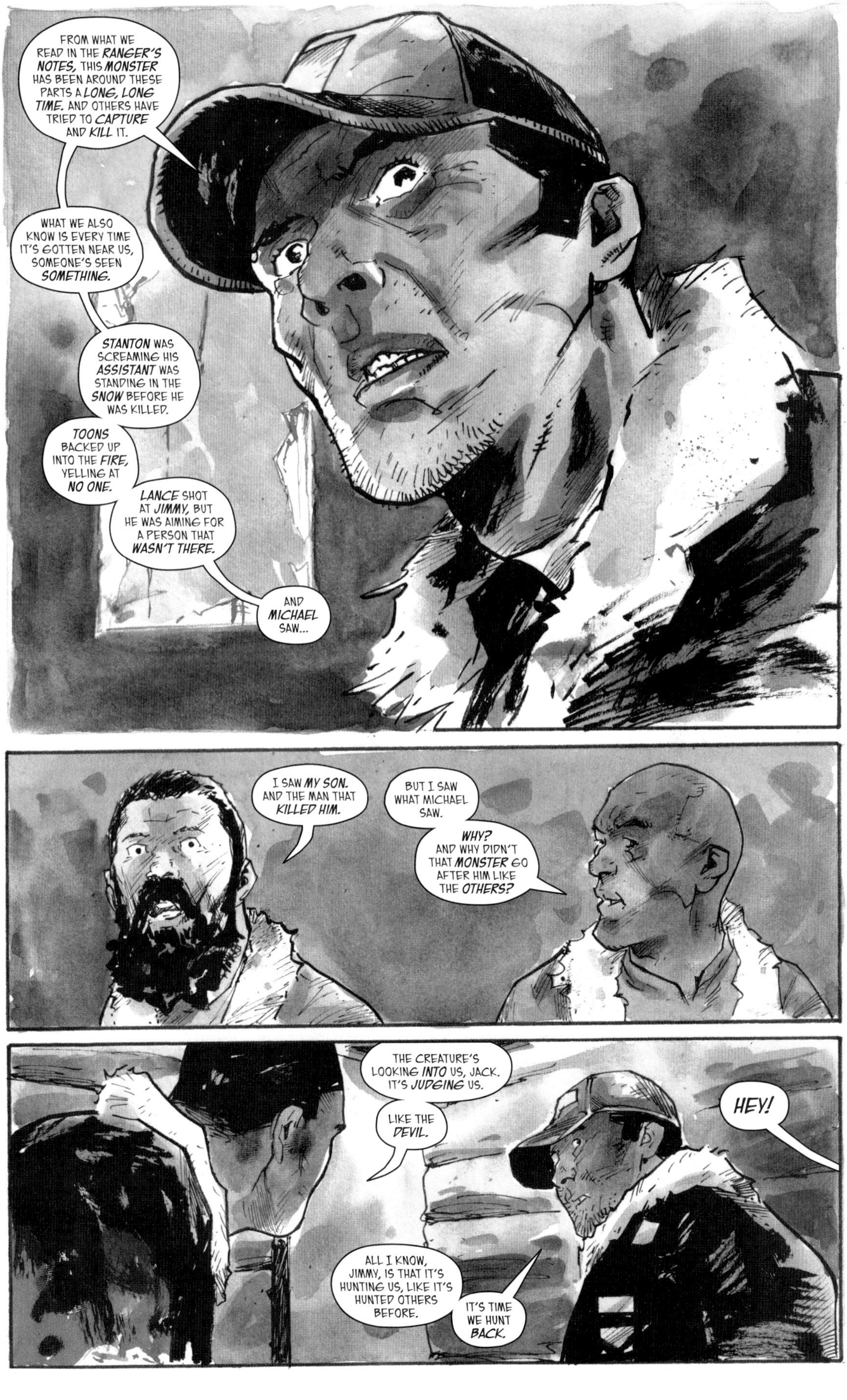
FROM WHAT WE READ IN THE RANGER'S NOTES, THIS MONSTER HAS BEEN AROUND THESE PARTS A LONG, LONG TIME. AND OTHERS HAVE TRIED TO CAPTURE AND KILL IT.
WHAT WE ALSO KNOW IS EVERY TIME IT'S GOTTEN NEAR US, SOMEONE'S SEEN SOMETHING.
STANTON WAS SCREAMING HIS ASSISTANT WAS STANDING IN THE SNOW BEFORE HE WAS KILLED.
TOONS BACKED UP INTO THE FIRE, YELLING AT NO ONE.
LANCE SHOT AT JIMMY, BUT HE WAS AIMING FOR A PERSON THAT WASN'T THERE.
AND MICHAEL SAW...
I SAW MY SON. AND THE MAN THAT KILLED HIM.
BUT I SAW WHAT MICHAEL SAW.
WHY? AND WHY DIDN'T THAT MONSTER GO AFTER HIM LIKE THE OTHERS?
THE CREATURE'S LOOKING INTO US, JACK. IT'S JUDGING US.
LIKE THE DEVIL.
HEY!
ALL I KNOW, JIMMY, IS THAT IT'S HUNTING US, LIKE IT'S HUNTED OTHERS BEFORE.
IT'S TIME WE HUNT BACK.

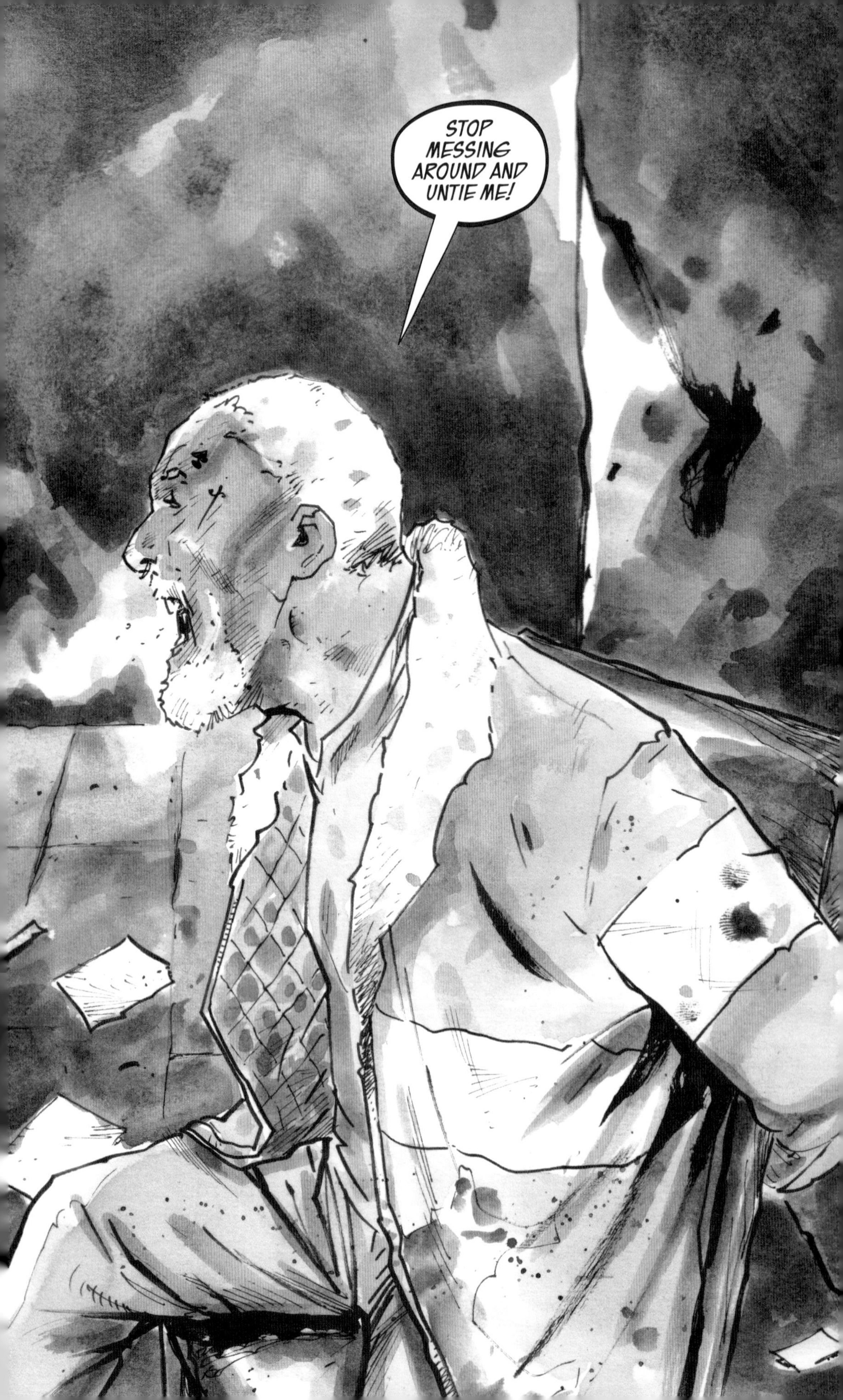
STOP MESSING AROUND AND UNTIE ME!

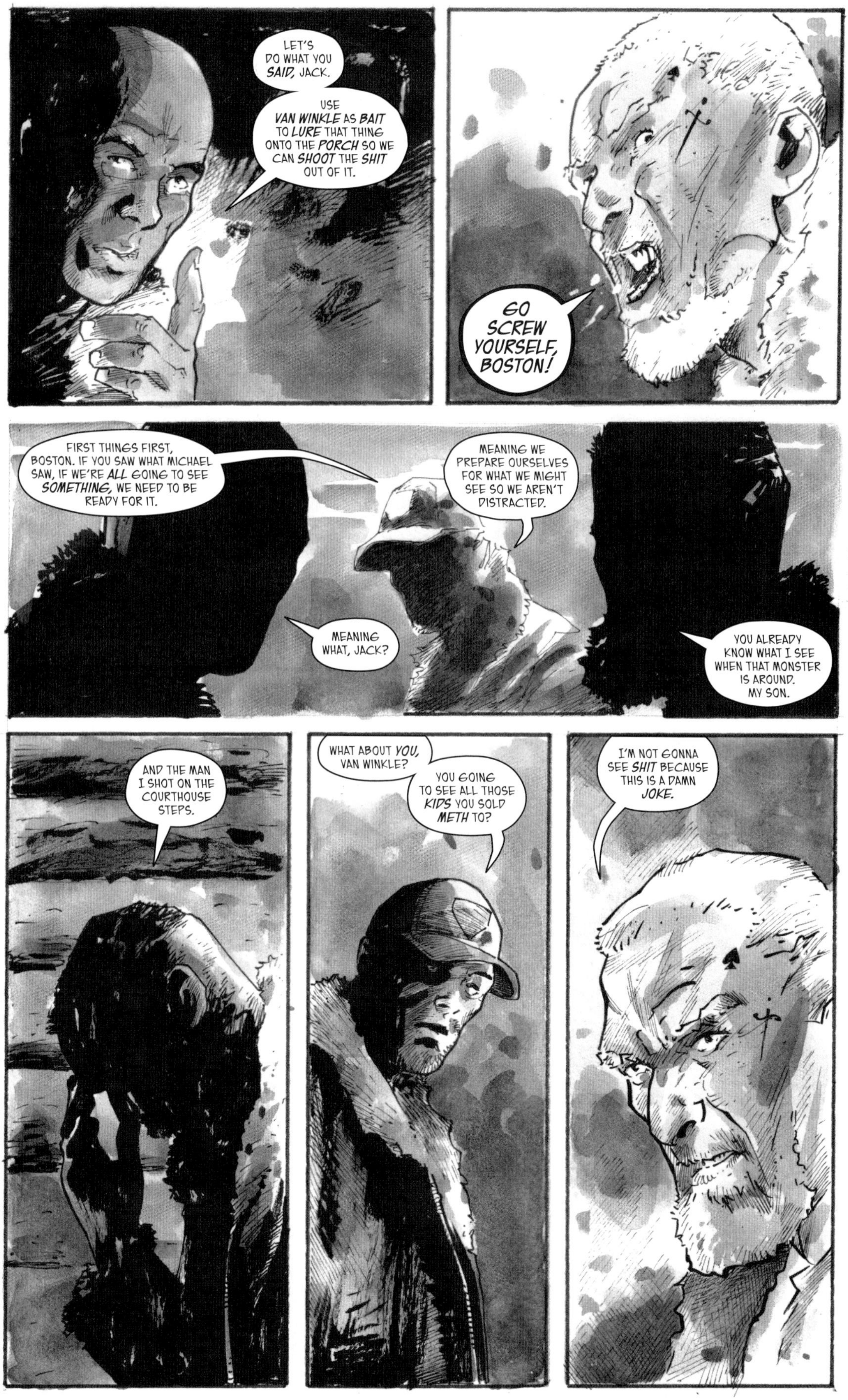
LET'S DO WHAT YOU SAID, JACK.
USE VAN WINKLE AS BAIT TO LURE THAT THING ONTO THE PORCH SO WE CAN SHOOT THE SHIT OUT OF IT.
GO SCREW YOURSELF, BOSTON!
FIRST THINGS FIRST, BOSTON. IF YOU SAW WHAT MICHAEL SAW, IF WE'RE ALL GOING TO SEE SOMETHING, WE NEED TO BE READY FOR IT.
MEANING WHAT, JACK?
MEANING WE PREPARE OURSELVES FOR WHAT WE MIGHT SEE SO WE AREN'T DISTRACTED.
YOU ALREADY KNOW WHAT I SEE WHEN THAT MONSTER IS AROUND. MY SON.
AND THE MAN I SHOT ON THE COURTHOUSE STEPS.
WHAT ABOUT YOU, VAN WINKLE?
YOU GOING TO SEE ALL THOSE KIDS YOU SOLD METH TO?
I'M NOT GONNA SEE SHIT BECAUSE THIS IS A DAMN JOKE.

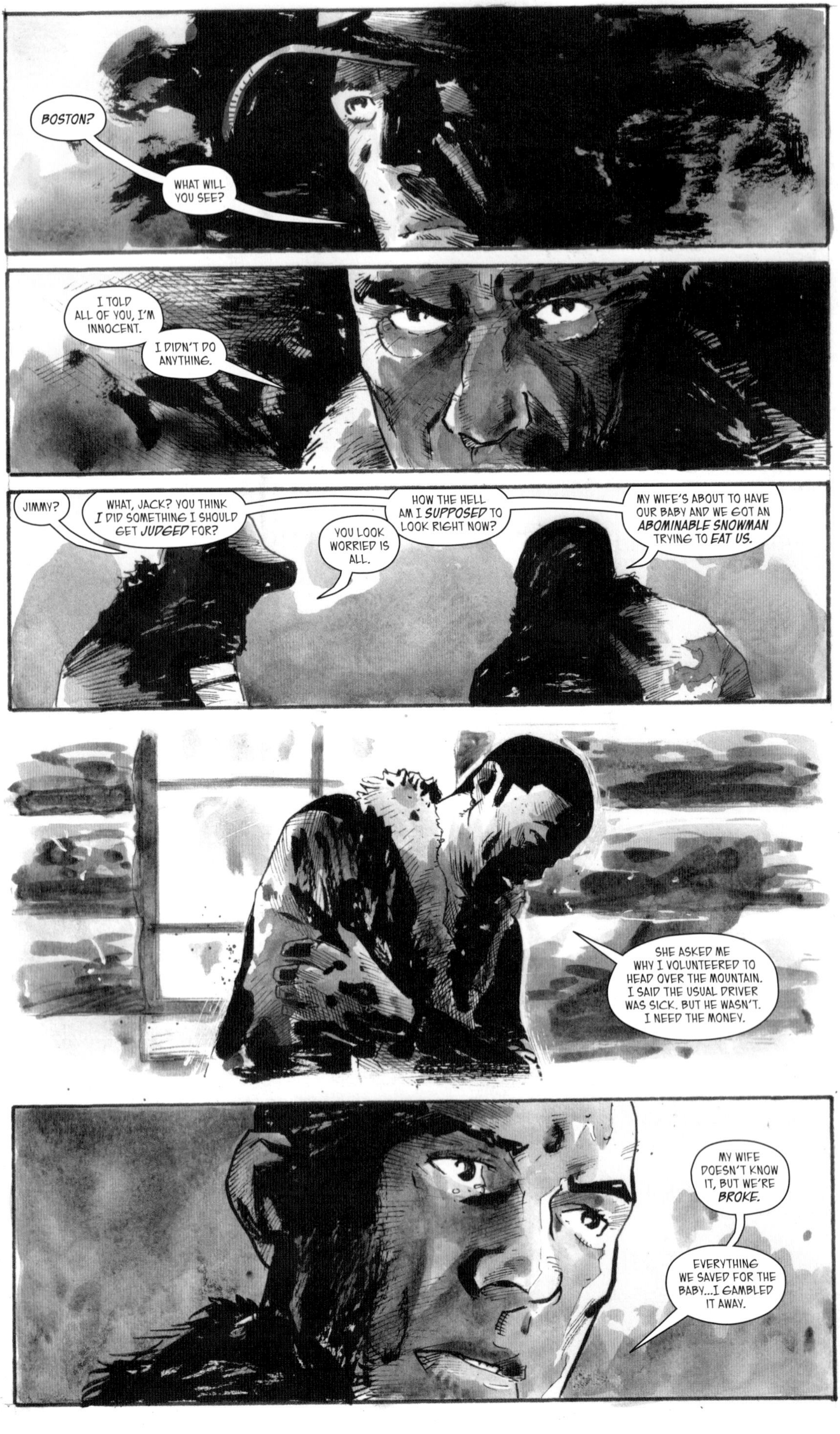
BOSTON?
WHAT WILL YOU SEE?
I TOLD ALL OF YOU, I'M INNOCENT.
I DIDN'T DO ANYTHING.
JIMMY?
WHAT, JACK? YOU THINK *I* DID SOMETHING I SHOULD GET *JUDGED* FOR?
YOU LOOK WORRIED IS ALL.
HOW THE HELL AM I *SUPPOSED* TO LOOK RIGHT NOW?
MY WIFE'S ABOUT TO HAVE OUR BABY AND WE GOT AN *ABOMINABLE SNOWMAN* TRYING TO *EAT US.*
SHE ASKED ME WHY I VOLUNTEERED TO HEAD OVER THE MOUNTAIN. I SAID THE USUAL DRIVER WAS SICK. BUT HE WASN'T. I NEED THE MONEY.
MY WIFE DOESN'T KNOW IT, BUT WE'RE *BROKE.*
EVERYTHING WE SAVED FOR THE BABY...I GAMBLED IT AWAY.

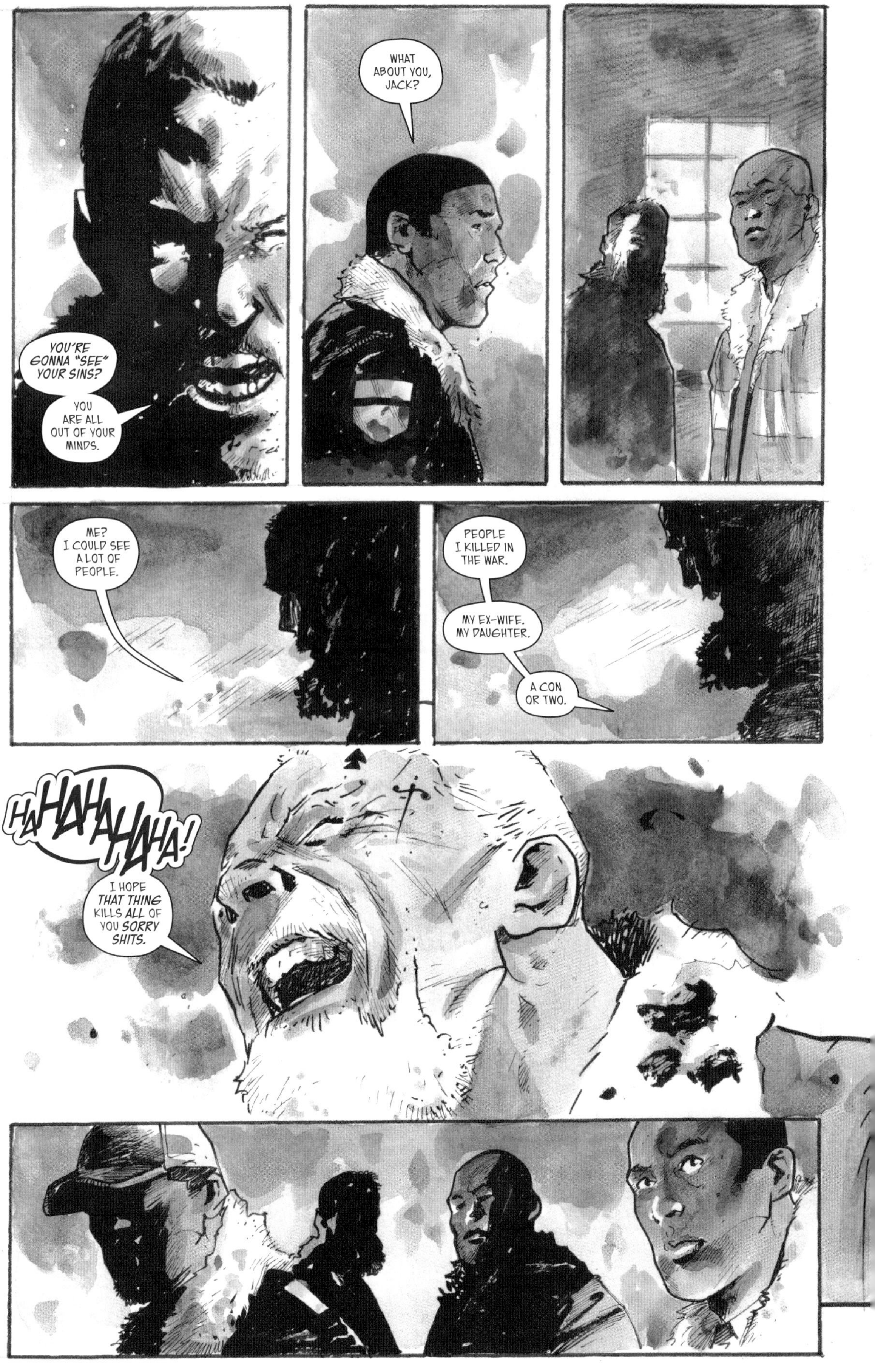

YOU'RE GONNA "SEE" YOUR SINS?
YOU ARE ALL OUT OF YOUR MINDS.
WHAT ABOUT YOU, JACK?
ME? I COULD SEE A LOT OF PEOPLE.
PEOPLE I KILLED IN THE WAR.
MY EX-WIFE. MY DAUGHTER.
A CON OR TWO.
HAHAHAHAHAHA!
I HOPE THAT THING KILLS ALL OF YOU SORRY SHITS.

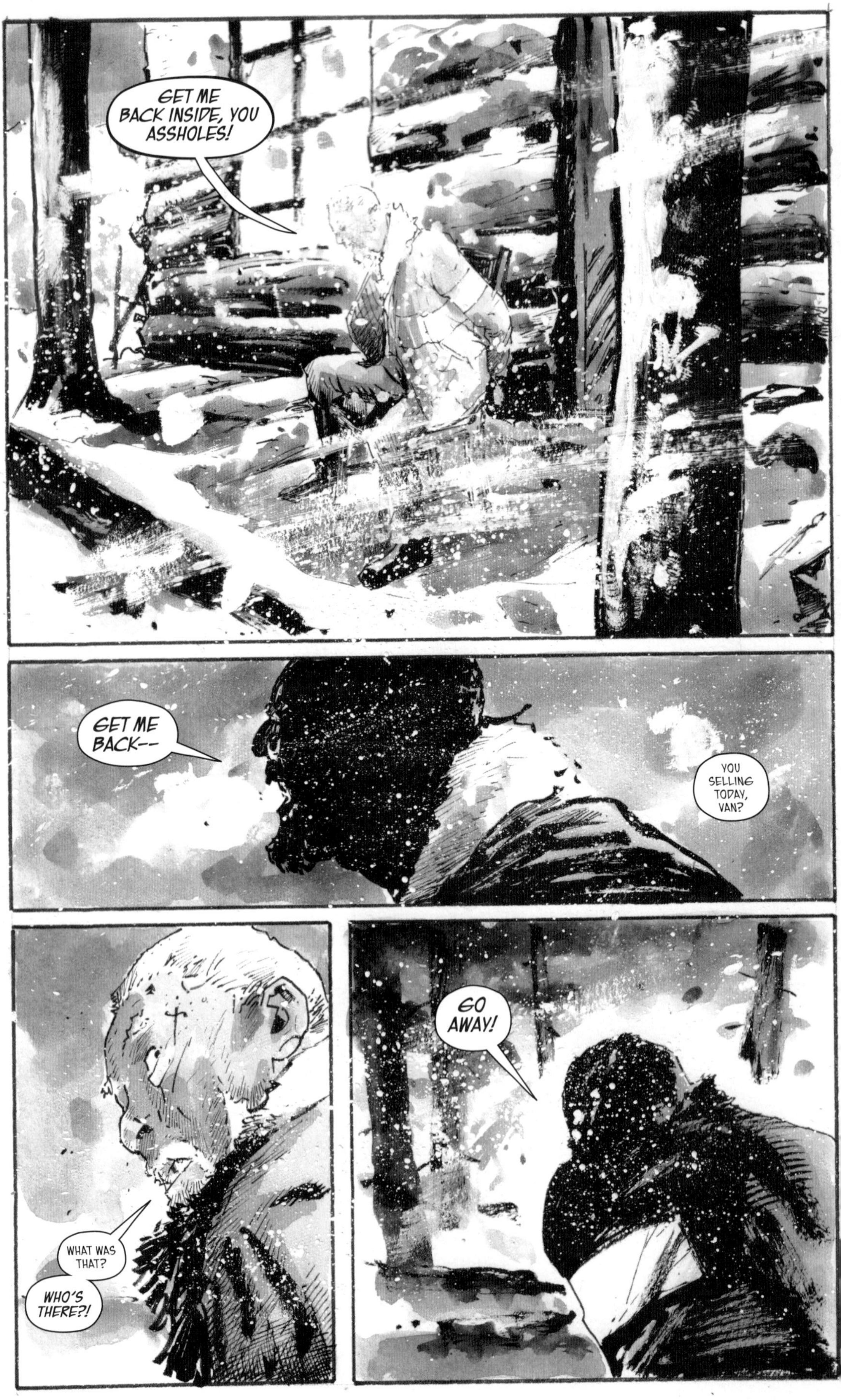
GET ME BACK INSIDE, YOU ASSHOLES!
GET ME BACK--
YOU SELLING TODAY, VAN?
WHAT WAS THAT?
WHO'S THERE?!
GO AWAY!

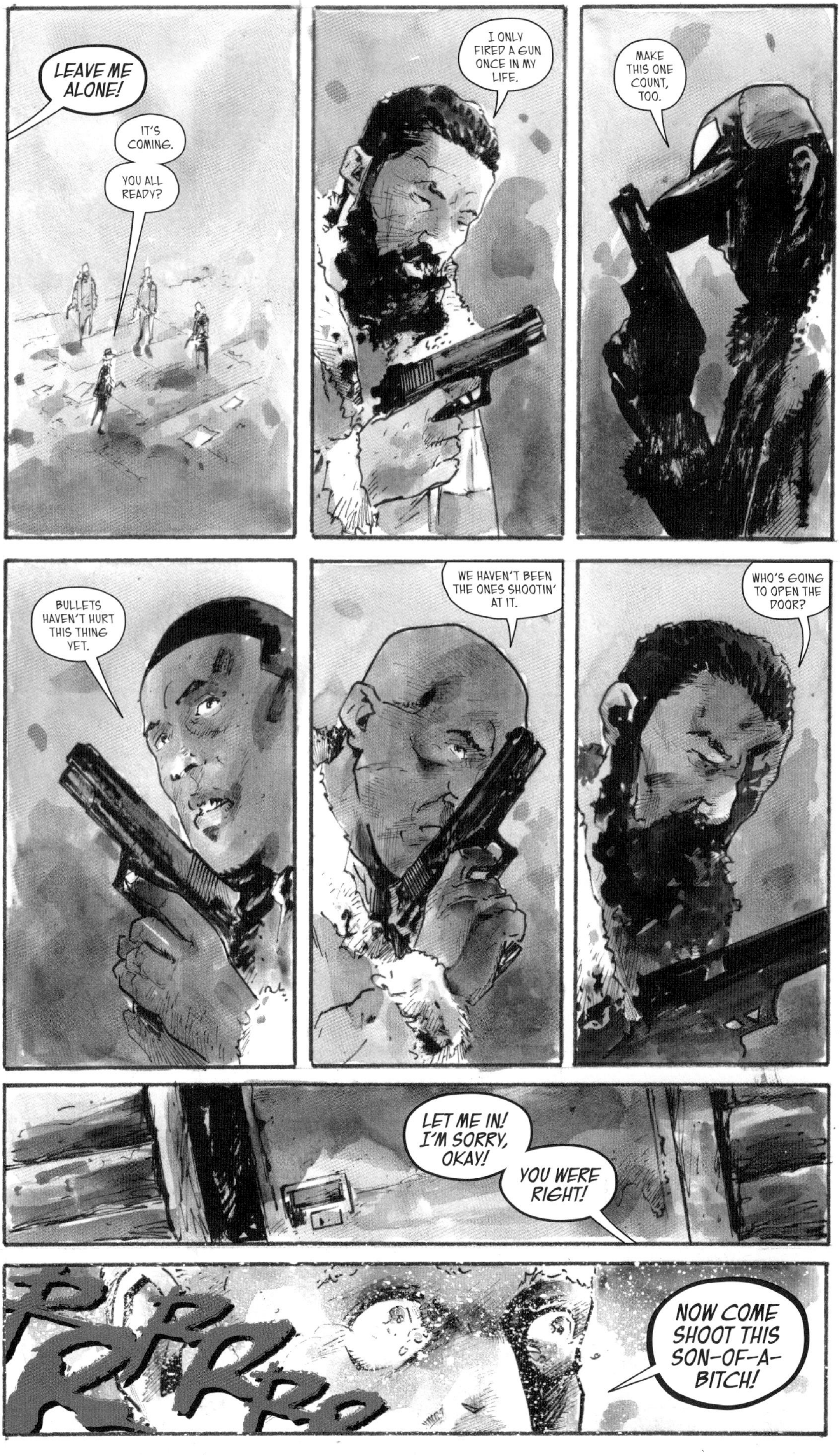
LEAVE ME ALONE!
IT'S COMING.
YOU ALL READY?
I ONLY FIRED A GUN ONCE IN MY LIFE.
MAKE THIS ONE COUNT, TOO.
BULLETS HAVEN'T HURT THIS THING YET.
WE HAVEN'T BEEN THE ONES SHOOTIN' AT IT.
WHO'S GOING TO OPEN THE DOOR?
LET ME IN! I'M SORRY, OKAY!
YOU WERE RIGHT!
NOW COME SHOOT THIS SON-OF-A-BITCH!

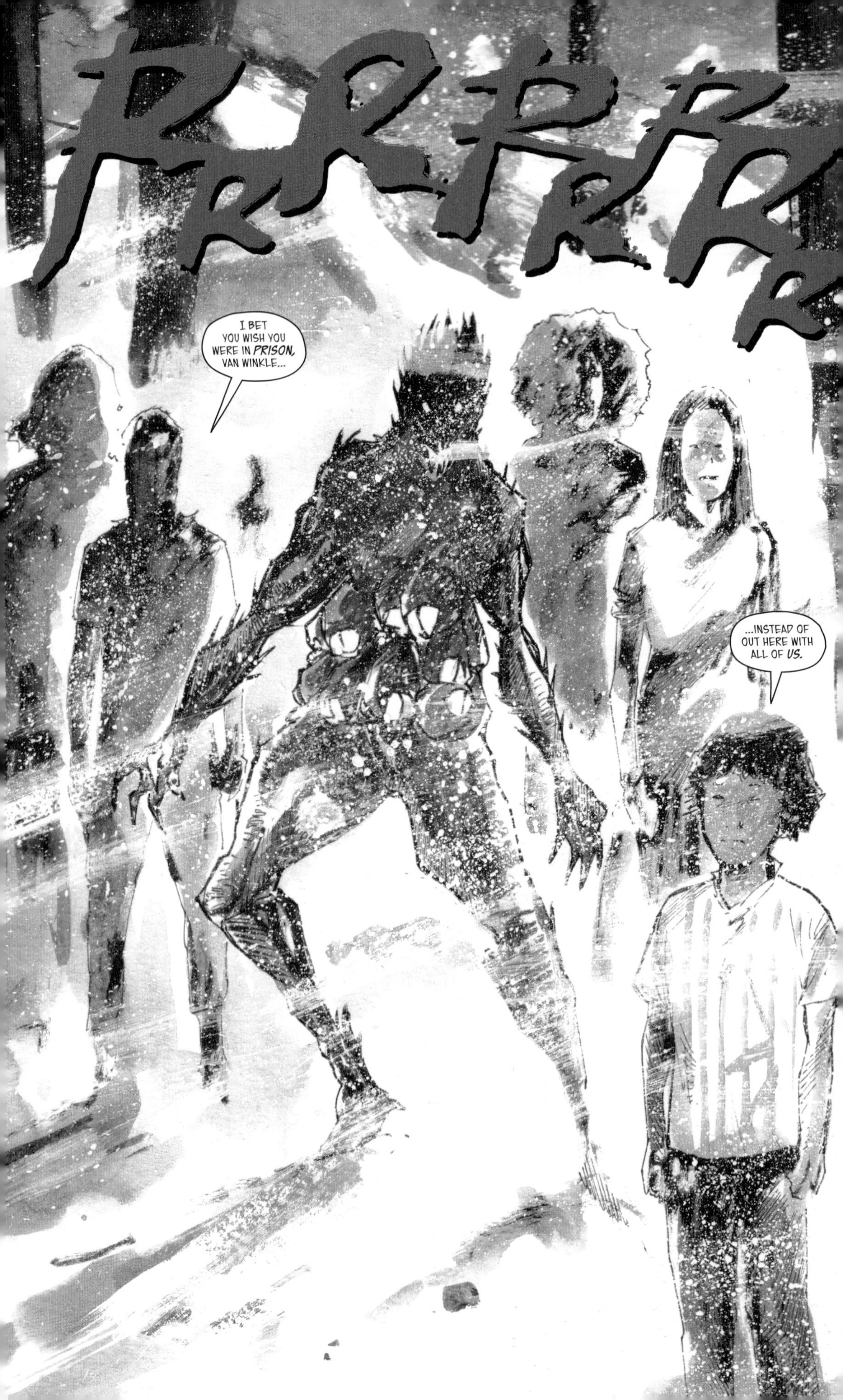
RRRRRRRRR
I BET YOU WISH YOU WERE IN PRISON, VAN WINKLE...
...INSTEAD OF OUT HERE WITH ALL OF US.

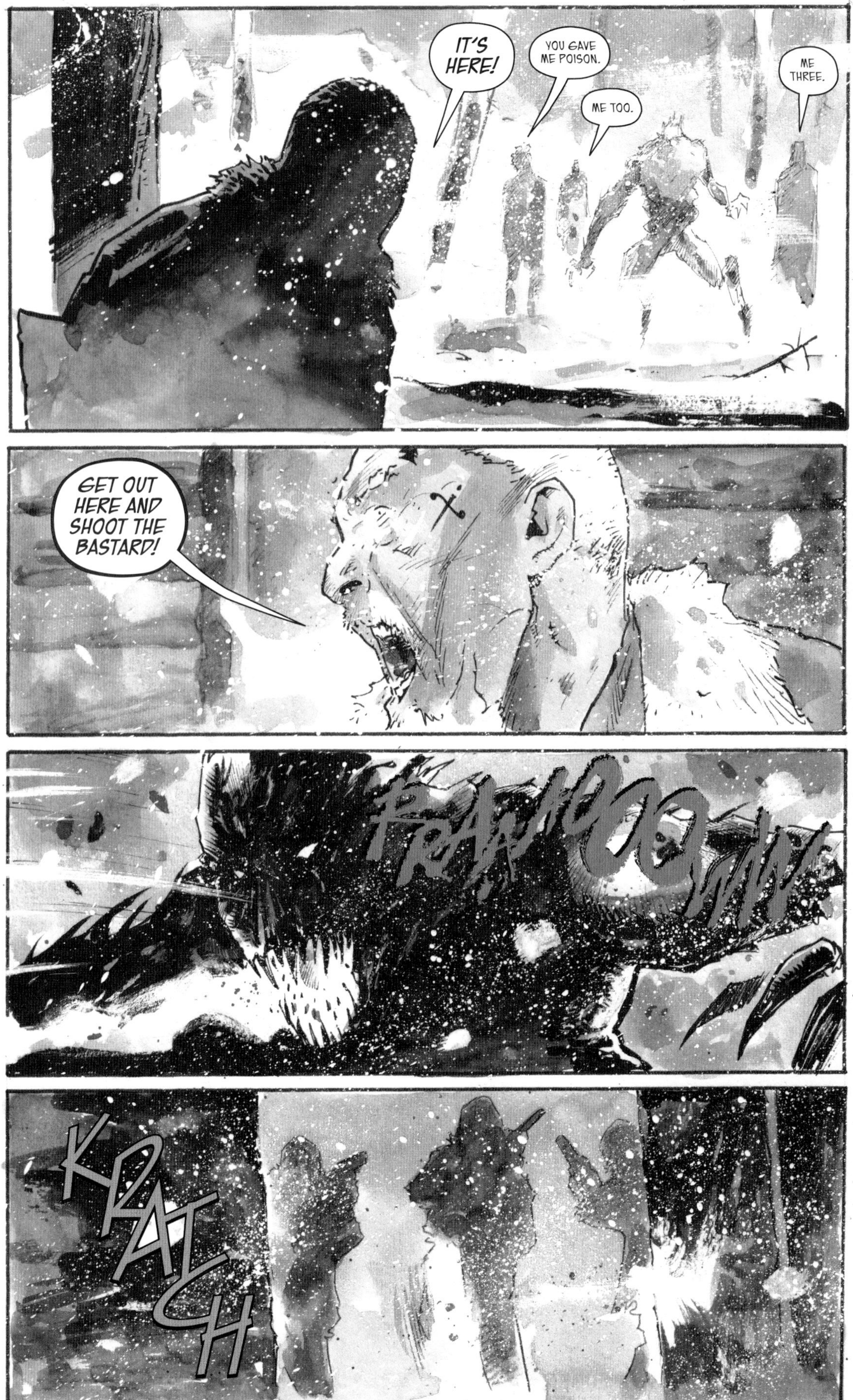
IT'S HERE!
YOU GAVE ME POISON.
ME TOO.
ME THREE.
GET OUT HERE AND SHOOT THE BASTARD!
FRAWOOOWW
KRAACH

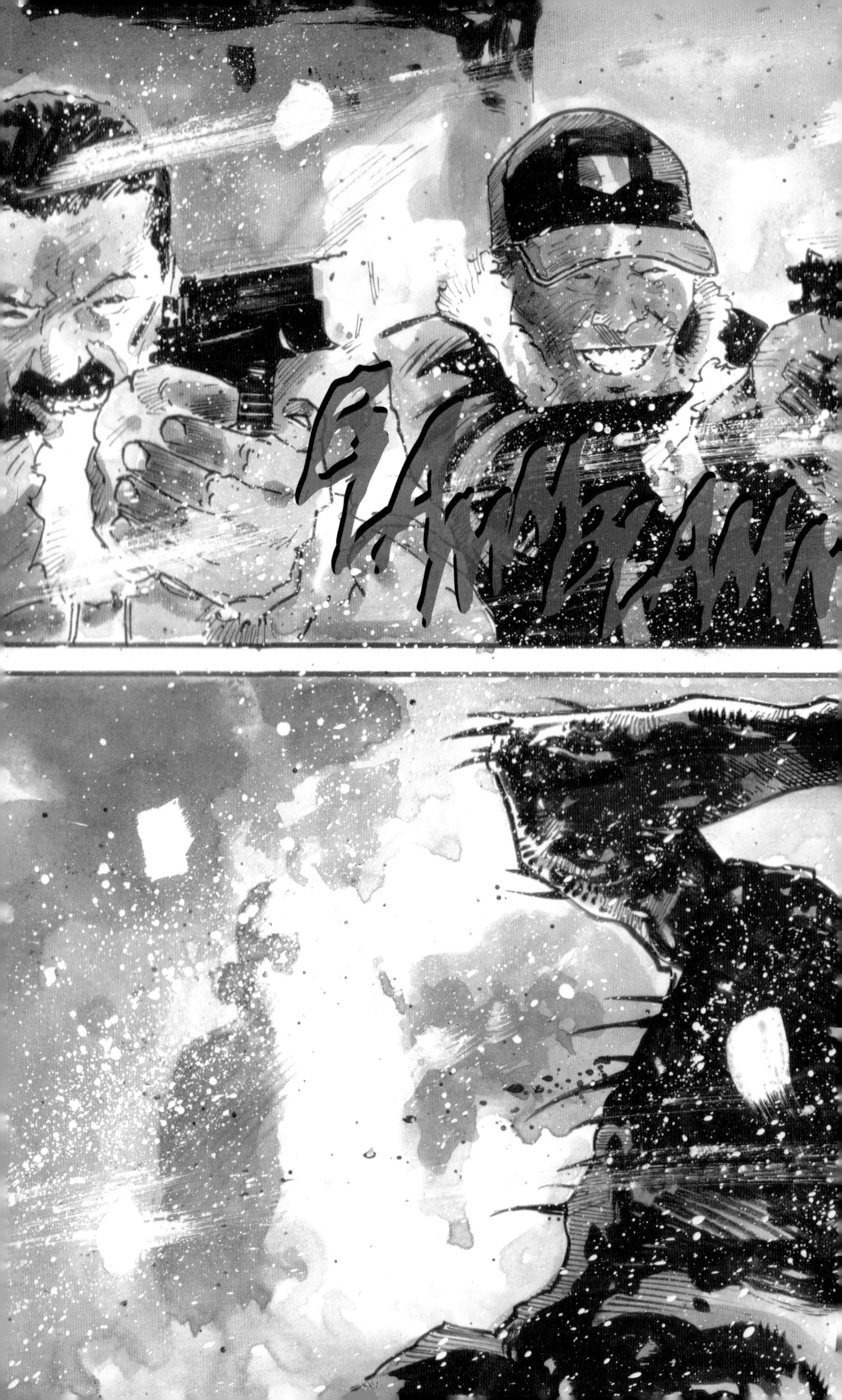

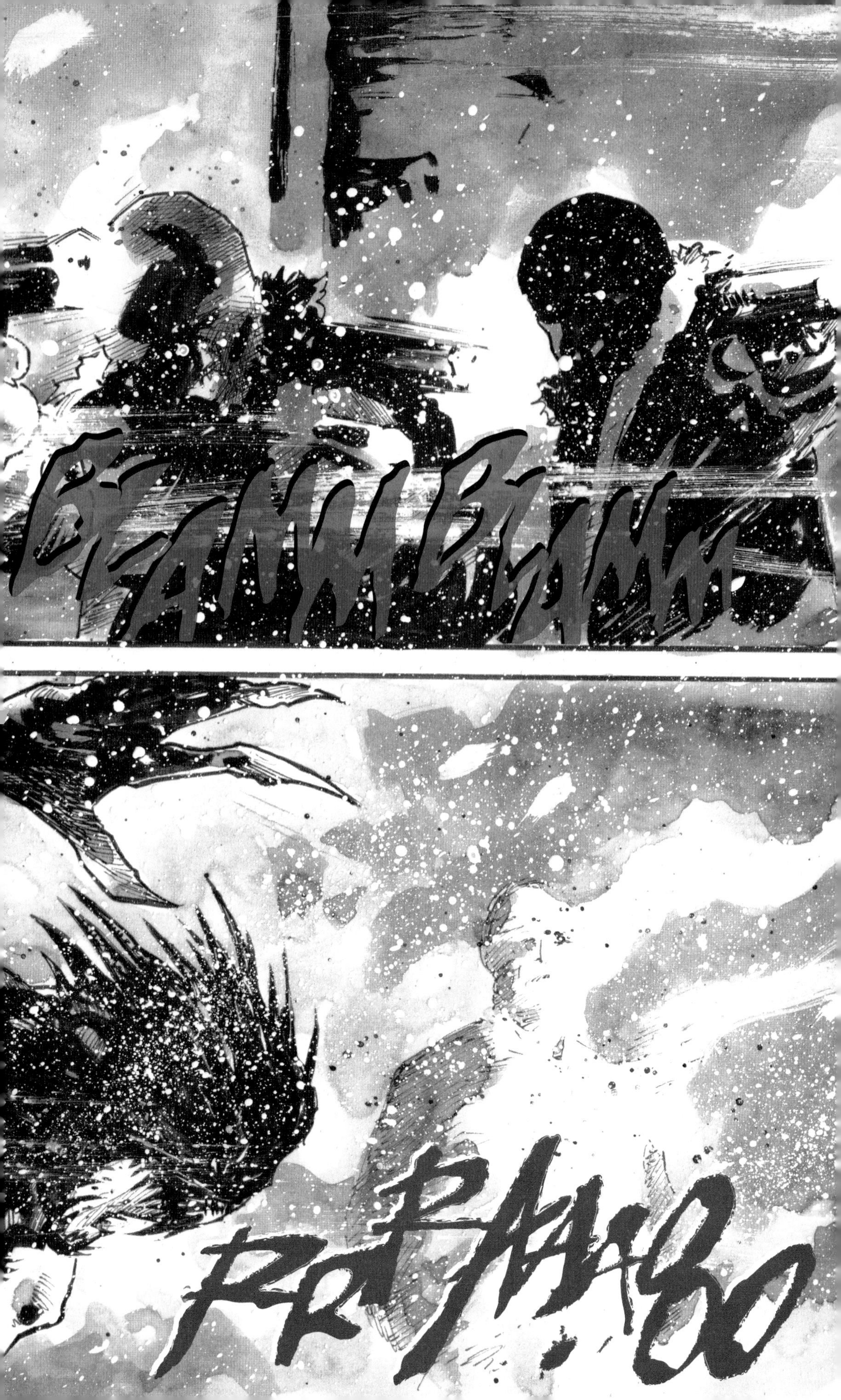
BLAMM BLAMM

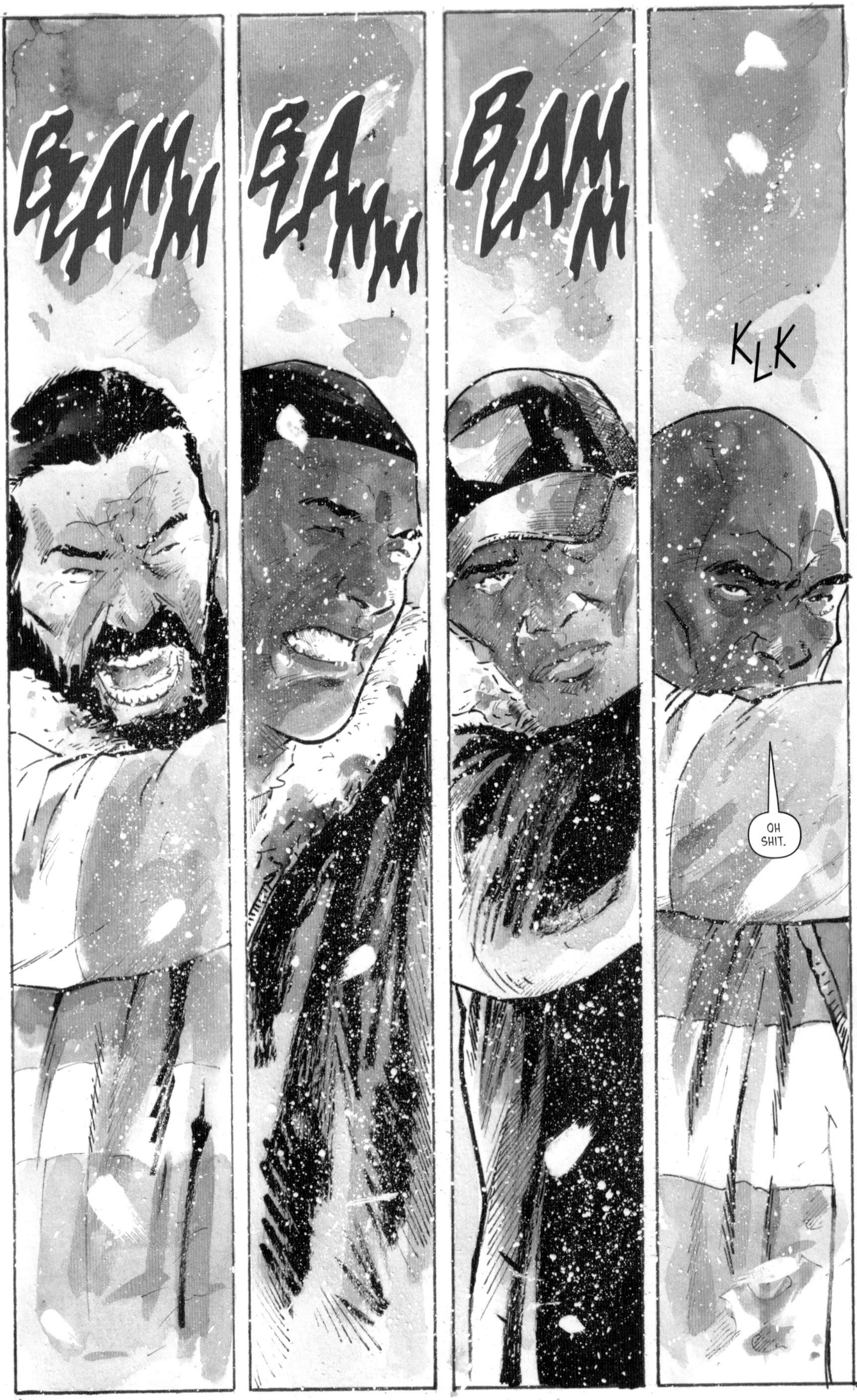
BLAMM
BLAMM
BLAMM
KLK
OH SHIT.

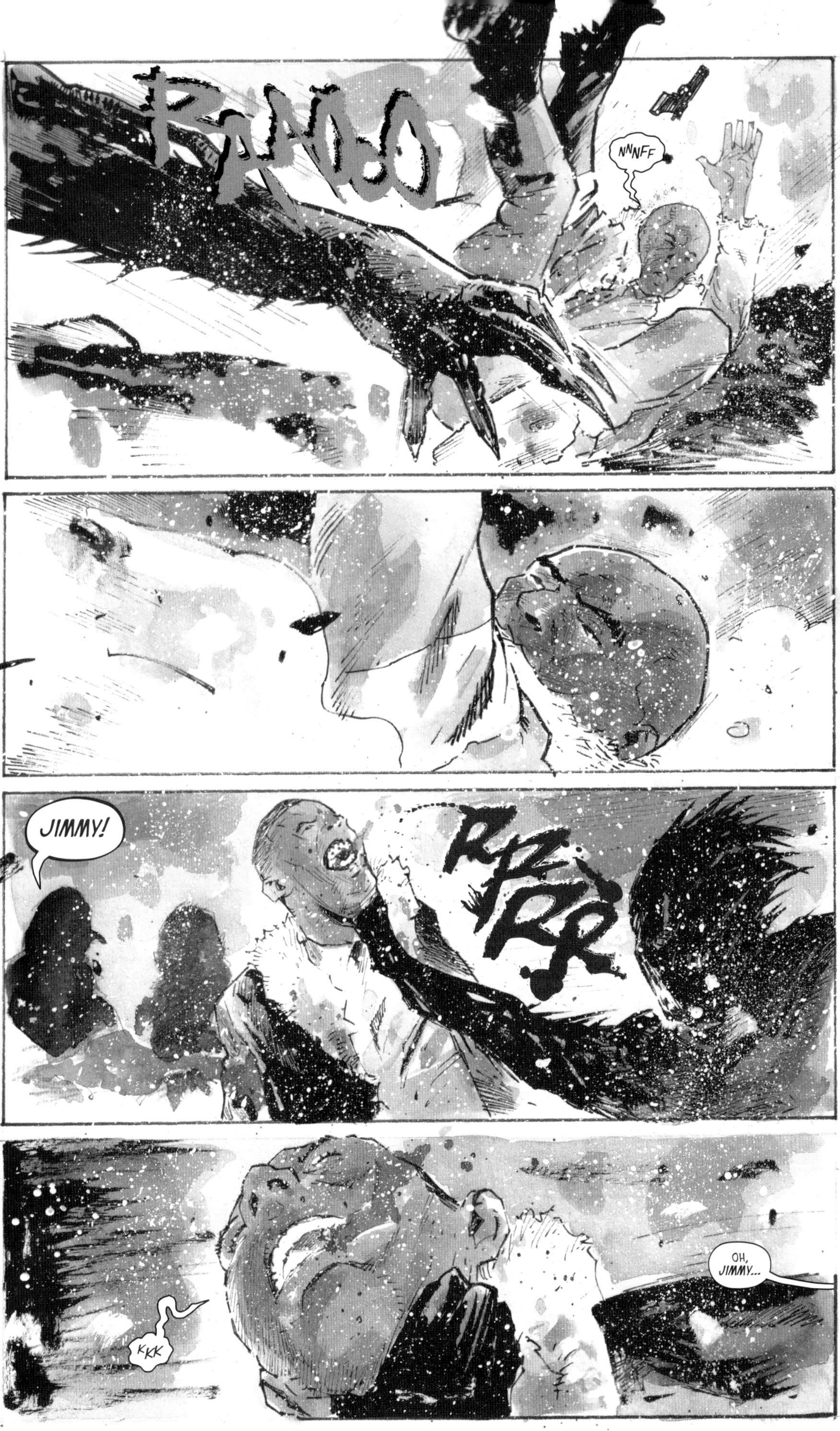
NNNFF
JIMMY!
KKK
OH, JIMMY...

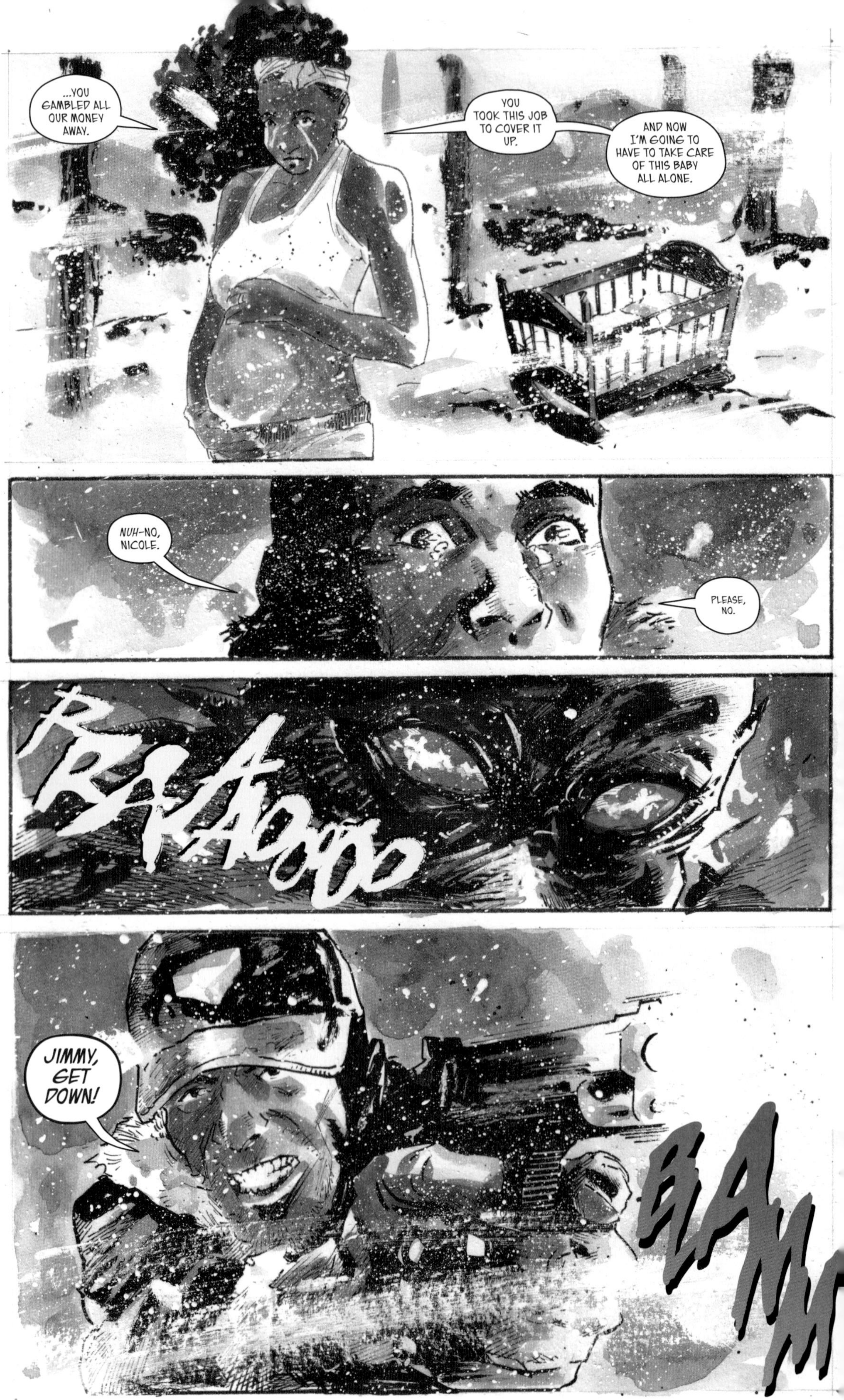
...YOU GAMBLED ALL OUR MONEY AWAY.
YOU TOOK THIS JOB TO COVER IT UP.
AND NOW I'M GOING TO HAVE TO TAKE CARE OF THIS BABY ALL ALONE.
NUH-NO, NICOLE.
PLEASE, NO.
BRAAOOOO
JIMMY, GET DOWN!
BAM

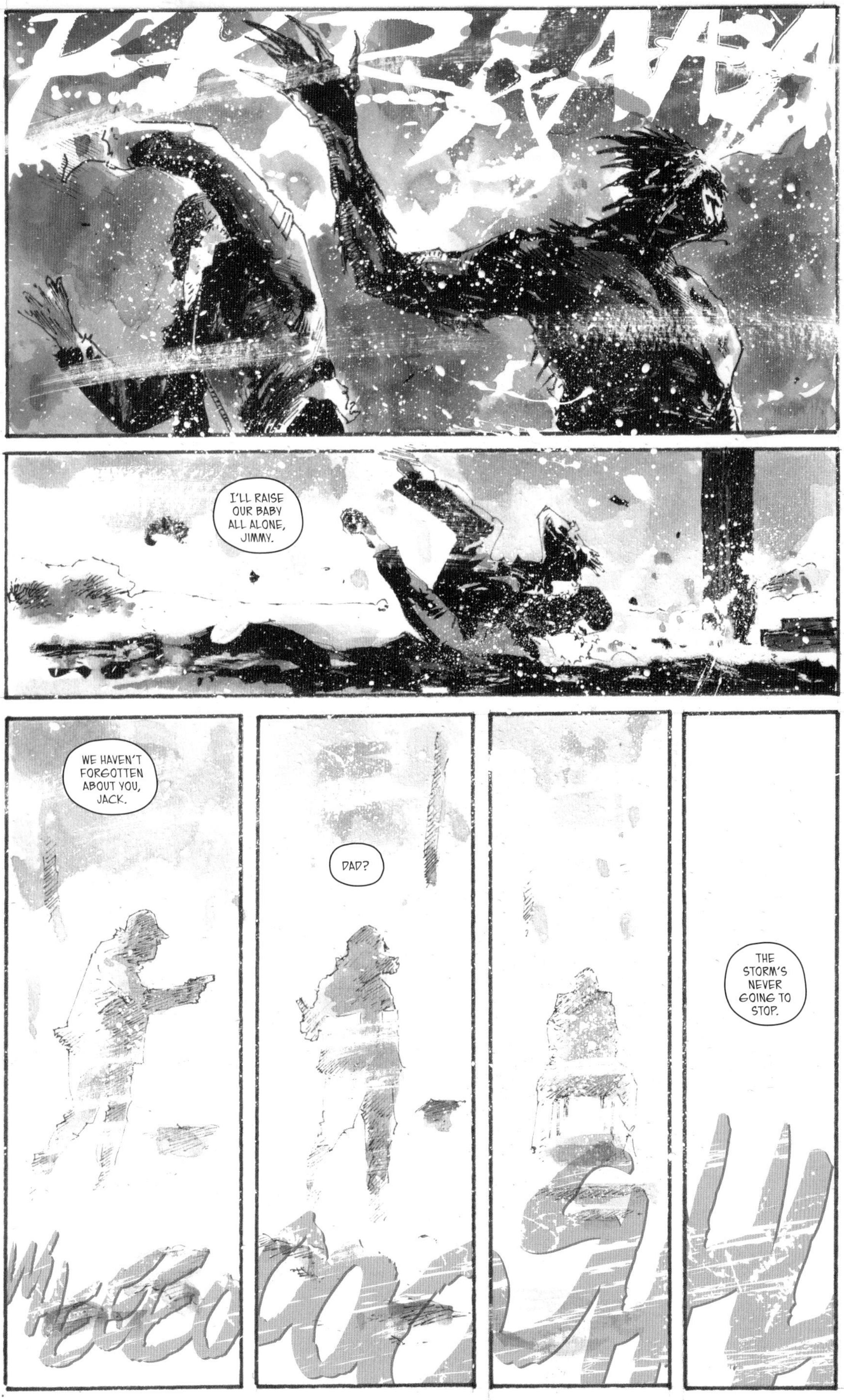
I'LL RAISE OUR BABY ALL ALONE, JIMMY.
WE HAVEN'T FORGOTTEN ABOUT YOU, JACK.
DAD?
THE STORM'S NEVER GOING TO STOP.

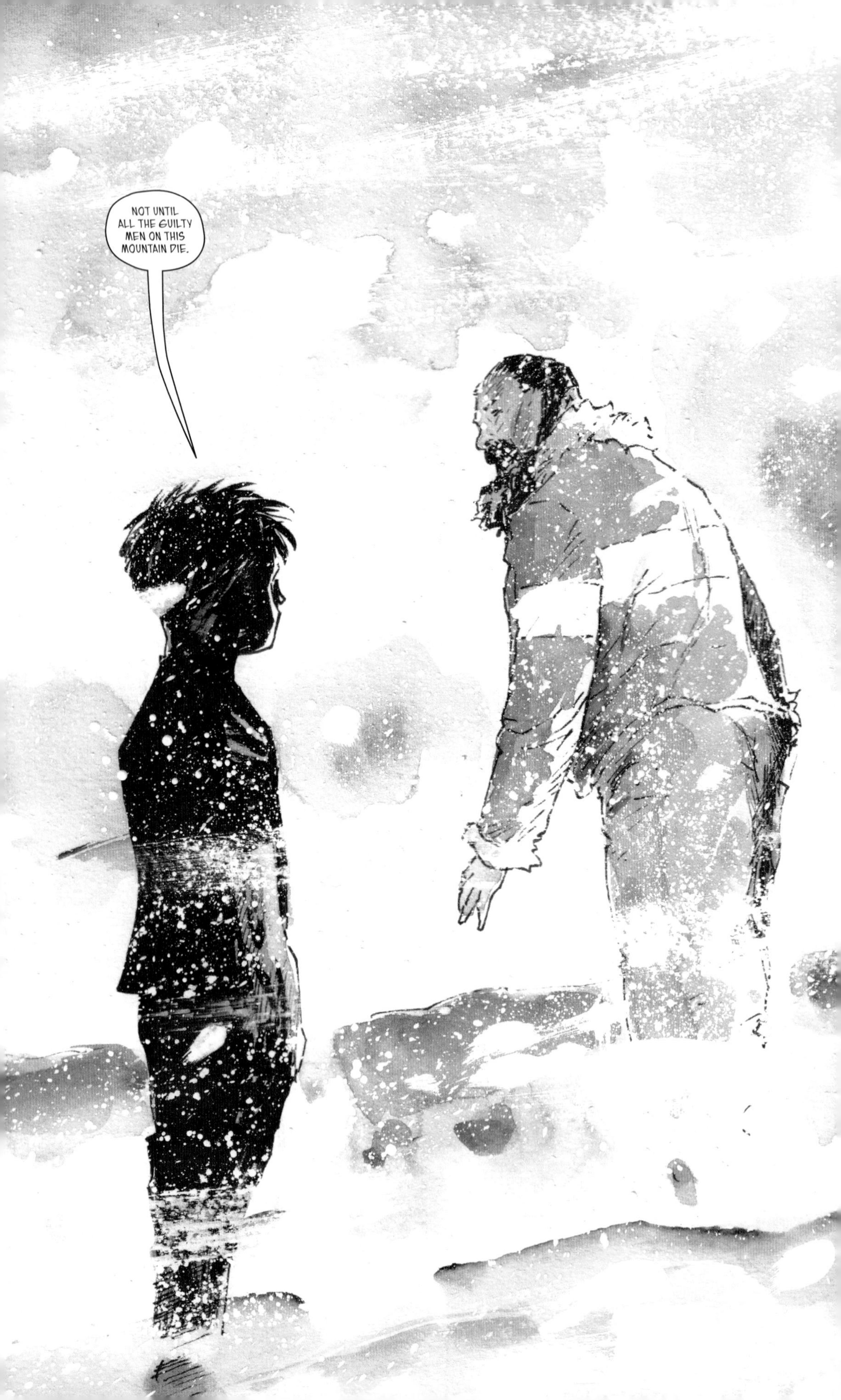
NOT UNTIL ALL THE GUILTY MEN ON THIS MOUNTAIN DIE.

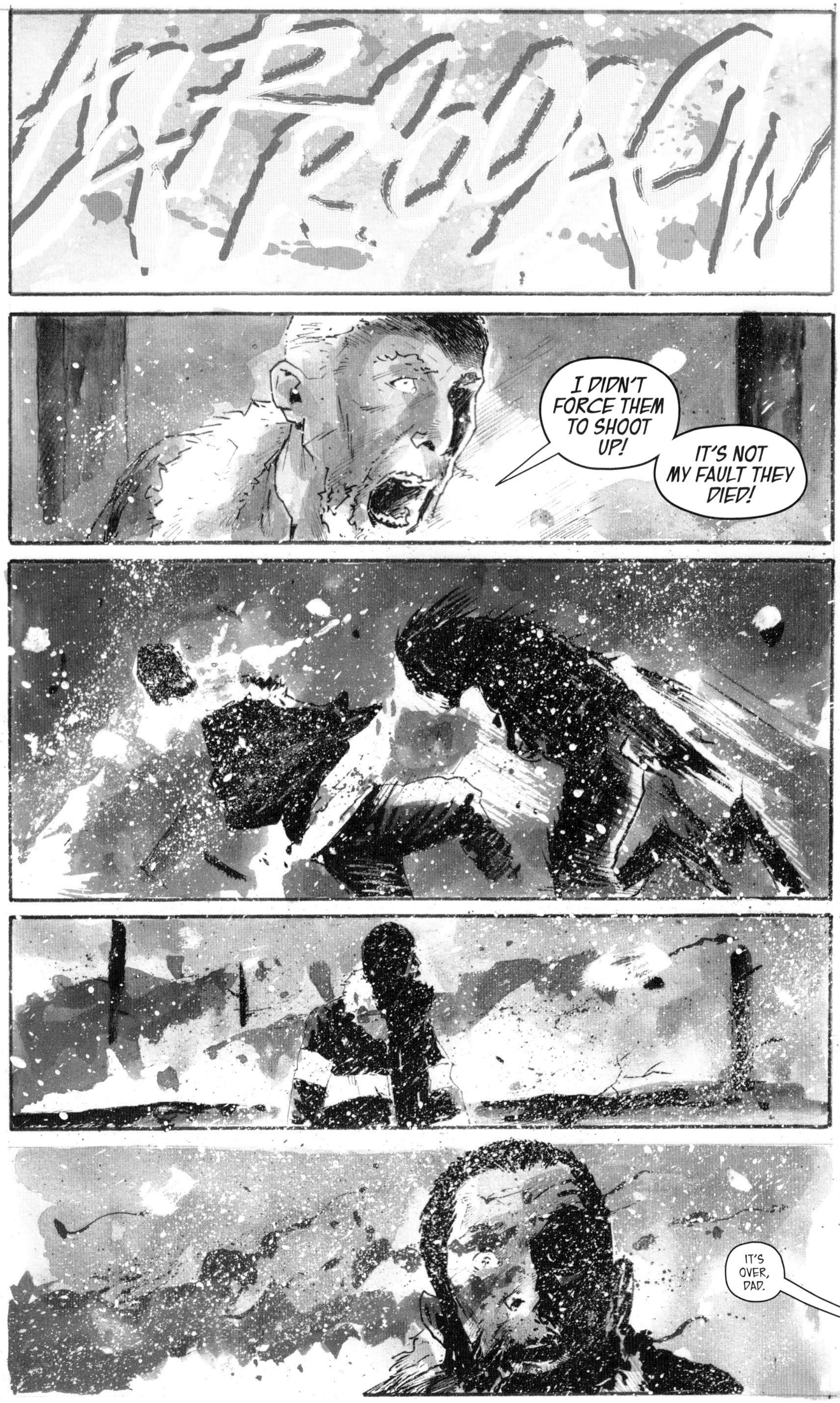
I DIDN'T FORCE THEM TO SHOOT UP!
IT'S NOT MY FAULT THEY DIED!
IT'S OVER, DAD.

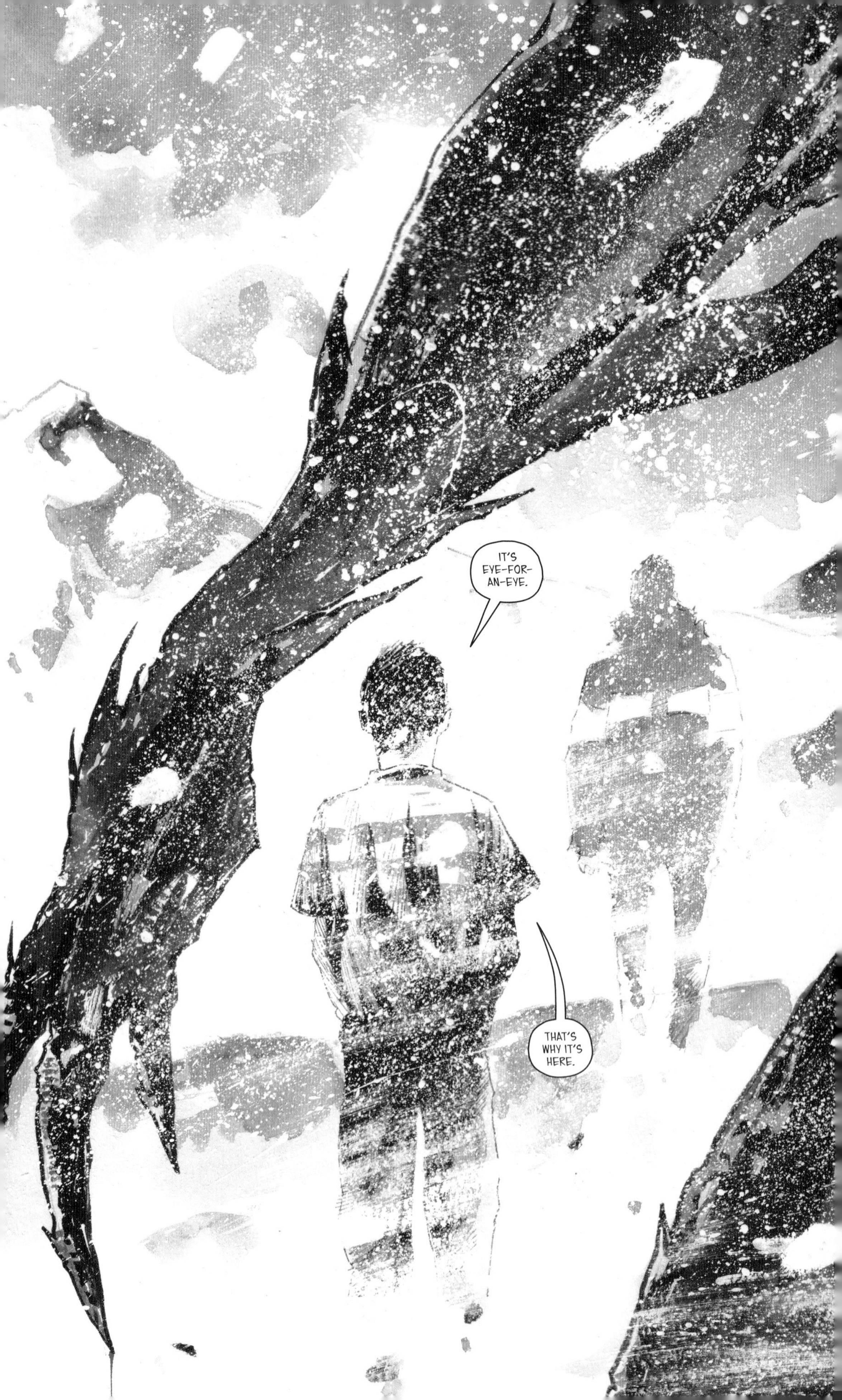
IT'S EYE-FOR-AN-EYE.
THAT'S WHY IT'S HERE.

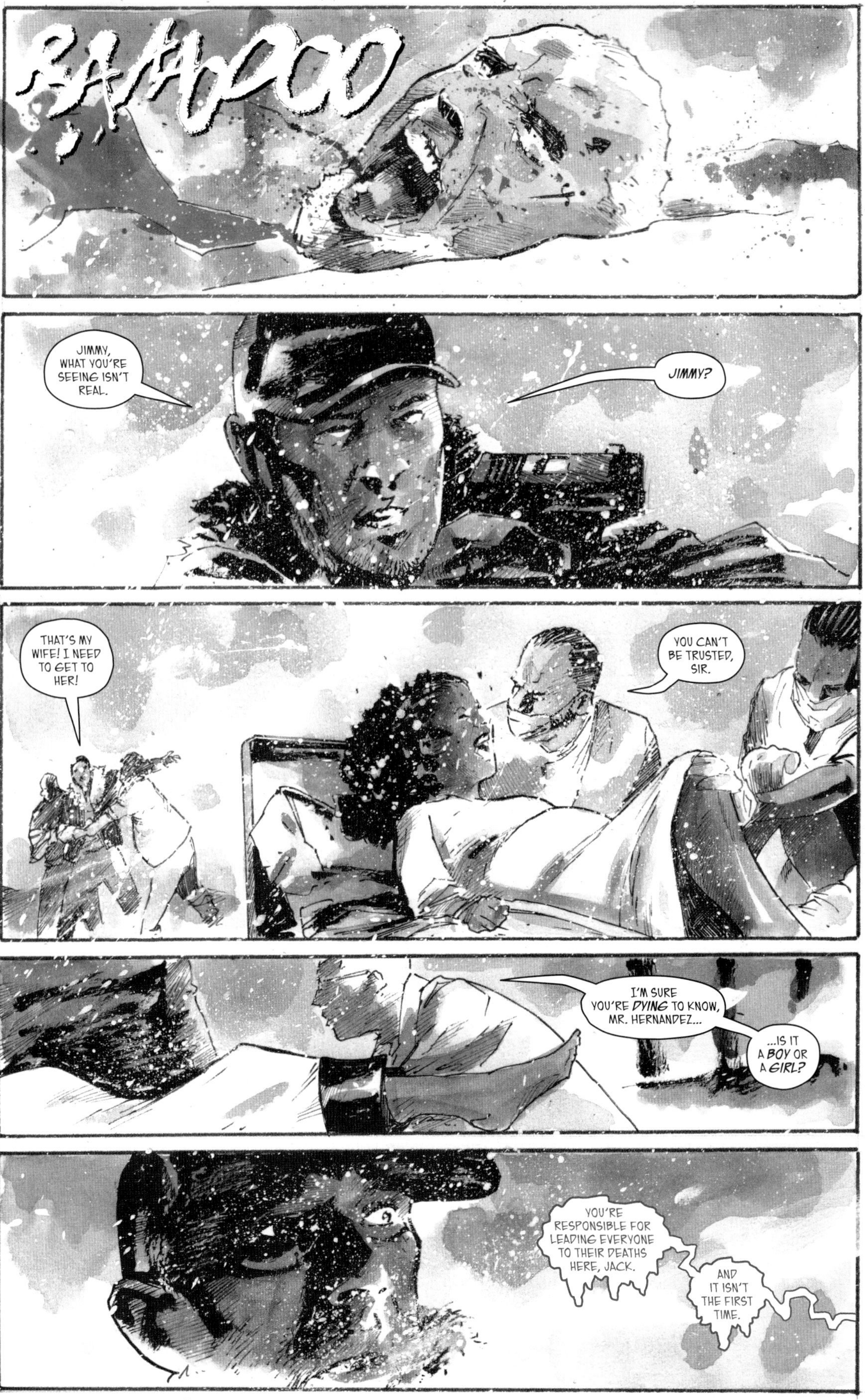
JIMMY, WHAT YOU'RE SEEING ISN'T REAL.
JIMMY?
THAT'S MY WIFE! I NEED TO GET TO HER!
YOU CAN'T BE TRUSTED, SIR.
I'M SURE YOU'RE DYING TO KNOW, MR. HERNANDEZ...
...IS IT A BOY OR A GIRL?
YOU'RE RESPONSIBLE FOR LEADING EVERYONE TO THEIR DEATHS HERE, JACK.
AND IT ISN'T THE FIRST TIME.

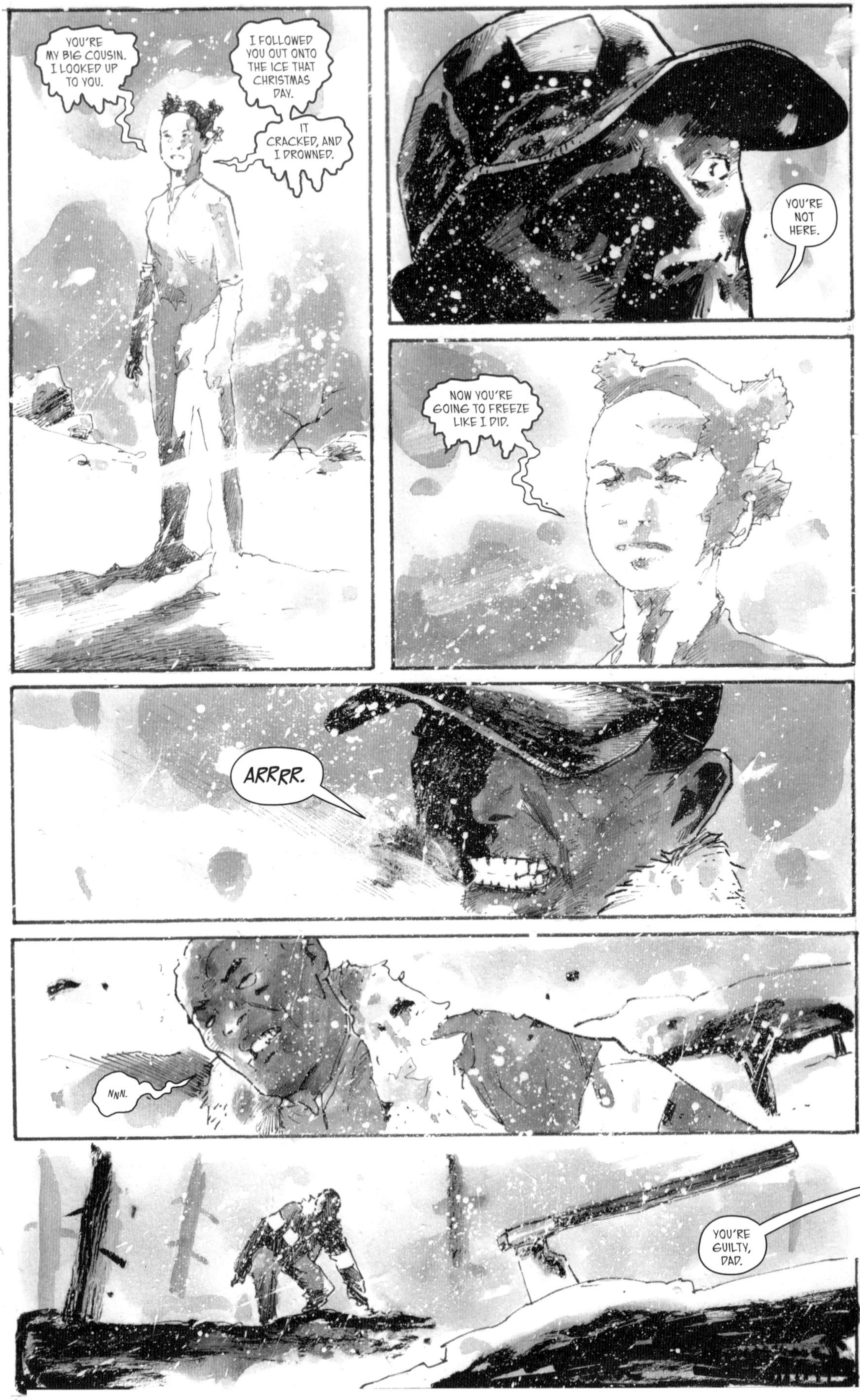
YOU'RE MY BIG COUSIN. I LOOKED UP TO YOU.
I FOLLOWED YOU OUT ONTO THE ICE THAT CHRISTMAS DAY.
IT CRACKED, AND I DROWNED.
YOU'RE NOT HERE.
NOW YOU'RE GOING TO FREEZE LIKE I DID.
ARRRR.
NNN.
YOU'RE GUILTY, DAD.

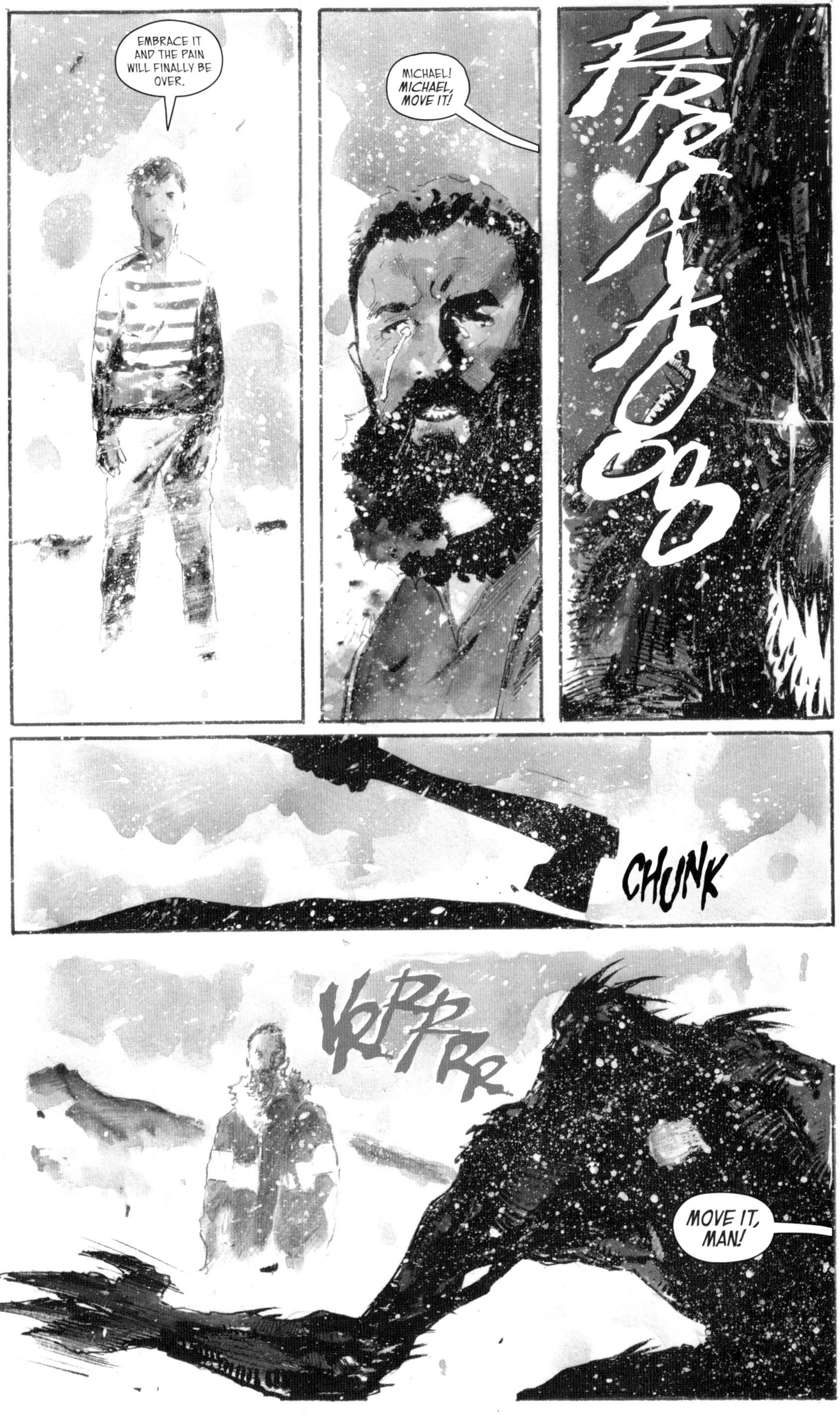
EMBRACE IT AND THE PAIN WILL FINALLY BE OVER.
MICHAEL! MICHAEL, MOVE IT!
CHUNK
MOVE IT, MAN!

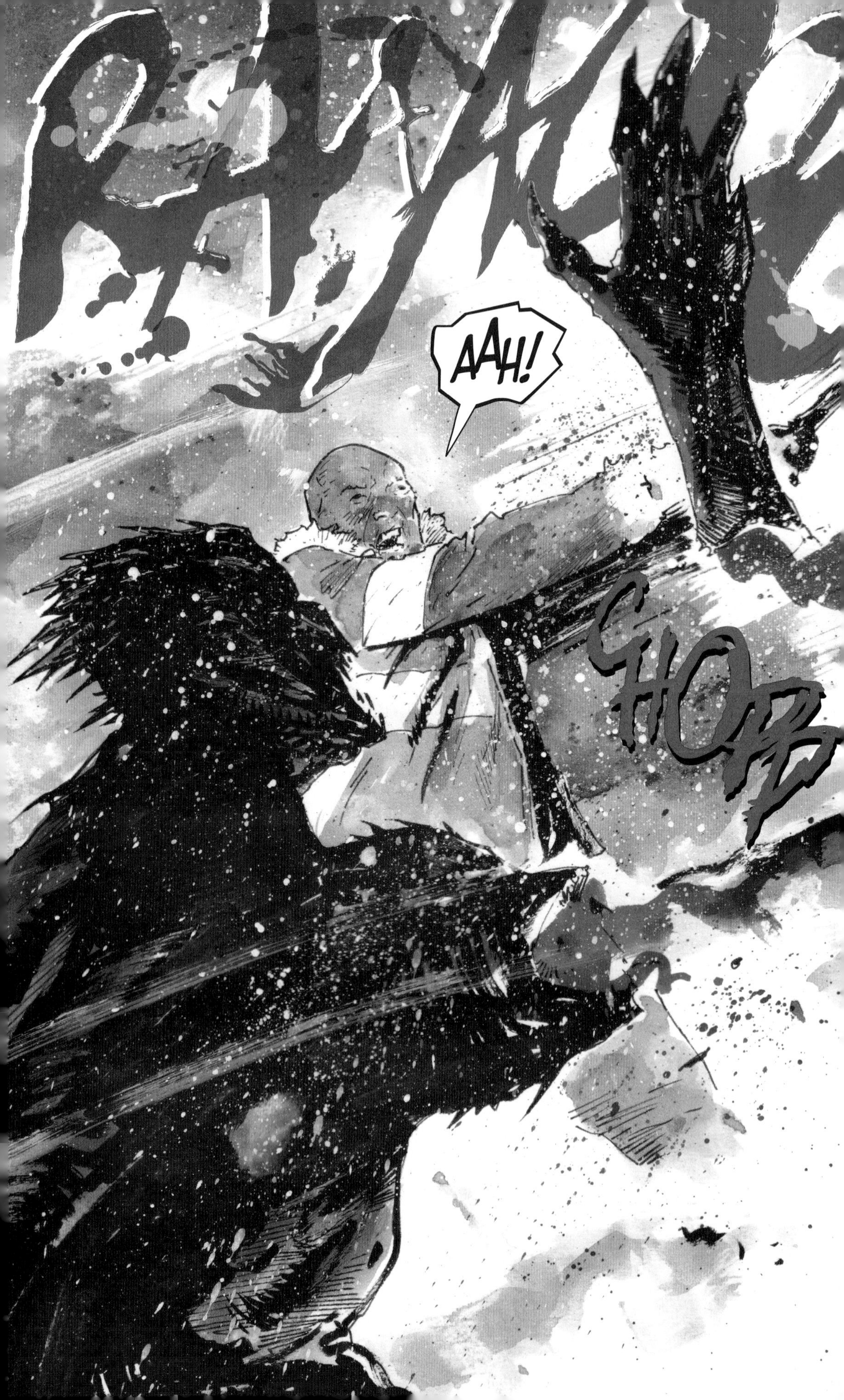
AAH!

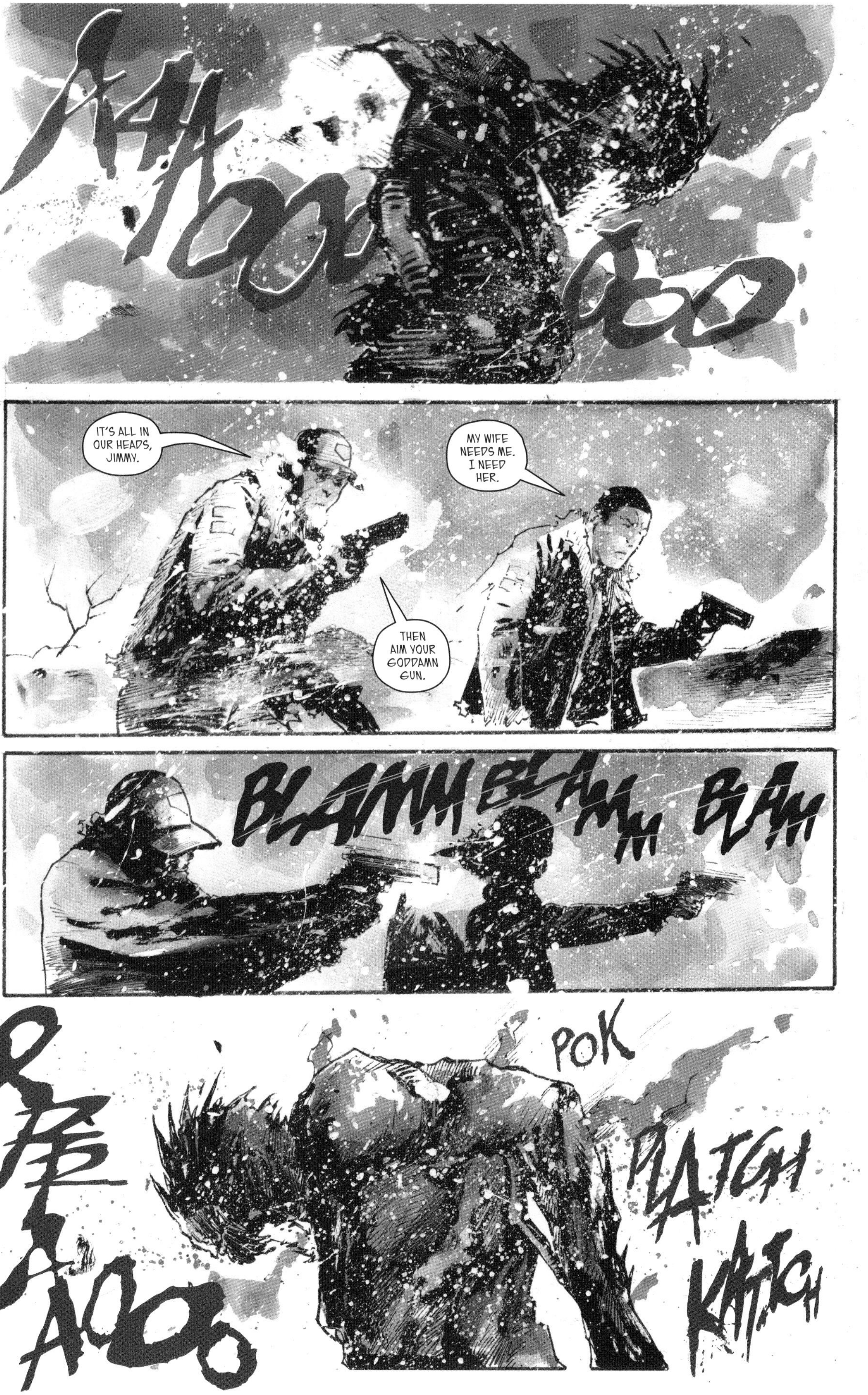
IT'S ALL IN OUR HEADS, JIMMY.
MY WIFE NEEDS ME. I NEED HER.
THEN AIM YOUR GODDAMN GUN.
BLAMM
BLAM
POK
PLATCH
KLATCH

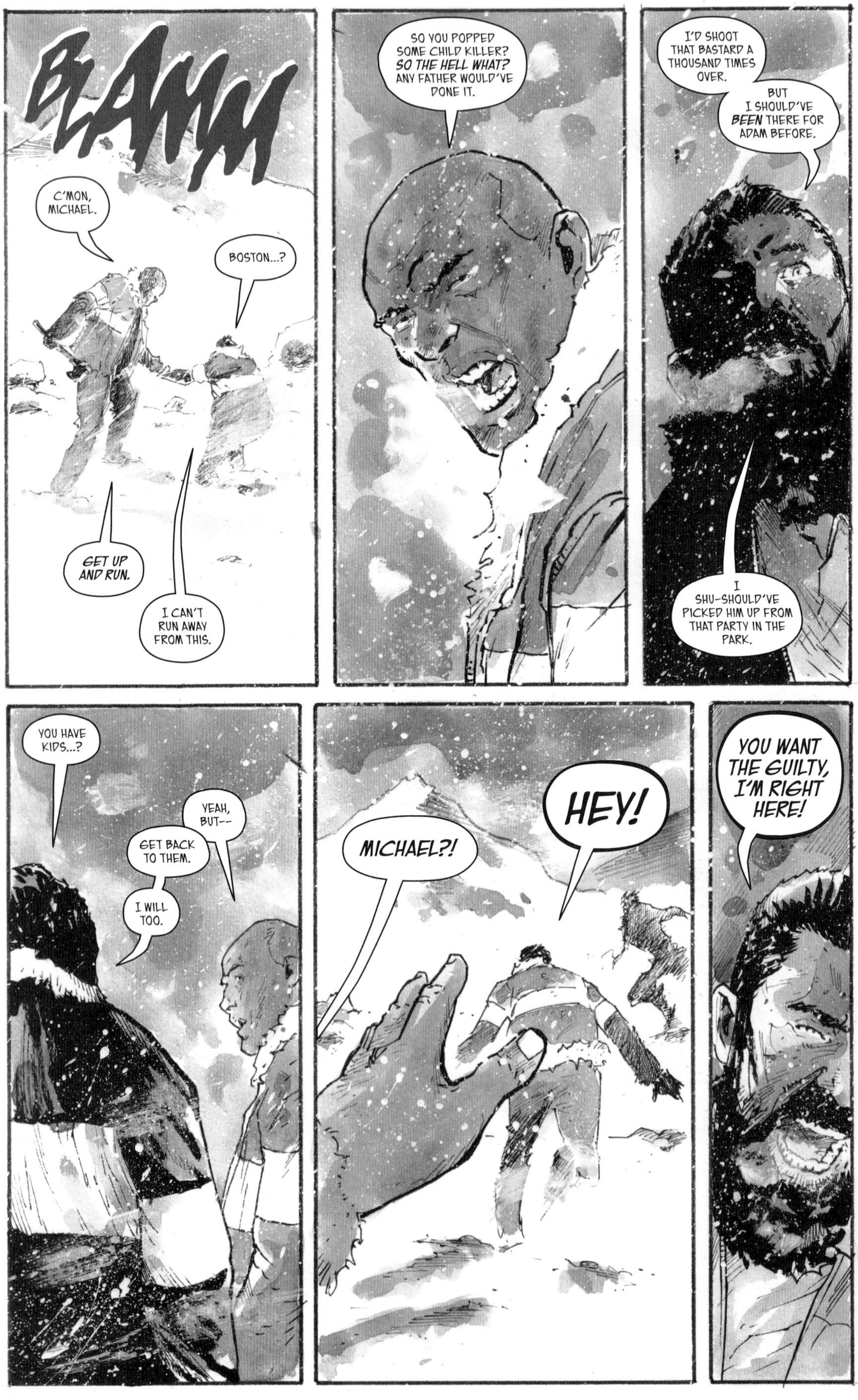
BLAMM
C'MON, MICHAEL.
BOSTON...?
GET UP AND RUN.
I CAN'T RUN AWAY FROM THIS.
SO YOU POPPED SOME CHILD KILLER? SO THE HELL WHAT? ANY FATHER WOULD'VE DONE IT.
I'D SHOOT THAT BASTARD A THOUSAND TIMES OVER.
BUT I SHOULD'VE BEEN THERE FOR ADAM BEFORE.
I SHU-SHOULD'VE PICKED HIM UP FROM THAT PARTY IN THE PARK.
YOU HAVE KIDS...?
YEAH, BUT--
GET BACK TO THEM.
I WILL TOO.
MICHAEL?!
HEY!
YOU WANT THE GUILTY, I'M RIGHT HERE!

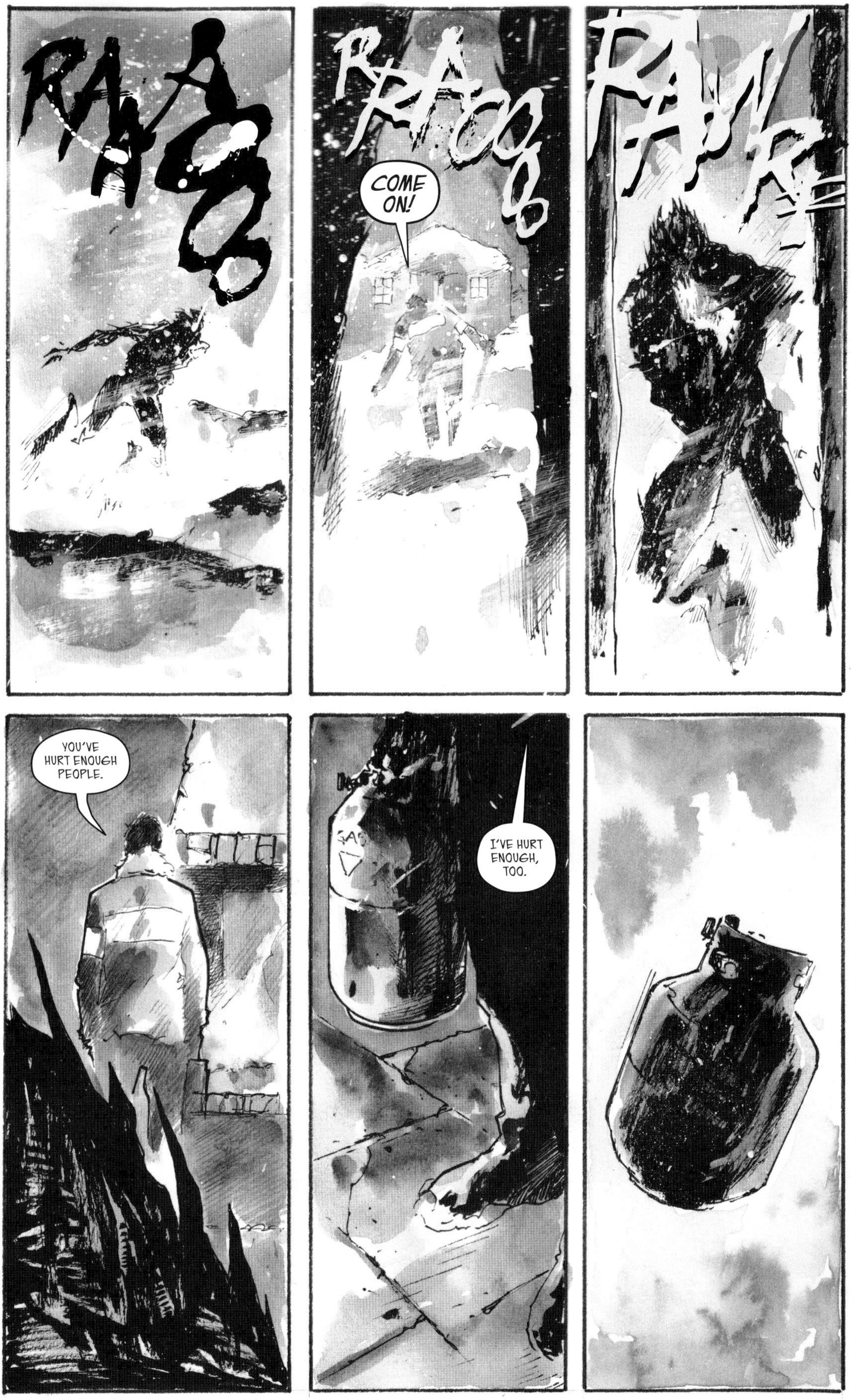
COME ON!
YOU'VE HURT ENOUGH PEOPLE.
I'VE HURT ENOUGH, TOO.

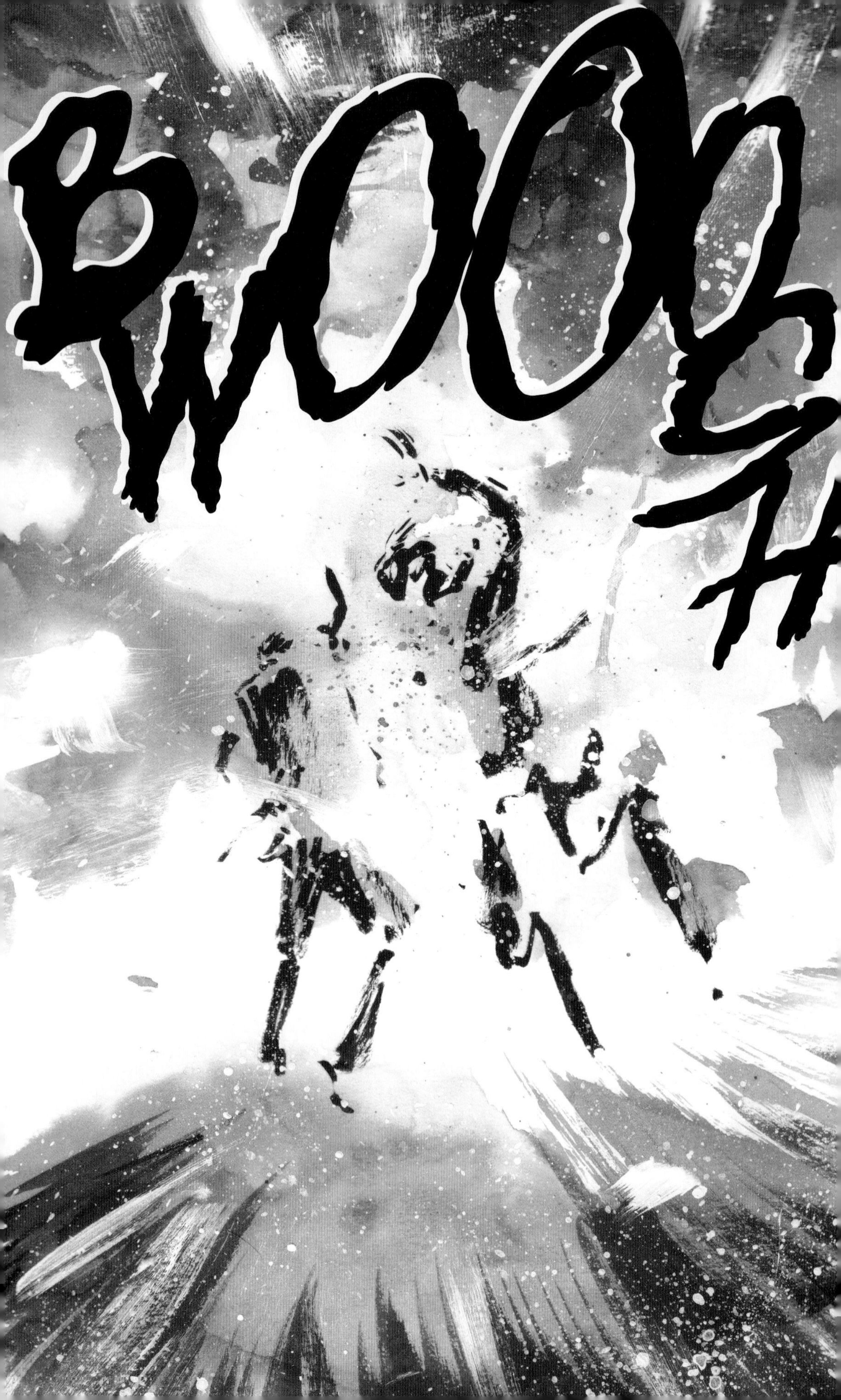
BWOOOSH

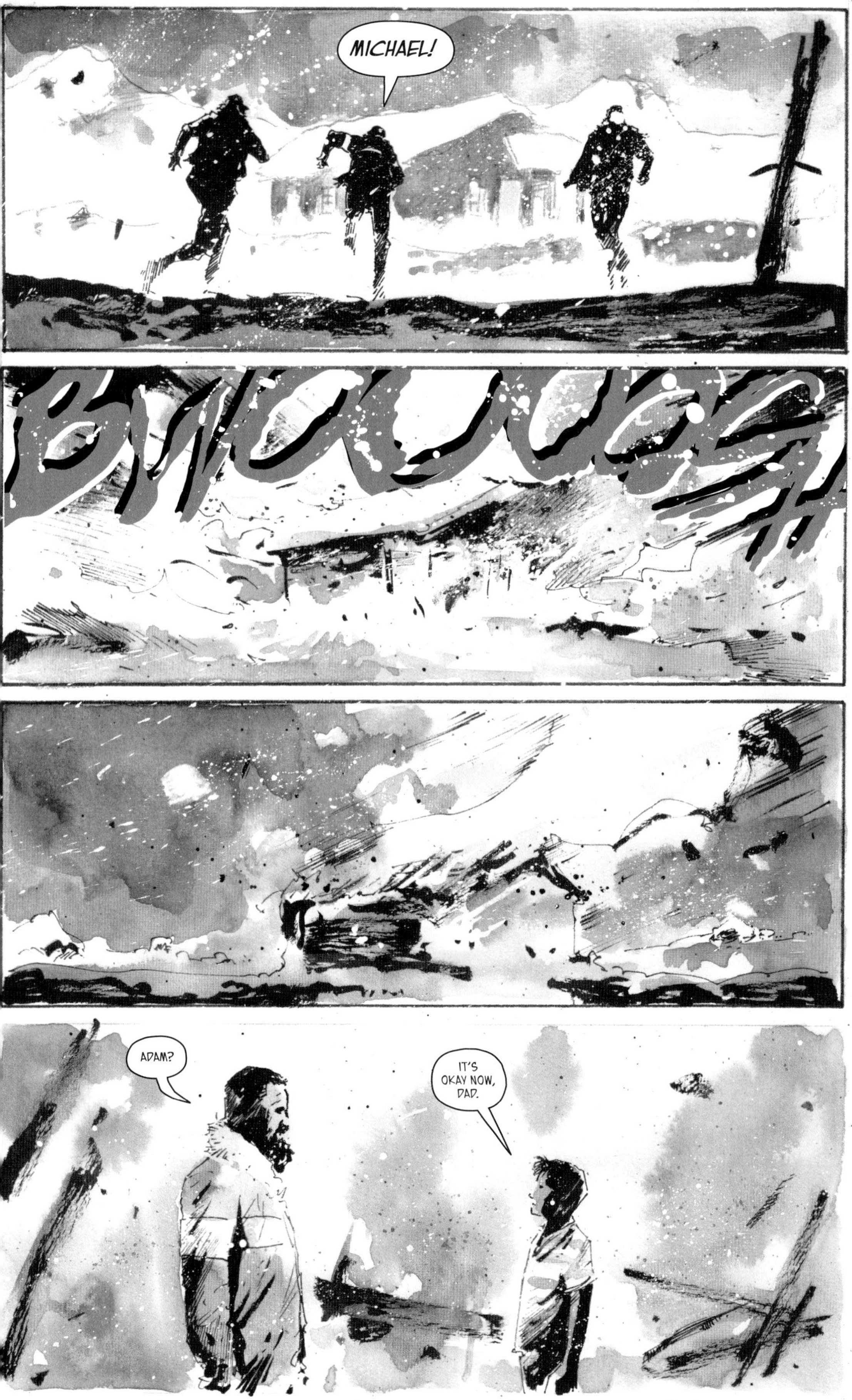
MICHAEL!
ADAM?
IT'S OKAY NOW, DAD.

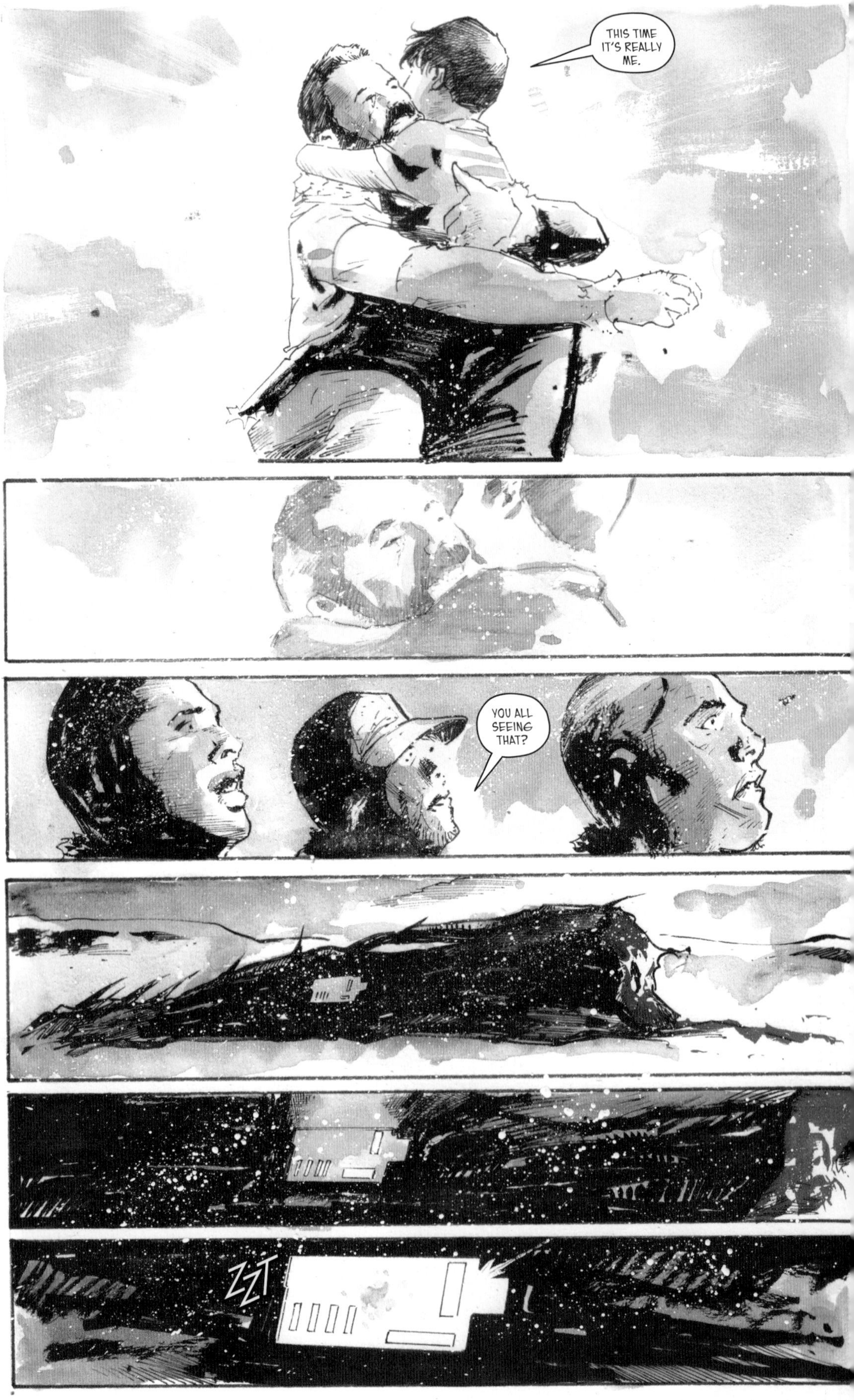
THIS TIME IT'S REALLY ME.
YOU ALL SEEING THAT?
ZZT

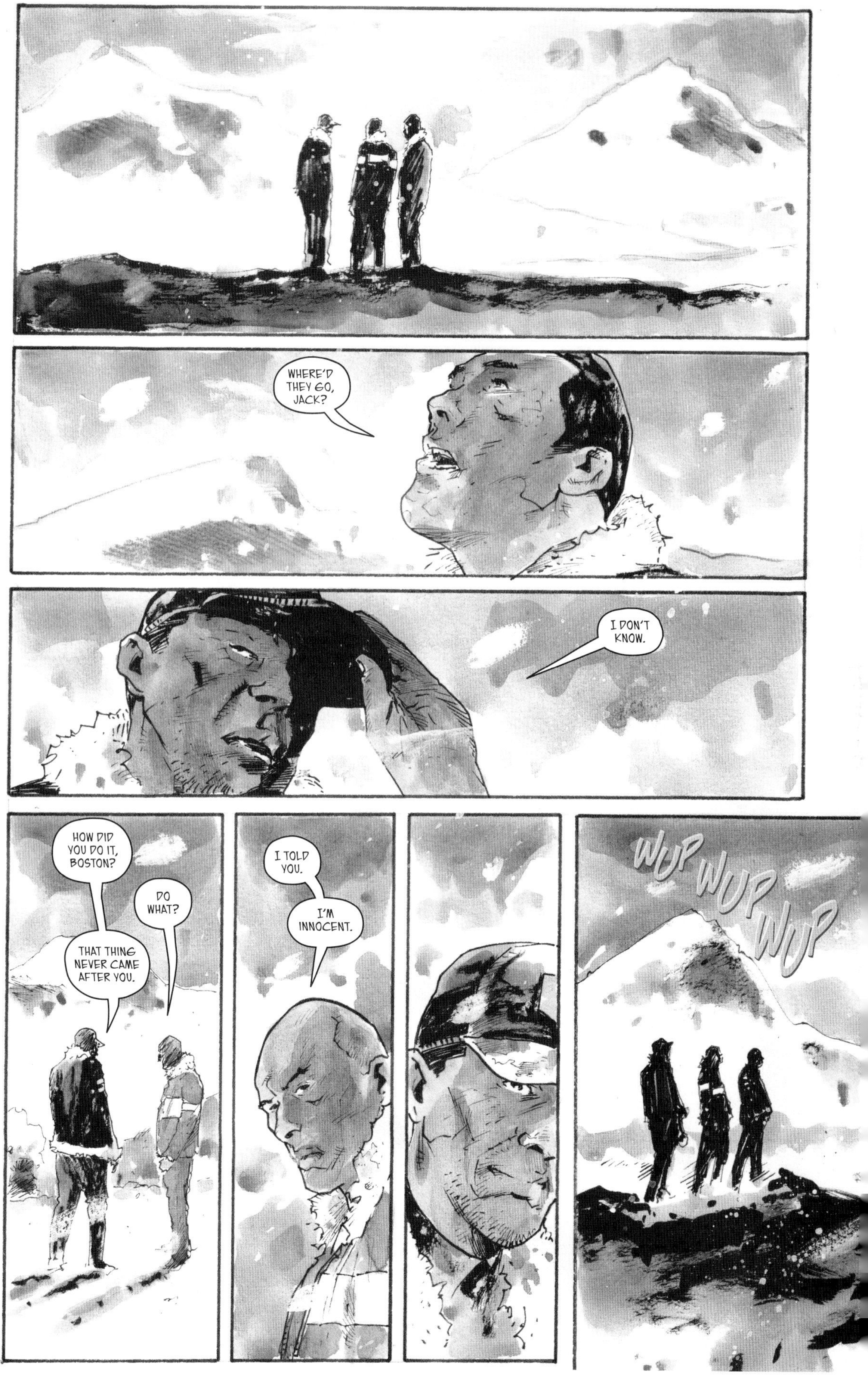
WHERE'D THEY GO, JACK?
I DON'T KNOW.
HOW DID YOU DO IT, BOSTON?
DO WHAT?
THAT THING NEVER CAME AFTER YOU.
I TOLD YOU.
I'M INNOCENT.
WUP WUP WUP

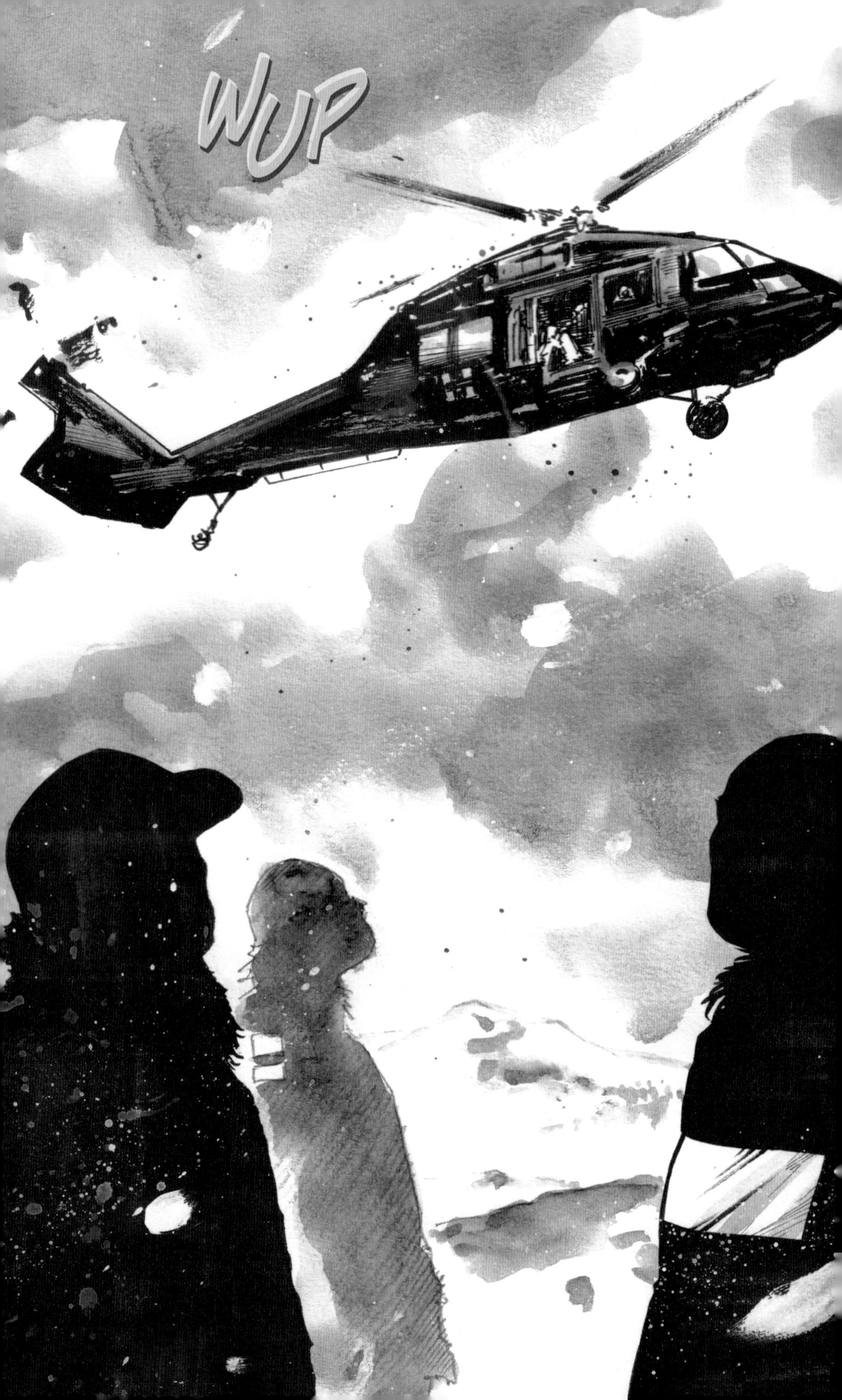
WUP

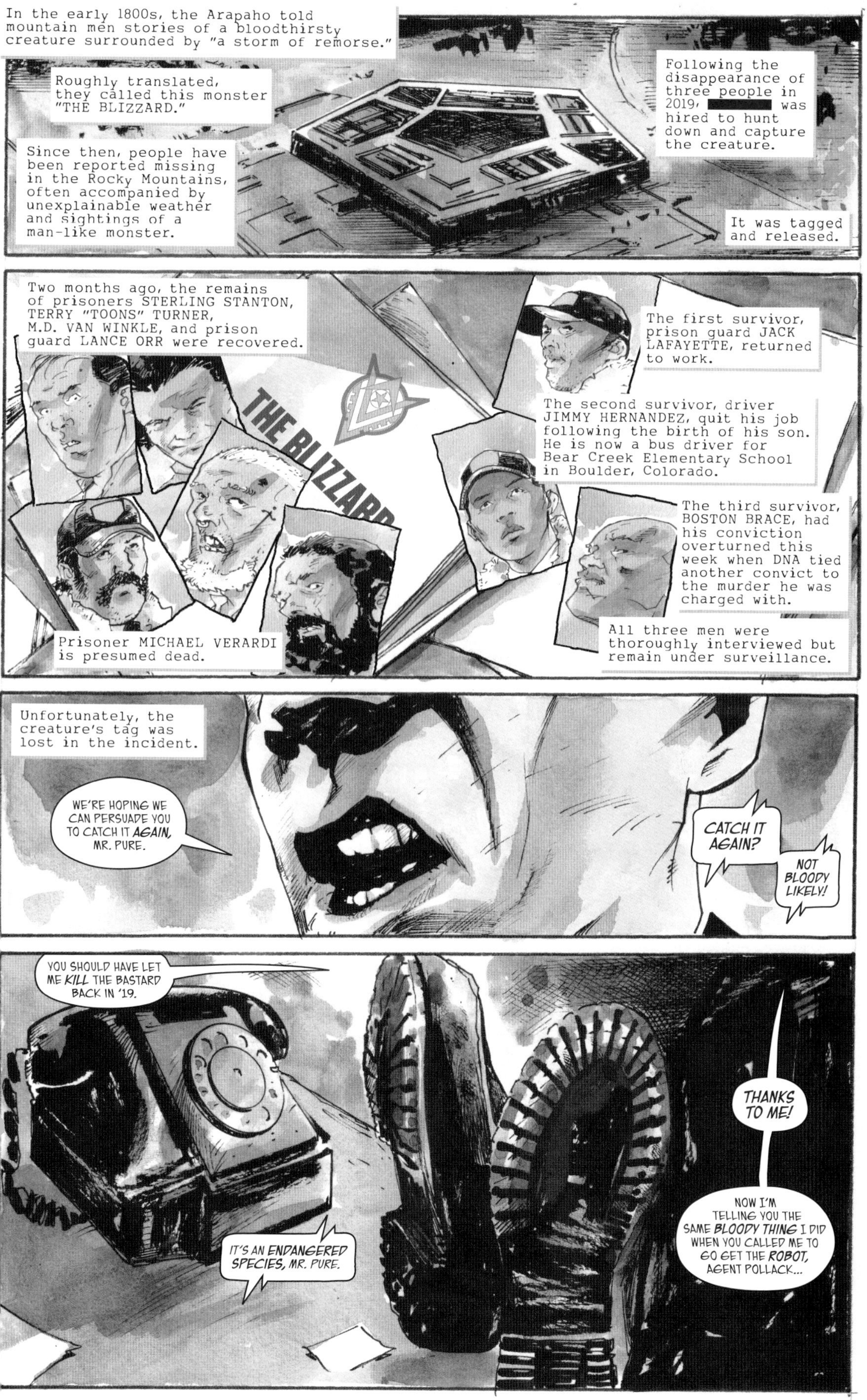

In the early 1800s, the Arapaho told mountain men stories of a bloodthirsty creature surrounded by "a storm of remorse."
Roughly translated, they called this monster "THE BLIZZARD."
Since then, people have been reported missing in the Rocky Mountains, often accompanied by unexplainable weather and sightings of a man-like monster.
Following the disappearance of three people in 2019, [redacted] was hired to hunt down and capture the creature.
It was tagged and released.
Two months ago, the remains of prisoners STERLING STANTON, TERRY "TOONS" TURNER, M.D. VAN WINKLE, and prison guard LANCE ORR were recovered.
THE BLIZZARD
The first survivor, prison guard JACK LAFAYETTE, returned to work.
The second survivor, driver JIMMY HERNANDEZ, quit his job following the birth of his son. He is now a bus driver for Bear Creek Elementary School in Boulder, Colorado.
The third survivor, BOSTON BRACE, had his conviction overturned this week when DNA tied another convict to the murder he was charged with.
Prisoner MICHAEL VERARDI is presumed dead.
All three men were thoroughly interviewed but remain under surveillance.
Unfortunately, the creature's tag was lost in the incident.
WE'RE HOPING WE CAN PERSUADE YOU TO CATCH IT AGAIN, MR. PURE.
CATCH IT AGAIN?
NOT BLOODY LIKELY!
YOU SHOULD HAVE LET ME KILL THE BASTARD BACK IN '19.
IT'S AN ENDANGERED SPECIES, MR. PURE.
THANKS TO ME!
NOW I'M TELLING YOU THE SAME BLOODY THING I DID WHEN YOU CALLED ME TO GO GET THE ROBOT, AGENT POLLACK...

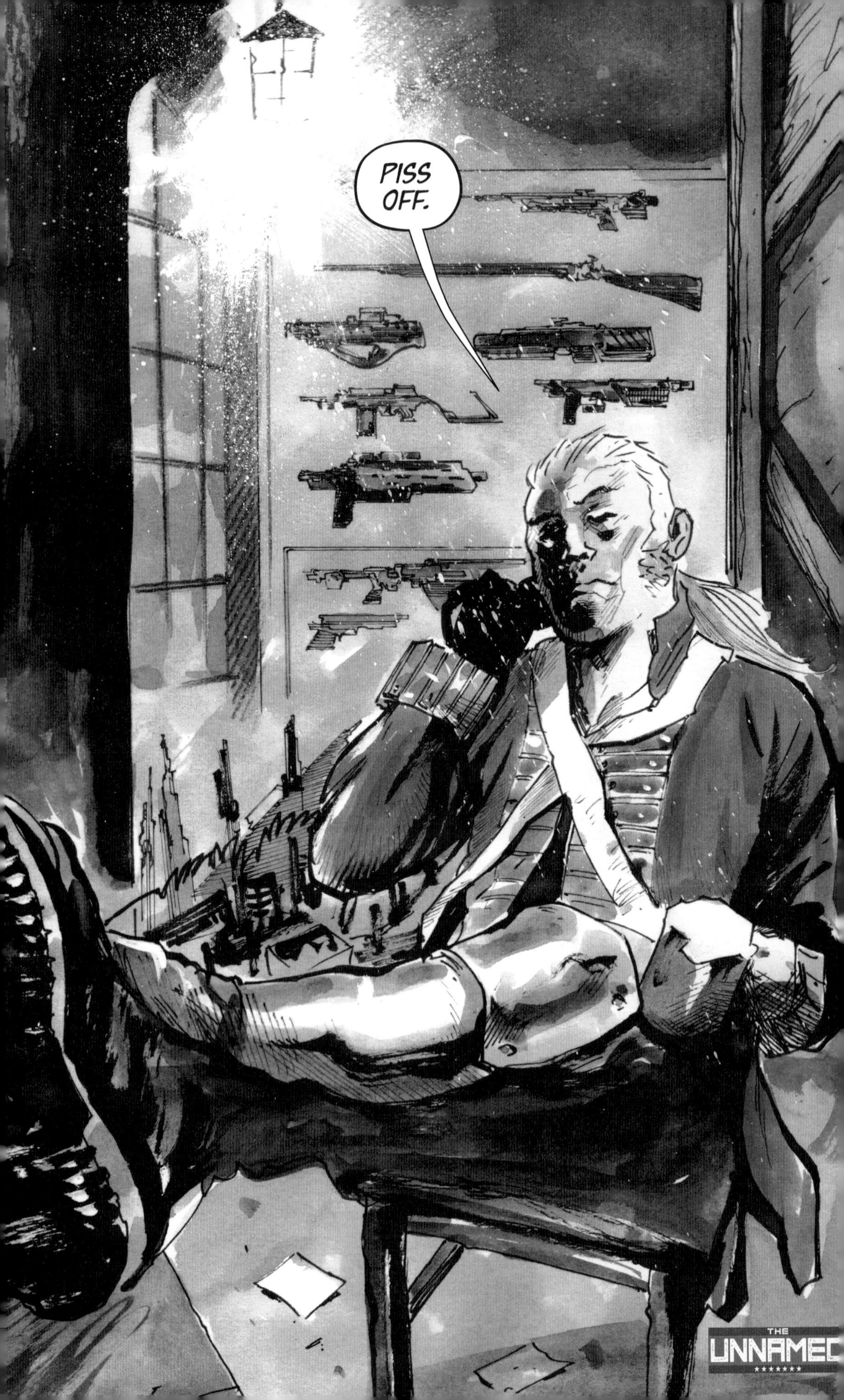
PISS OFF.
THE UNNAMED

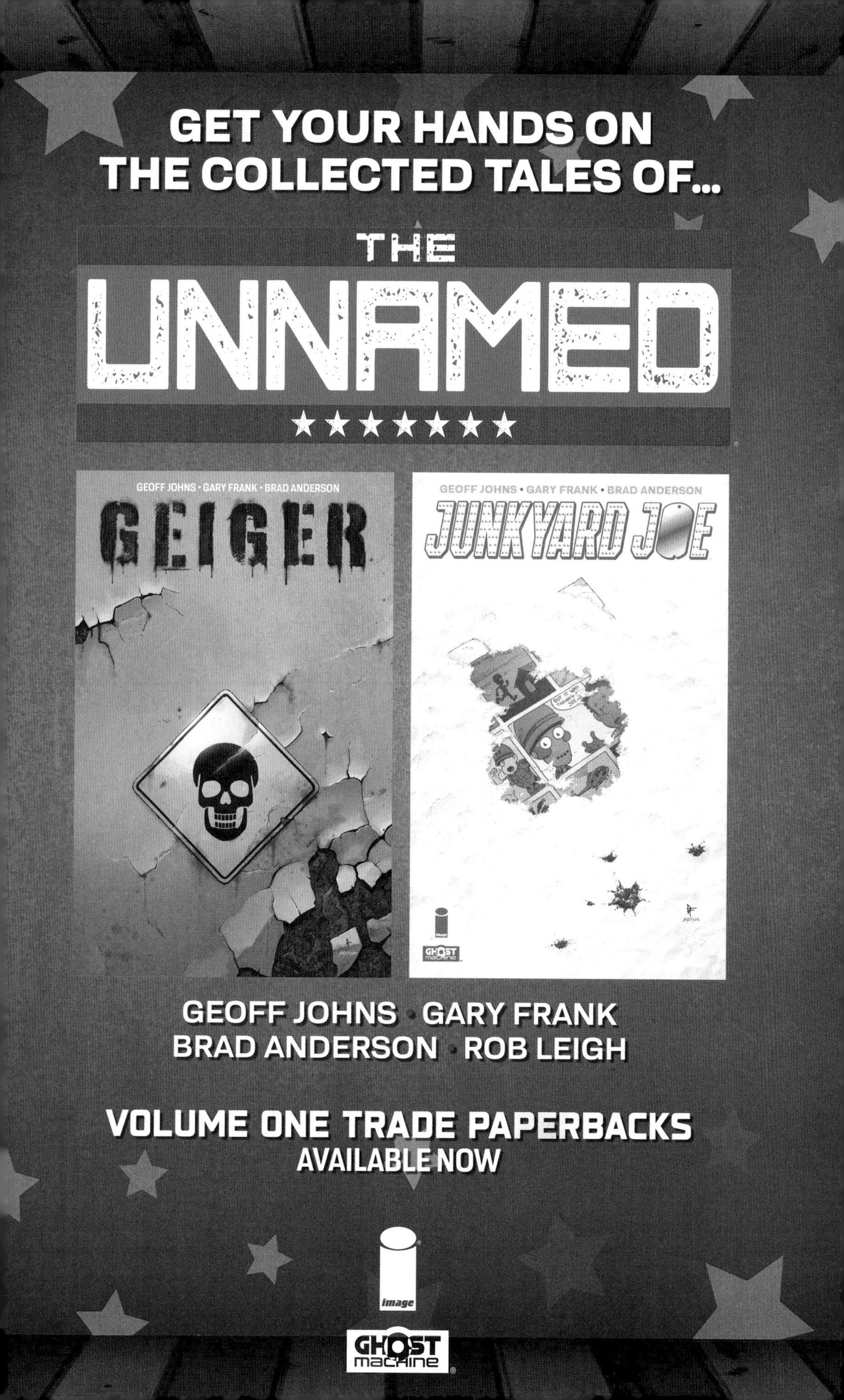
GET YOUR HANDS ON
THE COLLECTED TALES OF...
THE
UNNAMED
GEOFF JOHNS • GARY FRANK • BRAD ANDERSON
GEIGER
GEOFF JOHNS • GARY FRANK • BRAD ANDERSON
JUNKYARD JOE
image
GHOST machine
GEOFF JOHNS • GARY FRANK
BRAD ANDERSON • ROB LEIGH
VOLUME ONE TRADE PAPERBACKS
AVAILABLE NOW
image
GHOST machine

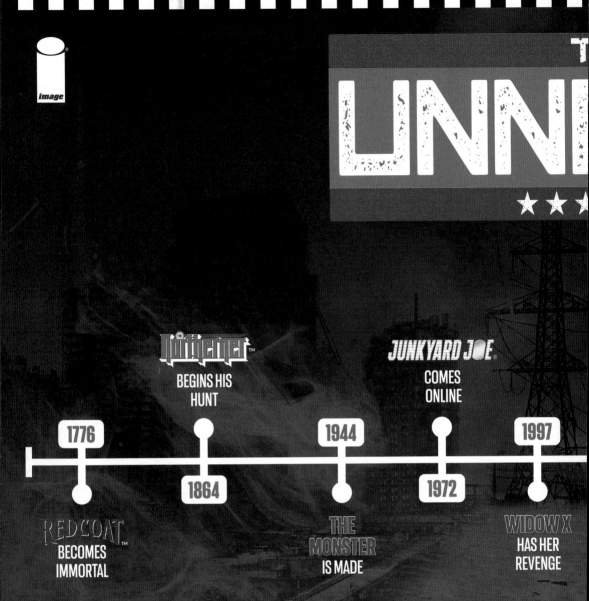

UNNI

★ ★ ★

THE NORTHERNER
BEGINS HIS
HUNT

JUNKYARD JOE
COMES
ONLINE

1776

1864

1944

1972

1997

REDCOAT
BECOMES
IMMORTAL

THE
MONSTER
IS MADE

WIDOW X
HAS HER
REVENGE

Throughout history unlikely and strange heroes have risen and fallen. These men and women are a mystery, their identities and lives a secret. But for a Great Evil to be stopped, their stories must be told. From a radioactive family man in the near future to a British assassin during the American Revolution to a robotic killing machine seeking its creator — and more — they are The Unnamed fighting The Unknown War.

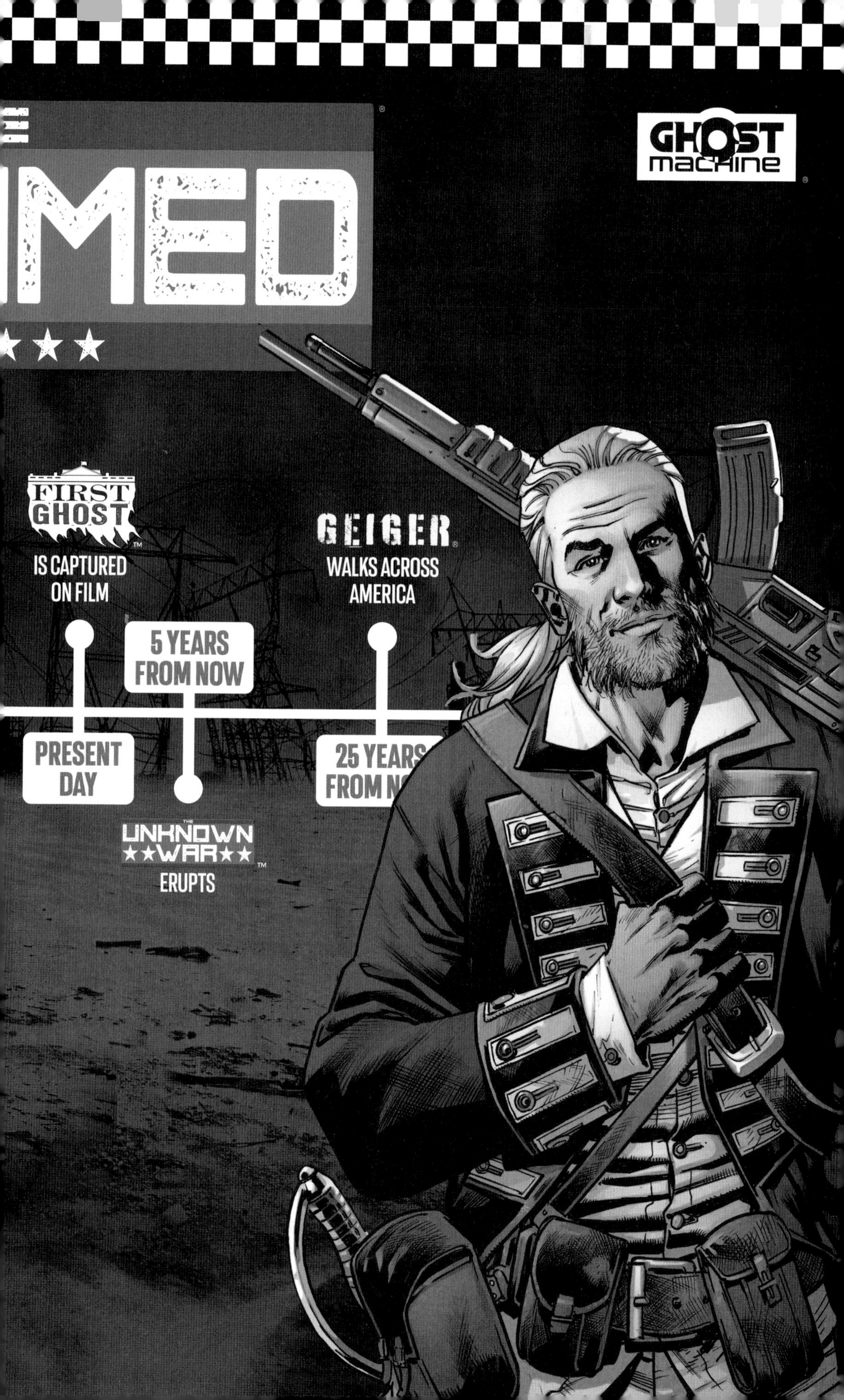
MED
GHOST machine
FIRST GHOST
IS CAPTURED ON FILM
GEIGER
WALKS ACROSS AMERICA
5 YEARS FROM NOW
PRESENT DAY
25 YEARS FROM NO
THE UNKNOWN WAR
ERUPTS

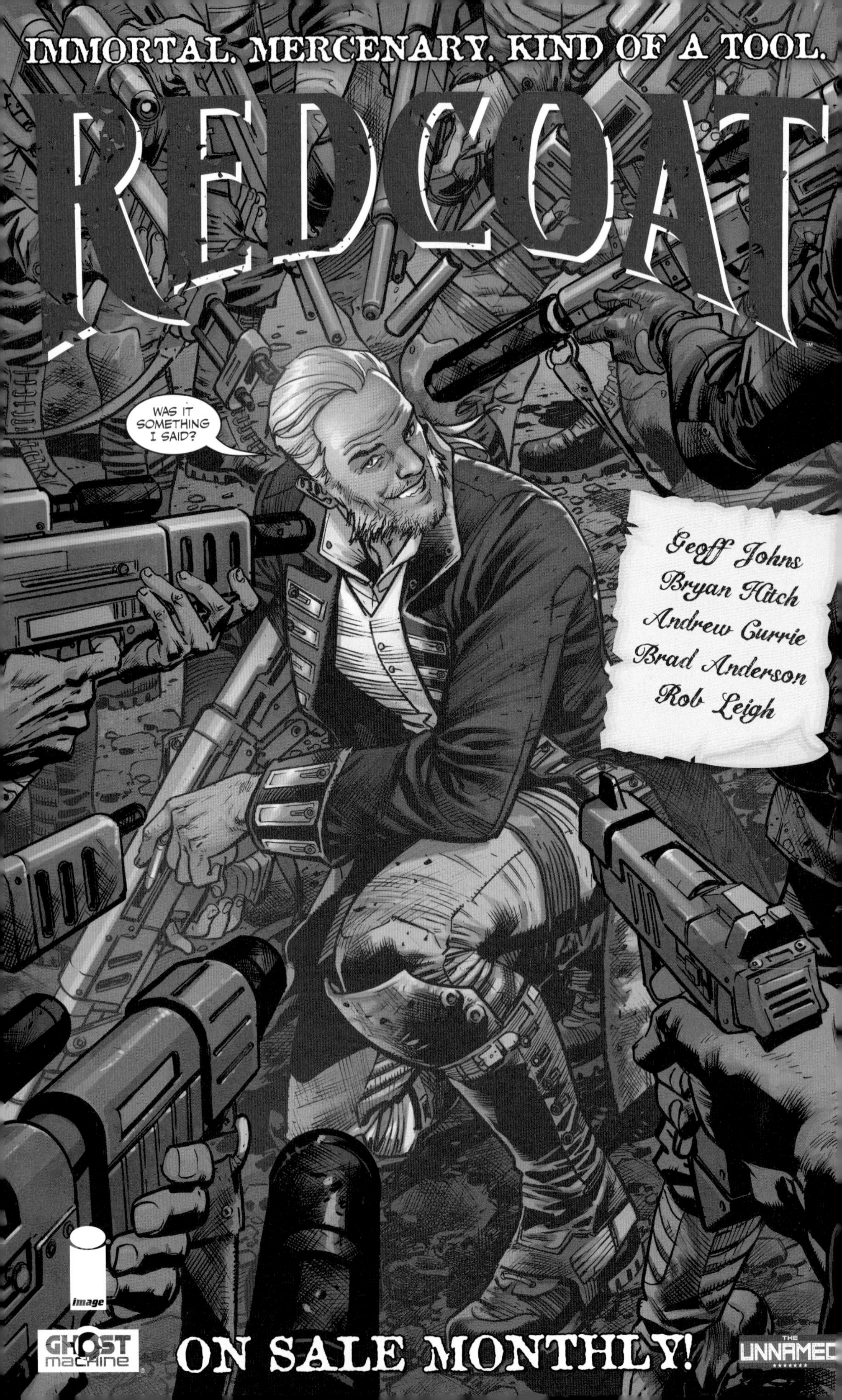
IMMORTAL. MERCENARY. KIND OF A TOOL.
REDCOAT
WAS IT SOMETHING I SAID?
Geoff Johns
Bryan Hitch
Andrew Currie
Brad Anderson
Rob Leigh
ON SALE MONTHLY!